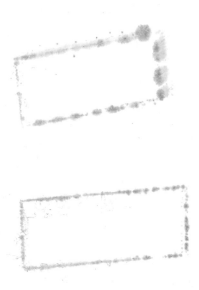

THE DIARY OF
VASLAV NIJINSKY

THE DIARY OF VASLAV NIJINSKY

UNEXPURGATED EDITION

TRANSLATED FROM THE RUSSIAN BY
KYRIL FITZLYON

EDITED BY

JOAN ACOCELLA

ALLEN LANE
THE PENGUIN PRESS

ALLEN LANE
THE PENGUIN PRESS

Published by the Penguin Group
Penguin Books Ltd, 27 Wrights Lane, London W8 5TZ, England
Penguin Putnam Inc., 375 Hudson Street, New York, New York 10014, USA
Penguin Books Australia Ltd, Ringwood, Victoria, Australia
Penguin Books Canada Ltd, 10 Alcorn Avenue, Toronto, Ontario, Canada M4V 3B2
Penguin Books (NZ) Ltd, Private Bag 102902, NSMC, Auckland, New Zealand

Penguin Books Ltd, Registered Offices: Harmondsworth, Middlesex, England

First published in France as *Nijinsky Cahiers* by Actes Sud 1995
First English-language edition published in the USA by Farrar, Straus and Giroux 1999
First published in Great Britain by Allen Lane The Penguin Press 1999
1 3 5 7 9 10 8 6 4 2

Printed and bound in Great Britain by The Bath Press, Bath

A CIP catalogue record for this book is available from the British Library

ISBN 0–713–99354–5

CONTENTS

INTRODUCTION

In December 1917, Vaslav Nijinsky, at that time the most celebrated male dancer in the Western world, moved into a villa in St. Moritz with his wife, Romola, and their three-year-old daughter, Kyra. His relations with Serge Diaghilev's Ballets Russes, the company in which he had made his name, were now severed, and with a war on, it was impossible for him to seek other engagements. So he and Romola had decided to retreat to neutral Switzerland and wait for peace. By the time of the armistice, however, Nijinsky had begun to go insane. The diary that follows, written in six and a half weeks, from January 19 to March 4, 1919, is the record of his thoughts as that was happening. To my knowledge, it is the only sustained, on-the-spot (not retrospective) written account, by a major artist, of the experience of entering psychosis. Other important artists have gone mad—Hölderlin, Schumann, Nietzsche, Van Gogh, Artaud—but none of them left us a record like this.

Nijinsky was born in Kiev around 1889 to a pair of Polish dancers who made their living on the touring circuit—opera houses, summer theaters, circuses—in Poland and Russia. His parents were his first dance teachers. At age seven he made his professional debut in a circus in Vilno, playing a chimney sweep who rescued a piglet, a rabbit, a monkey, and a dog from a burning house and then put out the fire. The following year, the father, Thomas, abandoned the family (his mistress was pregnant), and the mother, Eleanora, moved with her three children to St. Petersburg. At age nine, Nijinsky entered the Imperial Theatrical School, the same school that was to produce Michel Fokine, Anna Pavlova, Tamara Karsavina, George Balanchine, and Alexandra Danilova—most of whom, like Nijinsky, began their Western careers with Diaghilev's Ballets Russes—plus, more recently, Rudolf Nureyev, Natalia Makarova, and Mikhail Baryshnikov. He was a poor student (his younger sister, Bronislava, often did his homework), but, as soon became clear, he was a phenomenally gifted ballet dancer. By the time he appeared in school productions, the press was already calling him a prodigy, and when he graduated from school in 1907, at age eighteen, he was taken into St. Petersburg's Imperial Ballet not as a member of the corps de ballet, the usual starting rank, but as a *coryphée*, one rank higher. The company's foremost ballerina, Mathilde Kschessinska, requested him as her partner.

In those days in Russia there was a heavy sexual trade in ballet dancers. Some dancers actually accepted fees from interested ballet patrons for making introductions. In 1907 one such dancer introduced Nijinsky to the thirty-year-old Prince Pavel Lvov, a wealthy sports enthusiast, and Nijinsky entered upon what was probably his first sexual relationship, with the blessing of his mother, who, though she discouraged his heterosexual interests—she felt that marriage would impede his career—was proud to see her son with so fine a figure as Prince Lvov, and was also grateful for Lvov's financial help. (The Nijinskys had very little money.) But Lvov soon tired of Nijinsky and began introducing him to others, including, in 1908, Sergei Pavlovich Diaghilev.

Diaghilev, then thirty-five, was one of the most prominent figures in the St. Petersburg art world. With his friends, he was part of the capital's so-called World of Art group, a loosely organized fraternity of artists, musicians, critics, and other writers who set themselves the goal of liberating Russian artistic culture from the narrow political dictates (realism, nationalism, social criticism) that had dominated it since the 1860s. The group's most influential project was its journal, *Mir iskusstva (The World of Art*, 1898–1904), edited by Diaghilev. By publicizing in Russia the avant-garde art of the European fin de siècle, *Mir iskusstva* was instrumental in converting Russian painting from an exhausted realism to the freer, more imaginative symbolist style of the early twentieth century. Having brought Western art to Russia, Diaghilev then began bringing Russian art to the West, using Paris as his base. There, in 1906, he presented a lavish exhibition of Russian painting and sculpture; in 1907, a series of concerts of Russian music, most of it unknown to Europeans of that period; in 1908, a triumphant production, the first in the West, of Mussorgsky's *Boris Godunov*, starring Feodor Chaliapin.

For 1909 Diaghilev was planning to bring to Paris not just Russian opera but Russian ballet as well. Prince Lvov, Nijinsky writes in his diary, "forced me to be unfaithful to him with Diaghilev because he thought that Diaghilev would be useful to me. I was introduced to Diaghilev by telephone." He went around to the hotel where Diaghilev was staying, and was bedded, and presumably hired, the same day.

For both men, it was a fateful meeting. Diaghilev's 1909 Paris ballet season was so successful that he soon established a permanent company. That company, the Ballets Russes, was to be the most glamorous and influential theatrical enterprise in Europe in the 1910s and 1920s, and during its crucial pre–World War I period, Nijinsky's dancing was a great part of its fame. Conversely, it was the Ballets Russes that made Nijinsky famous. In St. Petersburg he had been a locally celebrated dancer. With the Diaghilev company, in the ballets of the troupe's house choreographer, Michel Fokine—*Les Sylphides, Scheherazade, Le Spectre de la Rose, Petrouchka*, others—he became an international star and, by all accounts, a great artist. That he was a virtuoso of unprecedented achievement is clear from the descriptions of his dancing in the memoirs of his younger sister, Bronislava Nijinska. (She too was a ballet dancer and a member of the Diaghilev troupe. Later, in her choreographic career, she would build on Nijinsky's experiments.) Apparently, he was also an extraordinary actor, not so much realistic as classical, in the Racinian sense. To quote one eyewitness, the ballet historian Cyril Beaumont, "He does not seek to depict the actions and gestures of an isolated type of the character he assumes; rather does he portray the spirit or essence of *all* types of that character."[1] Add to this the fact that most of the people attending the Ballets Russes had never before seen a good, let alone a great, male ballet dancer. Though still flourishing in Russia, ballet had been in decline for more than half a century in Europe, and male classical dancing was all but dead as an art. (In most Western ballet theaters, leading male roles were often taken by women *en travesti*.) To his audiences, Nijinsky was something utterly unforeseen, a miracle.

Augmenting his glamour was the atmosphere of scandal that, wherever he went, his whole life long, was always attached to Nijinsky's name. In the pre–World War I years, this was probably due to the fact that he lived openly as Diaghilev's lover— they shared hotel suites—and that the roles Fokine created for him were often ambisexual, and strongly sexual. The best example is the Golden Slave in *Scheherazade*, where he appeared in brown body paint, and grinning, and wound with pearls— not so much a sex object as sex itself, with all the accoutrements of perversity that the fin de siècle imagination could supply: exoticism, androgyny, enslavement, violence. Offstage too,

Nijinsky looked exotic. He had a Tartar face, with prominent cheekbones and slanted eyes. (At school, he was known as the "little Japanese.") Finally, there was his personality. So present and forceful onstage, he was the opposite offstage: naive, shy, recessive—blank, almost. Anything could be projected onto him, and anything was. In her memoirs the Bloomsbury hostess Ottoline Morrell, one of the Ballets Russes' English patrons, recalled that in the prewar years Nijinsky was the subject of "fantastic fables": "that he was very debauched, that he had girdles of emeralds and diamonds given him by an Indian prince."[2] During performances, people snuck into his dressing room and stole his underwear.

The note of scandal became more pronounced when, with Diaghilev's encouragement, Nijinsky began his choreographic career. From 1912 to 1913 he produced three ballets—*The Afternoon of a Faun*, *Jeux*, and *The Rite of Spring* (to Stravinsky's now-famous score)—that were like nothing that had ever been called ballet before. The lovely, noble three-dimensional shapes of the academic ballet, the five positions of the legs and arms, the turned-out feet: all were gone. Under Nijinsky's direction, the dancers moved in profile, slicing the air like blades (*The Afternoon of a Faun*), or they hunched over, hammering their feet into the floorboards (*The Rite of Spring*). The approach was analytic, the look "ugly," the emotions discomforting. Of these works, only one, *The Afternoon of a Faun*,[3] survives today, but it is enough to show that Nijinsky ushered ballet into modernism. That fact, however, was not widely recognized until much later, when Nijinsky was long dead. At the time when they were first performed, the crucial point about these ballets was that they caused an uproar. *The Rite of Spring*, as is well known, set off a riot in the Théâtre des Champs-Elysées in Paris. The police had to be called. All this added to Nijinsky's notoriety.

Nijinsky may have been unstable from his youth. His older brother, Stassik, was mentally unsound and had to be hospitalized as a teenager. If, as Bronislava Nijinska suggests, Stassik's troubles began when he fell out of a window as a child, his condition would have had little to do with Nijinsky's. But there were other circumstances. Peter Ostwald, in his 1991 psychiatric biography *Nijinsky*, speculates that the dancer may have had a genetic predisposition to depression, through his mother. (Her mother, upon being widowed, had starved herself to death.) Ostwald also raises the possibility that Nijinsky may have suffered brain damage as a result of a serious fall that he took at age twelve.[4] In any case, it is clear that at least by late adolescence Nijinsky was not like other boys. At eighteen, during his first season in the Imperial Ballet, he stopped dancing one night in the middle of the Act I pas de trois of *Swan Lake* and began taking his bows while the orchestra was still playing. If he was unbalanced at this point, the fame that now began gathering around his name may have unsettled him further. And if he was able to manage celebrity at that time, what was the effect on this quiet boy when, two years later, upon his debut with the Ballets Russes, the Parisians began referring to him as *le dieu de la danse*, the god of dance? Theater artists must always have some difficulty factoring into their minds the fantasies that they arouse in the audience, but in Nijinsky's case the fantasies were more elaborate and the mind more vulnerable. It is not impossible that his idea, endlessly reiterated in the diary, that he was God began with the experience of being called a god by the Parisian audiences.

To most people who knew him as an adult, the oddest thing about Nijinsky was his social incompetence. The dancer Lydia Sokolova, who began working with him in 1913, says that "when addressed, he turned his head furtively, looking as if he might suddenly butt you in the stomach. . . . He hardly ever spoke to anyone, and seemed to exist on a different plane."[5] Sokolova's statement, together with all other descriptions of Nijinsky written after he went mad, must be understood as colored by that fact. Furthermore, the memoirs of certain of his colleagues suggest that he was more forthcoming with people whom he knew well, and who spoke Russian. Still, by most accounts, he was remarkably introverted. At parties he would sit silently and pick his fingers. Even his wife, so protective of his reputation, reports that the dancers called him "Dumb-bell" behind his back.[6]

These social difficulties made his choreographic career a nightmare at many points. The Ballets Russes dancers had been trained in the academic style. To induce them to forget all that and move like figures in an antique frieze or aborigines around a campfire required tact, patience, and excellent communication skills: precisely what he lacked. Sokolova says that when, in rehearsing *Faun*, he told her to move through rather than to the music, she burst into tears and ran out of the theater. Others stayed but loathed his work and let him know it. *Faun*, an eleven-minute ballet, is said to have required over a hundred hours of rehearsal. And Nijinsky had to deal with opposition not just from the dancers but also from his collaborators— Debussy, the composer for *Faun* and *Jeux*, disliked both ballets and said so—not to speak of critics and audiences. During the premiere of *The Rite of Spring* the uproar in the theater was so great that the dancers could not hear the music. Nijinsky stood in the wings, sweat coursing down his face, screaming the musical counts to the performers—a terrible image. Whatever the stresses of his career as a dancer, those of his choreographic career were probably greater.

At the same time, his relationship with Diaghilev was deteriorating. By the time of *The Rite of Spring*, their love life was apparently over. Worse, Diaghilev seemed to be abandoning

Nijinsky as an artist. The company's next major ballet, *The Legend of Joseph*, with music by Richard Strauss, was to have been choreographed by Nijinsky. Diaghilev, perhaps dismayed by the scandal over *The Rite of Spring* or, more probably, concerned over the strain that Nijinsky's ballets imposed on the company, now reassigned *The Legend of Joseph* to Fokine, Nijinsky's rival, who was also demanding to dance Nijinsky's major roles. "Perhaps he [Nijinsky] should simply leave the Ballets Russes and not dance for a year," Diaghilev blandly suggested to Bronislava Nijinska, who was delegated to carry such messages to her brother. Nijinska recalls that Nijinsky was now in "a heightened state of nervousness . . . , as if he felt that a net was being woven around him."[7]

These last events help to explain the extraordinary thing Nijinsky did next. He got married. In the summer of 1913, shortly after the premiere of *The Rite of Spring*, the Ballets Russes embarked on a tour of South America. Diaghilev did not accompany them, but someone else did: Romola de Pulszky (1891–1978), a wealthy, headstrong, socially ambitious Hungarian, twenty-two years old, the daughter of Hungary's foremost classical actress, Emilia Márkus. Romola had seen Nijinsky dance in 1912. She thereupon decided to marry him and attached herself to the company, as a sort of groupie, for that purpose. On the ship, she made her interest in Nijinsky known, and two weeks out of port, without having exchanged more than a few words with her (at that time they had no language in common), he proposed. They were married in Buenos Aires two weeks later.

That was the beginning of a series of crises that culminated five years later in Nijinsky's madness. First, Diaghilev fired him. This is understandable; whatever the state of their relationship, Diaghilev still considered Nijinsky his companion, and he was undone by the younger man's defection. (Diaghilev's friend

Misia Edwards—later Misia Sert—was with Diaghilev when he received the news. He became hysterical, "sobbing and shouting," she wrote.[8]) Nijinsky, on the other hand, was apparently mystified by Diaghilev's reaction. He wrote Stravinsky begging him to "please ask Serge what is the matter." "If it is true that Serge does not want to work with me," he added, "then I have lost everything." Stravinsky later described this letter as "a document of such astounding innocence—if Nijinsky hadn't written it, I think only a character in Dostoievsky might have."[9] Nevertheless, Nijinsky's assessment of the situation was correct: he had lost everything. In order to dance, he did not need the Ballets Russes. Any ballet company would have been delighted to engage this great star to dance its standard repertory. But Nijinsky by this time was not a dancer of standard repertory. He had been through that stage with the Imperial Ballet. He was different now—an experimental artist. He needed roles that would extend his gifts, and above all, he needed to choreograph. For these things he did need the Ballets Russes, which at that time was the only forward-thinking ballet company in the world. While Nijinsky's later psychosis was probably, in part, biologically based, even the firmest adherents of the biological theory of schizophrenia agree that constitutional vulnerability must be combined with some potent psychological stress in order for the illness to develop. In Nijinsky's case, the major stress was unquestionably his inability, after his dismissal from the Ballets Russes, to do what he regarded as his work. By his marriage, Nijinsky probably thought that he was extricating himself from a difficult situation, his relationship with Diaghilev. He did not understand that his life as an artist depended on Diaghilev.

Nor, with his personality, could he manage a company of his own, as he soon learned. The following March, with the help of the loyal Bronislava, Nijinsky undertook to mount a ballet season, with a company of seventeen, at a music hall in London, but he soon fell ill from overwork, and what was to have been a two-month engagement was canceled after two weeks—a humiliating and expensive failure. Ostwald believes that at this point Nijinsky suffered his first "nervous break-down."[10] He couldn't sleep, was plagued by fears, went into screaming rages—a condition that was probably made worse by an increase in his responsibilities: the Nijinskys' first daughter, Kyra, was born in June 1914. Soon afterward, the family traveled to Budapest, to visit Romola's mother, at which point World War I broke out and Nijinsky, as an enemy alien, was placed under virtual house arrest in the home of Emilia Már-kus. There he remained for a year and a half—never dancing, trying to devise a system of dance notation, reporting to police headquarters once a week—while Romola quarreled with her mother. Emilia Márkus was a temperamental woman, and she did not relish the prospect of having houseguests for the duration of the war. In his diary Nijinsky bitterly recalls the cold welcome she gave his family.

In 1916 Nijinsky was released, thanks to Diaghilev and his important friends, because Diaghilev now needed him for a season at the Metropolitan Opera House in New York. The dancer returned to his old company, though his reunion with Diaghilev was poisoned by a quarrel over money. (Romola had decided that Diaghilev owed Nijinsky several years' worth of unpaid salary. At her behest, Nijinsky had sued Diaghilev in 1914.) When that first American season was over, Otto Kahn, the chairman of the Metropolitan Opera board, engaged the Ballets Russes for a second New York season, to be followed by a cross-country tour (1916–17), and he unwisely decided that the company should be directed during this period by Nijinsky, not Diaghilev. What followed was probably the most chaotic and demoralized tour the Ballets Russes ever undertook. A four-month journey, stopping in fifty-two cities, with over a hundred dancers and musicians: it was a huge administrative assignment, and Nijinsky had no administrative skills. By this time, furthermore, he had come under the influence of two members of the company, Dmitri Kostrovsky and Nicholas Zverev, who were followers of the religious philosophy of Leo Tolstoy. Night after night he would remain shut up in his train compartment with these two "moujiks,"[11] as Romola characterized them, while Kostrovsky, with shining eyes, called him to the faith. Born a Roman Catholic (though he received some Russian Orthodox training in school), Nijinsky had long had a religious turn of mind—Romola records that as a teenager he had dreamed of being a monk[12]—and he had been studying Tolstoy for years. Now he embraced Tolstoy's teachings with a whole heart. He became a vegetarian; he preached nonviolence; he tried to practice "marital chastity." He took to wearing peasant shirts and told Romola that he wanted to give up dancing and return to Russia, to plow the land—an announcement that prompted her to abandon him for the last leg of the tour. He tried to run the company in accordance with his new beliefs. For example, he began to practice democratic casting, giving lesser-known dancers leading roles, including his own roles, often without announcing the cast changes to the public.

After this dreadful tour, on which the Metropolitan Opera lost a quarter of a million dollars,[13] Nijinsky performed with the Ballets Russes for a few months more, in Spain and South America, in 1917. By now he was caught up not only in the quarrel between Romola and himself over his Tolstoyanism but also in a struggle between Romola and Diaghilev over what she saw as Diaghilev's plot to destroy Nijinsky. When the dancer stepped on a rusty nail, when a weight fell from a pulley backstage, these events were not regarded as accidents. Romola arranged to have Nijinsky guarded by detectives. In September, the Montevideo newspaper *El Día* printed what may have been Nijinsky's last interview. "After I left school," he was quoted as saying, "webs of intrigue were woven around me; people who had no other reason than envy for their hostilities began to appear."[14] (Since Romola often distributed typed "interviews" with Nijinsky to journalists, these may be her words, not his.) On September 30, 1917, after the end of the Ballets Russes' South American tour, Nijinsky performed with Arthur Rubinstein at a Red Cross benefit in Montevideo. According to Rubinstein's memoirs, Nijinsky, who was to have been second on the program, delayed and delayed his appearance, while the management threw on hastily assembled acts—the municipal band playing national anthems, a local intellectual declaiming an essay on dance—to give him time. Finally, after midnight, Nijinsky came onstage, looking, says Rubinstein, "even sadder than when he danced the death of Petrushka,"[15] and performed some steps to Chopin. Rubinstein burst into tears. This was Nijinsky's last public performance. He was twenty-eight. He then moved with his family to St. Moritz.

According to Romola, all went well during their first year in Switzerland. (This seems doubtful, but for 1918 she is our only witness.) Nijinsky, she says, did his exercises every day on the balcony of their house, Villa Guardamunt, just up the hill from the village of St. Moritz. He laid plans to start a school in Russia for choreographers, composers, and scenic artists. He plotted new ballets, made drawings, and worked on his notation system. Around the end of the year he received an unhappy letter: Bronislava, who had returned to Russia, wrote that their brother, Stassik, had died—news to which Nijinsky responded with a strange smile, Romola reports.

Then, around January of 1919, Nijinsky began to fall apart. He began closeting himself in his studio all night long, producing drawing after drawing, at furious speed. As a young man

Crayon drawing by Nijinsky, c. 1919. Romola, in her *Nijinsky*, says that the drawings Vaslav produced at this time made her shudder. "What are those masks?" she asked him. "Soldiers' faces," he replied. "It is the war"
Courtesy of Tamara Nijinsky

in St. Petersburg, he had studied drawing under the painter and Ballets Russes designer Léon Bakst. He drew "like a child," reports Marc Chagall, who was in the same class.[16] The drawings he made now were also childlike (or modernist), but above all obsessive. They were mostly of eyes, Romola reports: "eyes peering from every corner, red and black." When she asked him what they represented, he replied that they were soldiers' faces.[17] Others of his drawings, Romola says, showed butterflies with his own face or spiders with Diaghilev's face. When he and Romola took walks together, he would stop and fall silent for long periods, refusing to answer her questions. One day he went down to St. Moritz with a large gold cross over his necktie and stopped people on the street, telling them to go to church. He also had spells of violence. He drove his sleigh into oncoming traffic. He threw Romola (holding Kyra) down a flight of stairs. Once, when he asked Kyra's nurse, Mrs. Grant, to find something for him and she did not immediately comply, he leapt at her and seized her by the throat. She fled the house and never returned.[18]

He also gave a final dance concert, before an invited audience, at a nearby hotel, the Suvretta House. As Romola describes the performance, Nijinsky began by taking a chair, sitting down in front of the audience, and staring at them for what seemed like half an hour. Eventually he unrolled two lengths of velvet, one white, one black, to form a cross on the floor. Standing at the head of the cross, he addressed the audience: "Now I will dance you the war, . . . the war which you did not prevent."[19] He then launched into a violent solo, presumably improvised, and at some point stopped. On that same day, January 19, 1919, between finishing his lunch and going to Romola's dressmaker to pick up his costume for the concert, he began his diary.

After the performance at the Suvretta House, says Romola, "I never felt the same again."[20] Apparently, she had already confided in a doctor, a friend of the family. She does not give his name, but Nijinsky's diary does. He was Hans Curt Frenkel, a young physician attached to one of St. Moritz's resort hotels. According to Ostwald, Frenkel's specialty was sports injuries, but during his medical training in Zurich he had attended lectures by the renowned psychiatrist Eugen Bleuler, who in 1911 had invented the term "schizophrenia."[21] Frenkel was also familiar with Jungian theories of psychopathology. Thinking that he might be able to help Nijinsky, he began visiting him almost every day. He tried to induce him to reveal his private thoughts;

he warned him that his behavior was upsetting Romola. But Nijinsky only got worse. Day after day, he would retreat to his study to make drawings of staring eyes or to write in his diary, which he would not let Frenkel or Romola see. (In any case, it was in Russian, a language that neither of them could read.) Finally, Frenkel wrote to his old professor, Bleuler, asking if he would see Nijinsky. Bleuler agreed. Meanwhile, Romola had apparently summoned her mother and stepfather to come from Budapest and help her take Nijinsky to Zurich. They arrived, and the group—Nijinsky, Romola, Emilia Márkus, and her husband, Oscar Párdány—departed for Zurich. The diary ends on that day, March 4, 1919, as Nijinsky is waiting for the cab to take them to the train station.

In Zurich Romola first went to Bleuler alone. After listening to her account of Nijinsky's behavior, he told her, "The symptoms you describe in the case of an artist and a Russian do not in themselves prove any mental disturbances." But the next day, when he saw Nijinsky, he changed his mind. After what Romola says was an interview of ten minutes, Bleuler described Nijinsky in his notes as "a confused schizophrenic with mild manic excitement."[22] The doctor showed Nijinsky out of his office, asked Romola to come in, and told her that her husband was incurably insane. When she returned to the waiting room, the dancer looked up at her and uttered the words now famous in the Nijinsky legend: "*Femmka* [little wife], you are bringing me my death-warrant."[23]

Had it been a death warrant, it might have been more merciful. The couple returned to their hotel, and that night Nijinsky locked himself in his room, refusing to come out. After twenty-four hours, the police were called, and they forced open the door. Nijinsky was taken without protest to the Burghölzli University Psychiatric Hospital, where Bleuler was the director. Three days later he was sent to nearby Kreuzlingen, to the

Bellevue Sanatorium, a luxurious and humane establishment directed at that time by Ludwig Binswanger, one of the founders of existential therapy. Within three months at Bellevue, Nijinsky was hallucinating, tearing his hair out, attacking his attendants, declaring that his limbs belonged to someone else, not him. It is impossible to know whether this decline was part of the natural course of his illness or whether it was the result of hospitalization. In his lucid periods, according to the Bellevue records, he would cry out, "Why am I locked up? Why are the windows closed, why am I never left alone?"[24] Romola later claimed that Nijinsky's deterioration was brought on by the episode of the police breaking open his hotel room door and taking him to Burghölzli. She said that her mother had engineered this behind her back.[25] But Nijinsky records at the end of the diary that when they were about to leave for Zurich, Romola came to him and asked him to tell Kyra that he would not be coming back. If that is true, then hospitalizing Nijinsky was part of Romola's plan for the trip. Nijinsky does not seem to have understood this fully. He took his diary with him on the journey, for, as he says, he intended to find a publisher for it in Zurich. Instead, it was turned over to the doctors of Burghölzli, who copied out passages of it into their records to support their diagnosis.

As noted, Nijinsky began the diary on the day he was to give the performance at the Suvretta House. This was probably no coincidence. As the early pages of the diary indicate, he already had Frenkel in the house, "analyzing" him; it had already been suggested to him that he go see the "nerve specialist" in Zurich. At one point Romola had also hired a male nurse to watch him. (She told Nijinsky that the man was a masseur. Nijinsky was not fooled, she says.) In other words, Nijinsky knew that the people around him had doubts about his sanity, and he must also have known that the performance he was going to give that evening would alarm them further. He may well have embarked on the diary as a last chance to show that he was not mad but, on the contrary, had ascended to a higher plane of understanding. He had joined his soul to God—on the drive to the Suvretta House, he told Romola, "This is my marriage with God"[26]—and from God he was bringing a message to the world: that people should not think but feel. This, he believed, was the source of the problems between him and Romola. She was trying to understand him through her intellect ("I want to destroy her intellect"), not through feeling. Failure of feeling was also the cause of the war. David Lloyd George, the British prime minister, operated via intellect; Woodrow Wilson (whose pacifism Nijinsky, as a Tolstoyan, naturally supported) relied on feeling, but Lloyd George undermined him. The war, how-ever, was only one problem. As Nijinsky describes the situation in his diary, the entire world is being laid waste by materialism and opportunism. Scientists are claiming that human beings are descended from apes. Industrialists are despoiling the planet. The stock exchange, the manufacturers, the shops are robbing the poor. This is what he has understood from God. Indeed, he is now God, and he is going to convert the world back to feeling. (That is the "aim" of which he speaks repeatedly.) His primary means will be the diary. Once it is published, he will have it distributed for free. He is hoping to have it reproduced in facsimile rather than printed, because he feels that the man-uscript is alive and will transmit feeling directly, off the page, to readers.

He knows that his message will be opposed. In his descrip-tions of the harm done by the strong to the weak, and by "thinkers" to "feelers," there are certain names that come up repeatedly, notably those of Lloyd George and Diaghilev: "They are eagles. They prevent small birds from living." Emilia Márkus is also in this group. But as the diary proceeds, the list of enemies lengthens, for he fears that he will be punished for the truths he is revealing. (He is convinced that Zola was gassed to death for telling the truth in the Dreyfus affair. He also thinks that William Howard Taft has been assassinated.) He is afraid that the English will send people to shoot him because of what he has written about Lloyd George. When he complains about his fountain pen and accuses the manufacturers of fraud, he imagines that they will sue him and have him put in prison. As noted, the drawings that he was making at this time were filled with eyes.

There are several other themes in the diary. His bodily processes—eating, digestion, elimination—are on his mind. This is related to his refusal to eat meat, a source of bitter conflict between himself and Romola, probably because to her it symbolized his Tolstoyanism, which, at times, she saw as the source of all their troubles. In addition, he is very concerned about sex, which he views with revulsion. (It was partly in order to suppress lust that he refused to eat meat.) He guiltily recalls his childhood sex play and his pursuit of prostitutes before and after his marriage. He imagines that his servants are having sex with animals. He accuses the four-year-old Kyra of masturbating, a practice that he believes causes mental and physical breakdown. (This was a common assumption at the time.) He also meditates on various projects. He wants to build a bridge from Europe to America, presumably to help in uniting the world. He plans to invent a new kind of fountain pen; he will call it "God." He has a cure for cancer.

One feels a frantic struggle for control underlying much of the diary. In a larger sense, this is Nijinsky's effort to right the balance of power in the world, to wrest authority from the thinkers, return it to the feelers. At the same time, however, he is fighting for control over his own life. If he felt that eyes were watching him, they were—Romola's, Frenkel's—and he knew where this was leading. Apart from his campaign for feeling, no theme in the diary is more important than his fear of being hospitalized, as his brother was. He mentions this already on the first night of the diary: "I will not be put in a lunatic asylum, because I dance very well and give money to anyone who asks me." As events gather, he guesses that this is what the trip to Zurich is about. A little over halfway through the diary, there is a break in the text. Nijinsky signs off—as "God Nijinsky"—on the material he has already written. Then he starts what he calls Book II, entitling it "On Death," and begins recording terrible thoughts. Suddenly he is separated from God, and filled with evil: "I am not God, I am not man. I am a beast and a predator." He feels ruin closing in on him. "Death came unexpectedly," Book II begins, "for I wanted it." But it was not death that was coming; it was Emilia Márkus. As he notes, she is arriving at his house the next morning at eleven o'clock. He disliked her already because of her unkind treatment of his family during their internment in Budapest. But his reaction here is more than dislike; it is a catastrophic fear. He knows that her arrival will be followed by the trip to Zurich—that she has come to help Romola place him in an institution.

Nijinsky's struggle against the people who think he is going mad would be painful enough, but the situation is worse, for he too knows that he is going mad, or at times he does: "I am standing in front of a precipice into which I may fall." "My soul is sick . . . I am incurable." Soon, however, he is God again. This is the most wrenching thing about the diary. He knows that something extraordinary is going on in his brain, but he does not know whether this means that he is God or that he is a madman, abandoned by God.

While that drama is transpiring in his mind, a parallel drama is going on in the household—what to do with him?—and it is the counterpoint between the two that makes the diary read at times like a novel. Nijinsky's recording could not be more immediate. At one point, he actually writes while lying in bed with Romola. We get to hear her breathing. As the crisis escalates, we hear phones ringing, people running, Romola weeping somewhere in the house, Dr. Frenkel comforting her. Nijinsky can't make out what they are saying. He has to guess, and so do we. It's like a French *nouveau roman*. Before us, we have the man, and, in the background, the muffled sounds of his fate being decided. It is not impossible that Nijinsky was trying to create a work of literature. Each of the three notebooks in which the diary was recorded has an ending that sounds like an ending (even though, in the case of the first two notebooks, the ending was imposed arbitrarily, by the paper running out). The last lines of the first notebook, in which he describes his daughter singing, are actually beautiful. The last lines of the final notebook are not beautiful, but mordant, ironic, and they thereby provide a perfect close for this otherwise passionate and headlong document.

Nijinsky's diary was first published in 1936, in an English-language version translated by Jennifer Mattingly and edited by Romola Nijinsky. This book, which is still in print—it has become a classic of confessional literature—represents Nijinsky's text poorly. To begin with, Romola extensively rearranged the sequence of the diary. For example, she took the beginning of the first notebook and used it to open the final section of her version. (As a result, the Suvretta House concert comes *after* the trip to Zurich.) To make an ending for that final section, she used the conclusion of the first notebook. Then she created an "epilogue" out of some material that she sliced off the front of the third notebook. The effect of these changes is to obscure the grim march of events carrying Nijinsky from the Suvretta House concert to Dr. Bleuler's office in Zurich. It is unlikely, however, that Romola was trying to suppress that story. (She told it plainly enough in her first biography of her husband, *Nijinsky*, published two years before the diary.) Most of her rearrangements seem to be in the service of making the diary more respectable. Nijinsky begins his first entry by saying what he had for lunch, after which he veers off into a description of how the Swiss are as dry as the beans he just ate. To Romola, I believe, this was too humble, and too crazy, a beginning, so she started with a later, nobler passage. Likewise, the materials she moved to the end of her edition— Nijinsky's description of Kyra singing, his sign-off as "God Nijinsky"—make a nice ending, if not the true ending.

Romola also cut about 40 percent of the diary. For obvious reasons, she deleted all references to defecation and much of the copious material on sex. As for homosexuality, she rewrote Nijinsky's description of his first encounter with Diaghilev: "I immediately made love to him" became "At once I allowed him to make love to me."[27] This change, together with her blurring of his references to earlier homosexual contacts, converted him into an involuntary homosexual. In addition, she dropped a great deal of the domestic material. She disguised identities. Dr. Frenkel is more or less eliminated. When Nijinsky speaks of him, she either deletes the sentence or, if she needs it, replaces his name with "the doctor" or "the doctors" or "friends." She also had to deal with many uncomplimentary references to herself. Recalling the early days of their marriage, Nijinsky says, "She did not love me much. She felt money and my success. She loved me for my success and the beauty of my body." Romola translates this as "She loved me. Did she love me for my art and for the beauty of my body?"[28] When he says, "My wife is an untwinkling star," she just deletes it.

The many other cuts and revisions in Romola's edition can be summarized by saying that she tried to eliminate the less romantic aspects of Nijinsky's illness: the oddness, the illogic.

When he reverses cause-and-effect relationships ("The audience did not like me, because they wanted to leave"), she repairs them ("They did not like me, they wanted to go away"[29]). When he makes bizarre puns, or writes long, repetitious poems full of Russian wordplay, she excises them. When, without transitions, he begins writing now in his own voice, now in the voice of God, she italicizes God's statements and puts them in quotation marks, thus creating a distinction that Nijinsky did not make.

In addition, Romola dropped most of the so-called fourth notebook. Together with the diary, which was written in three school notebooks, Nijinsky left a fourth notebook in which he had written a series of increasingly wild-worded letters to various people. Of the sixteen letters in the fourth notebook, Romola chose six—the saner ones—which, after heavy editing, she inserted into the body of the diary. The remaining ten she discarded.

The subtle but wholesale change that Romola wrought can be seen by comparing two versions of a passage in which Nijinsky meditates on the danger he is in. Here is a more or less literal translation, by Kyril FitzLyon, of the Russian original:

> I know the love of my servants, who do not want to leave my wife by herself. I will not go to my wife, because the doctor does not want it. I will stay here and write. Let them bring me food here. I do not want to eat sitting at a table covered with a tablecloth. I am poor. I have nothing, and I want nothing. I am not weeping as I write these lines, but my feeling weeps. I do not wish my wife ill. I love her more than anyone. I know that if they separate us I will die of hunger. I am weeping . . . . I cannot restrain my tears, which are dropping on my left hand and my silk tie, but I do not want to restrain them. I will write a lot

because I feel that I am going to be destroyed. I do not want destruction, and therefore I want her love. I do not know what I need, but I want to write. I will go and eat and will eat with appetite, if God wills it. I do not want to eat, because I love him. God wants me to eat. I do not want to upset my servants. If they are upset, I will die of hunger. I love Louise and Maria. Maria gives me food, and Louise serves it. [The ellipses are his.]

The following is Romola's version:

I understand the love of my people, who do not want me to leave my wife alone. I am poor. I have nothing and I want nothing. I am not crying, but have tears in my heart. I do not wish any harm to my wife, I love her more than anyone else, and know that if we parted I would die. I cry . . . I cannot restrain my tears, and they fall on my left hand and on my silken tie, but I cannot and do not want to hold them back. I feel that I am doomed. I do not want to go under. I do not know what I need, and I dislike to upset my people. If they are upset, I will die. I love Louise and Marie. Marie prepares me food and Louise serves it.[30]

Romola has eliminated two critical elements. One is the connection between love and food. Nijinsky, as he makes clear, has been called to a meal, so that his grief over his alienation from Romola becomes attached to the idea of not getting food, of starving. Romola probably found this primitive. The other element missing from her version is the layering of events. Nijinsky's account has three things happening at once. In the dining room are the servants putting out the meal. In another room is Romola, probably weeping again. (Dr. Frenkel may or may not be with her.) In his studio sits Nijinsky, weeping too, and writing and listening. Romola may have felt that this polyphony was confusing or, again, that such details as the goings-on in the dining room were too prosaic. So she kept only what seemed to her central and noble, Nijinsky's tears.

Many passages of Nijinsky's original text are clearly the work of an artist. Some gleam like hellfire; others pierce to deep emotional truths. (The paragraphs on his relationship with Diaghilev—his disgust, for example, at the sight of the older man's pillowcases, blackened with hair dye—are an eloquent statement on the end of a relationship.) Other passages, however, are very hard to read: repetitious, obsessional, simultaneously searing and boring, as mad people often are. It was this problem, among others, that Romola set herself to eliminate. By the thirties, when she began work on her version, Romola made her living (lectures, books, loans, gifts) off the reputation of the genius-madman Nijinsky, who, out of a surcharge of visionary power, had severed his ties with ordinary humanity—"The manifestation of his spirit could only be approached humbly by us human beings," as she later put it[31]—but who might someday alight, and dance again. (When the diary was first published, it contained a plea for contributions to the costs of his care.) If the grim details of his illness were to become widely known, this might have made him, and her, a less appealing cause. At the same time, she was trying to protect Nijinsky, and she lived in a time when the preservation of an uplifting legend was more valued than textual integrity. That time has passed, however, at least as regards Nijinsky. The document that Romola published is in many ways an editorial achievement, and, compared with the original, it is comforting to read—clearer, nobler, shorter—but it is not what Nijinsky wrote.

Once Romola's English-language version was published, it became the basis for translations into other languages. Its distortions were thus perpetuated and compounded. The original notebooks were not released. Then Romola died in 1978, and in 1979 the three diary notebooks were sold at auction at Sotheby's. During the years that followed, they passed through the hands of various collectors. Meanwhile, the copyright remained the property of the Nijinsky daughters, Kyra and Tamara, and they did not choose to exercise it. Finally, in 1993, a French writer, Christian Dumais-Lvowski, who had already had extensive dealings with Tamara Nijinsky—he had created a play, *Nijinsky Monologues*, out of excerpts from Romola's edition of the diary—went to see Tamara in Phoenix, Arizona, where she lives, and prevailed upon her to release the copyright. (Kyra by this time was disabled by a stroke. For many years she had also had a psychiatric disorder that may have been related to her father's. She died in 1998.) Thus, with the family's blessing, the complete diary was at last published in 1995, by Actes Sud in Arles, in a French translation by Dumais-Lvowski and Galina Pogojeva. The text that follows, translated from Nijinsky's manuscript by Kyril FitzLyon, is the first complete English edition, and it is the first edition, ever, to contain the entire fourth notebook.

No argument needs to be made for its publication. At least since 1979, when Sotheby's, on the basis of a preliminary translation by FitzLyon, made known the extent of Romola's excisions, scholars have been longing to see the original diary. But it earns its keep, for it tells us some new things about Nijinsky, and elsewhere offers new evidence to support old suspicions. First, Nijinsky was not the idiot savant—genius of dance, helpless in all else—that he was often advertised as being. Both Romola and Bronislava, in their writings on Nijinsky, claimed that he was a cultivated man, but they were not disinterested witnesses, and as for Romola, she was one of the major purveyors of the Christ-like image of Nijinsky that ended up obscuring his sophistication. But as the diary makes clear, Nijinsky had read widely in Russian literature—Pushkin, Gogol, Tolstoy, Dostoevsky, Merezhkovsky—and he thought about what he read, applied it to his own life and work. He knew something about painting, probably because Diaghilev had taken him around the great museums of Europe. (He discusses the Old Masters' practice of making copies of their predecessors' paintings.) He was also up on current events. However mad his lucubrations on the war, they are not uninformed.

Nijinsky says relatively little about his ballets—he doesn't even mention *The Rite of Spring*—and most of what he says was included in Romola's edition. But he tells us other things that, though they were recorded several years after he made his ballets, and in the midst of a psychotic break, nevertheless reflect on his work. In Romola's abridged version the intensity of his spiritual concerns was already clear; in the unabridged version, we see the intensity of his sexual concerns. As Lincoln Kirstein pointed out in his *Movement & Metaphor*, the three ballets that Nijinsky created in 1912–13 constitute a sort of ontogeny of sex: "in *Faune*, adolescent self-discovery and gratification; in *Jeux*, homosexual discovery of another self or selves; in *Le Sacre du Printemps*, fertility and renewal of the race."[32] Most of the unproduced ballets that Nijinsky contemplated during his periods of enforced inactivity after 1913 also had to do with sex. (One was set in a brothel.) In confronting the abundance of sexual material in the diary, one must make certain subtractions. He was struggling at this time to quell his sex drive, in keeping with Tolstoyan dictates, so sex would have been on his mind. Furthermore, psychotic delusions often involve sexual guilt. Nevertheless, the sexual eruptions in the diary are no doubt an extension of his thoughts as an artist.

One suspicion about Nijinsky that the diary seems to confirm is that despite his early homosexual experience, he was primarily heterosexual by inclination. This point was made by Ostwald in 1991.[33] All the homosexual liaisons that Nijinsky mentions, first with Lvov, then with the men to whom Lvov introduced him, including a Polish count and Diaghilev, were connected with material or professional rewards (though it should be noted that he says he loved Lvov). When he describes sexual experiences in which the motivation is frankly sexual—when he fantasizes while masturbating, when he pursues prostitutes before and after his marriage, when he is excited by someone he sees in the street—the object is always a woman. As for his reputed androgyny, again there seems to be a difference between what he did for others and what he did for himself. While Nijinsky made his fame in the androgynous roles choreographed for him by Fokine (the "poet" in *Les Sylphides*, the Golden Slave in *Scheherazade*, the Specter of the Rose), the roles he created for himself in his own ballets were unequivocally male. Nevertheless, Nijinsky was clearly interested in exploring the boundary between male and female. He didn't just dance those sexually ambiguous roles that Fokine made for him; he triumphed in them. Romola, in her *Nijinsky*, recalls how good he was at impersonating female dancers. "He was able to place himself in the soul of a woman," she writes.[34] He himself says in the diary, "I am both wife and husband," and though at this point he imagines himself as just about everybody on earth, his choice of words is interesting.

Another sexual matter on which the diary casts some light is the long-repeated story that while Nijinsky was going insane, Romola was conducting a love affair with Dr. Frenkel. In some versions it is added that Romola's second daughter, Tamara, born in 1920, was Frenkel's child. There is no proof of the latter claim. Nijinsky was back at home, on a five-month leave from Bellevue Sanatorium, when Tamara was conceived. And Tamara, in her 1991 memoir *Nijinsky and Romola*, says that according to Emilia Márkus, Romola at this time made a determined effort to become pregnant by Nijinsky, in the hope that the birth of another child would jolt him back into sanity.

Yet there does seem to have been an affair between Romola and Frenkel. Nijinsky at this time was practicing chastity; it is not illogical that Romola would have sought attentions elsewhere. Furthermore, members of Frenkel's surviving family told Peter Ostwald that such a liaison occurred and that Frenkel, in his unhappiness over Romola's refusal to divorce Nijinsky, attempted suicide and became addicted to morphine.[35] I too have corresponded with Frenkel's family, and they have added to this account, as follows. One night in what was probably 1920, a year after Nijinsky was first hospitalized, Frenkel, distraught over his relationship with Romola, closeted himself in a shut-down hotel in St. Moritz and tried to kill himself by means of a drug overdose. His unfortunate wife found him in time to save him. The affair with Romola ended at that point, or before. In an effort to escape the ensuing scandal, Frenkel's wife changed the family name. Dr. Frenkel's morphine addiction stayed with him until his death from pneumonia in 1938, at age fifty-one[36]—a sad story.

Ostwald's hypothesis, however, was not just that the affair occurred but that Nijinsky suspected it, and that that knowledge was what precipitated the psychiatric emergency which caused him to be taken to Bleuler.[37] This latter part of Ostwald's argument seems to be contradicted by the diary, which Ostwald, who died in 1996, did not have the opportunity to examine in its correct sequence. In his notebooks Nijinsky gives no sign that he knows of anything improper going on between Romola and Frenkel. Now and then he expresses resentment of Frenkel, but only because the doctor has intruded into the

Nijinsky family's affairs ("I see that doctors meddle in things that are outside their duties") and because Romola seems to trust Frenkel's judgment more than her husband's ("Dr. Frenkel is not God. I am"). But the strongest evidence that Nijinsky had no suspicion of an affair between Romola and Frenkel is the tone in which he speaks of her. He sometimes accuses her of terrible things ("You are death"), but he sees her sin as a failure of sympathy, never as betrayal. His attitude is best judged not from his broad statements about her but from his offhand remarks. He likes her nose; he wants to take walks with her; he calls her by her pet name, Romushka. The whole diary is in some measure addressed to her. While he wants to save the world, most of all he wants to save his relationship with Romola. His loss of her understanding is his greatest sorrow. He also worries about having told her that she was the first woman he ever made love to, when in fact he had had long experience with prostitutes: "If my wife reads all this, she will go mad, for she believes in me." These are not the words of a man who thinks his wife is having an affair.

A final point that the diary makes clear is that Nijinsky was indeed suffering from what is called schizophrenia. Though schizophrenia, like other psychoses, affects most areas of behavior, it is regarded primarily as a thought disorder.* The current, fourth edition of the American Psychiatric Association's *Diagnostic and Statistical Manual of Mental Disorders*, or *DSM-IV*, lists five symptoms: delusions (false beliefs), hallucinations (false perceptions), disorganized language, disorganized or catatonic behavior, and "negative symptoms" (e.g., emotional flatness).[38] A patient must have at least two in order to be diagnosed as schizophrenic. To judge from the diary, Ni-

---

* Schizophrenia is not "split personality," formally known as multiple personality disorder or, more recently, as dissociative identity disorder. That is an entirely different condition.

jinsky had at least three: delusions, disorganized language, and disorganized behavior. Most striking are the delusions. Almost all the varieties of delusion discussed in *DSM-IV* as indicative of schizophrenia are present in the diary: delusions of grandeur, of persecution, of control (one's actions are being manipulated by an outside force), of reference (environmental events are directed specifically at oneself). Nijinsky also seems to have somatic delusions: he believes that the blood is draining away from his head, that the hairs in his nose are moving around. He may be hallucinating too. Twice he feels that someone is in his studio, staring at him behind his back. God speaks to him, seemingly out loud.

Even more than their content, however, the form of Nijinsky's thoughts is characteristically schizophrenic. Some researchers believe that the basic problem in schizophrenia is a breakdown in selective attention, with a consequent "loosening of associations." The person starts to say something but then makes a peripheral connection, pursues that, and consequently gets off the track repeatedly, issuing long chains of associations. The trouble may be compounded by "circumstantiality," in which the person becomes distracted from his or her train of thought by environmental details, as Nijinsky so often is by the mechanics of writing. In his 1911 monograph on schizophrenia, Bleuler reproduced a letter from a patient to illustrate the thought processes involved:

Dear Mother . . .

I am writing on paper. The pen which I am using is from a factory called "Perry & Co." This factory is in England. I assume this. Behind the name of Perry Co. the city of London is inscribed; but not the city. The city of London is in England. I know this from my school-days. Then, I always liked geography. My last teacher in that subject was Professor August A. He was a man with black eyes. I also like black eyes. There are also blue and gray eyes and other sorts, too. I have heard it said that snakes have green eyes. All people have eyes. There are some, too, who are blind. These blind people are led about by a boy. It must be very terrible not to be able to see. There are people who can't see and, in addition, can't hear. I know some who hear too much. One can hear too much.[39]

This sounds eerily like Nijinsky, not just in the circumstantiality and loosening of associations, but also in the underlying sense that the associations seem to make. One feels a drift toward terrible thoughts ("One can hear too much") and a struggle, in the short, tight sentences, to counter the drift. When, in the diary, Emilia Márkus arrives, Nijinsky unleashes a long spiral of associations, starting with Emilia's voice and veering off onto his nerves, the corns on his feet (he knows how to cure them), the extinction of the earth (he knows how to reverse it), and so on. It is a dizzying flight, but one senses its logic: his fear of harm to himself and his insistence that he, not others, not Emilia, has the answer to what is ailing him and the world.

The diary shows other schizophrenic traits as well—for example, "clanging," the connecting of words on the basis of sound (often rhyme) rather than sense, and perseveration, or persistent repetition. Both of these are especially notable in the poems that Nijinsky included in the diary and also in the letters in the fourth notebook. (They render the final letters almost unreadable.) The repetition also turns up in his drawings of this period. With obsessive consistency, they are composed of circles and arcs. As noted, the arcs seem to form eyes, and Nijinsky says they do: "I often draw one eye." Those "eyes" also look like the fish, ⌒×, the sign of Christ. Finally, they

Crayon drawing by Nijinsky, c. 1916–18. "I often draw one eye"
Courtesy of Tamara Nijinsky

also look like the female genitals, the thing that, in his conver-
sion to Tolstoyanism, he had renounced. That may be, at times,
the eye that is watching him.

To apply the term schizophrenia to Nijinsky's diary is to
imply that he was suffering from a disease comparable to an
organic disorder, with a known cause. In fact, schizophrenia is
simply a name that psychiatrists have applied to what they
think is a unified pattern of behavioral abnormalities. And
though it is now clear that organic factors are involved in what
is called schizophrenia, we do not know the extent of their

contribution, nor do we know whether the behavioral abnormalities in question constitute a single pattern, as opposed to several. (In the 1980 edition of the *DSM* this condition was listed as "schizophrenic disorders."[40]) The term "disorder" has itself been questioned, notably by the antipsychiatric writers of the 1960s and 1970s. In his 1976 book *Schizophrenia: The Sacred Symbol of Psychiatry*, Thomas Szasz argued that schizophrenia was not an illness at all but rather a pretext for depriving unconventional behavior of moral meaning and thus for controlling it (by locking the person up). Earlier, R. D. Laing had put forth his theory that schizophrenia was a strategy that people employed to shed the "false self" that society had compelled them to adopt. Such ideas have been applied to Nijinsky. Indeed, they have added to his fame, given him a reputation as a sort of seer. "It is *we* who are ill," not Nijinsky, said a 1974 article in *Dance Magazine*.[41] This view was anticipated in Colin Wilson's *The Outsider* (1956), where Nijinsky is included among the existential truth-seekers forced to live on the margins of a truth-denying society.

With advances in biochemical research in the past few decades, the antipsychiatric argument has been largely discredited, at least as regards schizophrenia. There does seem to be such an illness; the illness does seem to involve abnormalities of brain chemistry. Nevertheless, there are factors other than schizophrenia that may have helped to produce the qualities that seem schizophrenic in the diary. Ostwald points out that Dr. Frenkel was giving Nijinsky a sedative, chloral hydrate, that causes attention to wander, and also that Frenkel subjected Nijinsky to word-association tests, a possible spur to the bizarre associations we find in the diary.[42] As for repetition, elision, and odd juxtapositions, these were the stock-in-trade of early modernist artists, of whom Nijinsky was one. The conductor Igor Markevitch, who at one time was Nijinsky's son-in-law (he married Kyra), compared the diary's stream-of-consciousness narration to that of *Ulysses*.[43]

One must also keep in mind the intellectual trends of the day. Protests against nineteenth-century materialism and positivism, and calls for spiritual renewal, were commonplace. A number of writers of the turn of the century—Vladimir Solovyov, for example—aspired literally to join humankind to the Godhead. Such thinking influenced many artists of the prewar period, Nijinsky perhaps among them. Nijinsky's idea that Russia will be the world's spiritual instructor was a basic teaching of nineteenth-century Slavophilism; he could have gotten it from Gogol, Dostoevsky, Tolstoy, or any number of other sources. His vegetarianism, anarchism, and pacifism, together with his recoil from sex and what seems to be his repudiation of his past work ("all those dances are death"), are all connected to Tolstoy, whom many besides Nijinsky—Gandhi, for example—regarded as a great teacher. His knowing paradoxes ("I want to write the truth and therefore I lie") are a standard device of Christian writing. The paradox of the wise fool, "jester of God," sane madman, is also a standard Christian idea, and more than standard in Russia. Nijinsky mentions *The Idiot* and compares himself to Dostoevsky's hero.

Apart from intellectual currents, the particulars of Nijinsky's life must be taken into account. His burning focus on his bodily processes may seem regressive, but for a dancer, eating and digestion are professional concerns. We must also grant him the privilege of metaphor. If he says that he is God, he also says he is an Indian, and a seabird, and Zola. (And he is not the only one who is God; Dostoevsky is too.) Finally, not every strange circumstance that Nijinsky records is necessarily imagined. If he claims that his dessert was spiked with medication, perhaps it was.

But however much these factors may have affected Nijinsky's

thinking, they cannot have been responsible for the massive derailment that we see in the diary. He himself notices how he gets off the track, and he tries in vain to bring himself back. He is also suffering terribly, and if Romola is telling the truth, he was violent. Her decision to take him to Bleuler was certainly justified. Ostwald, who was a psychiatrist, points out that Nijinsky met the diagnostic criteria not only for schizophrenia but also for bipolar disorder, or manic-depressive illness. (The manic trend can be seen in the rush of his thoughts, in the forced jocularity of his wordplay, and in his ability to write all night.) Ostwald consequently renders the *DSM* diagnosis that combines these two conditions: schizoaffective disorder.[44] In the diary, however, the evidence for schizophrenia appears far more prominent than the signs of manic-depressive illness. Bleuler's description of Nijinsky—"confused schizophrenic with mild manic excitement"—seems exactly correct.

There remains the question of a connection between Nijinsky's madness and his art. The idea of the genius-madman is a tiresome one: sentimental, tautological, demeaning to artists. In the case of Nijinsky, in particular, one hesitates to invoke it, for it has been applied to him often, with little gain in understanding. (Indeed, it puts an end to understanding, places him beyond our poor powers.) Nevertheless, many of the characteristics that seem bizarre in his diary—repetition, obsession, "ugliness," extreme states of mind—are what seem striking in his art. The quality of abstraction that made his acting so remarkable may have been rooted in the same traits of mind as his communication problems. That is, realistic acting, with its agreed-upon gestures, may have been as unavailable to him as the agreed-upon manners of social intercourse. Likewise, the experimentalism of his ballets, his *analysis* of movement—and the fact that he began this analysis in his very first professional ballet, with no preparatory, imitating-his-elders period (Marie

Rambert: "Everything that he invented was contrary to every-thing he had learned"[45])—may have been connected to some neurological idiosyncrasy. Nijinsky's ballets, wrote Kirstein, demonstrated "theories as profound as had ever been articu-lated about the classical theatrical dance."[46] Other artists have profound theories too, but to transform them into art, they have to fight their way past formidable barriers: custom, ad-vice, the anxiety to please, the wish to be understood. If, as seems likely, such things were not as real to Nijinsky as to others, he would have been able to go more directly to the bottom of his thought. Why should he worry about being un-derstood? He was seldom understood.

This is not to say that the diary forms part of the same arc of invention as the ballets. In the diary all the things besides profundity that made Nijinsky an artist—shaping, compres-sion, the sense of rhythm and climax, the acts of control—are gone, or going. It is the same instrument, but unstrung.

Nijinsky was almost thirty years old when he was diagnosed as schizophrenic. He lived for thirty years more, during which time his reputation grew. The myth that had collected around him as a dancer—that he was a flame, a vision, a messenger from the beyond—seemed merely confirmed by the news of his illness. It was as if the beyond had reclaimed him. Movies and ballets were based on his story. (*The Red Shoes*, in some mea-sure, is about him.) He became a symbol for that part of us that, in fantasy, takes off for the high hills, as opposed to the part that stays home. Nijinsky had always been famous for his jump. As witnesses describe it, he would rise and then pause in the air before coming down. Now, it seemed, he had declined to come down.

Such ideas have been applied to other dancers, for example, Olga Spessivtseva, a Russian ballerina who also performed with the Diaghilev troupe and who went insane in her forties. Indeed, madness and its allied states—obsession, ecstasy, self-immolation—are often associated with dancing in the public mind. In any case, the idea of Nijinsky as a bolt from the beyond was based almost wholly on his dancing, not on his choreography, which very few people estimated at what seems to have been its true worth until the 1970s, with the publication of Richard Buckle's biography and, above all, Lincoln Kirstein's *Nijinsky Dancing*. (Perhaps not coincidentally, these reevaluations came shortly after Stravinsky, who had long disparaged Nijinsky's choreography, declared that he had been wrong.) Nor could an image of Nijinsky as a mind beyond intelligence have been based on his choreography. While it is possible, as I have said, to relate the experimentalism of his ballets to his later insanity, the first and strongest impression one gets from his one extant ballet, *The Afternoon of a Faun*, is of a steely intelligence: strict, analytic, even ironic. The appreciation of Nijinsky's choreography is an aesthetic matter; one has to think about it. The appreciation of *him*, or of what he was said to be, was an emotional matter, connected to our fascination with sex, madness, and transfiguration. It was automatic.

While Nijinsky's romantic image was building, he himself was living a life that could not have been less romantic. From 1919 onward, he was basically a chronic schizophrenic. He was helpless; he could not brush his teeth or tie his shoelaces by himself. When Romola settled in a place where she could keep him, she took him home. The rest of the time, he lived in institutions. Usually he was gentle and passive, though occasionally he would throw his food tray at the wall or assault someone. Tamara Nijinsky, in her memoir, recalls watching him one day, at Emilia Márkus's villa in Budapest, reduce an antique chair to kindling with his bare hands.[47] (It was Emilia's favorite chair.) For the most part he was mute, but Ostwald's review of the Bellevue records suggests that Nijinsky could speak when he wanted to: "If someone tried to approach him, he would say, quite coherently, 'Ne me touchez pas' (Don't touch me)."[48]

On April 8, 1950, during a visit with Romola to London—they were living at that time in Sussex—Nijinsky died quietly of kidney failure. His death probably aided in the growth of his legend. Before, the press would occasionally publish photographs of this portly, balding older man, with the vacant smile. Now, with that distraction eliminated, his story, the *meaning* of Nijinsky, took on new force. The books, the plays, the ballets are still coming. Within the last few years, there have been at least four new one-man shows based on his life. Another movie is in the works.

This, then, is a strange story. Nijinsky has become one of the most famous men of the century, but never was so much artistic fame based on so little artistic evidence: one eleven-minute ballet, *Faun*, plus some photographs. A large part of his reputation rests on the diary, which, apart from the fact that until recently all available versions misrepresented Nijinsky's text, is not artistic evidence, but something more like a personal letter—"a huge suicide note," as Thomas Mallon called it [49]—and one very likely to appeal to our sentimentality about those cut off in the prime of life. By now, Nijinsky is less a man than a saint, his genius less a fact than a tradition, like the lives of the saints. Actually, most great reputations in dance are a matter of belief, for in most cases the dance is gone. But with Nijinsky the belief required is more absolute, in proportion to the claims. Such faith is probably not misplaced, though. On the small artistic evidence that we have—above all, on the evidence of *Faun*—Nijinsky probably was a genius. Hence the diary becomes a truly terrible document, a record not just of his loss but of ours.

Joan Acocella

NOTES

1. Beaumont, *Bookseller at the Ballet*, p. 135.
2. Morrell, *Memoirs of Lady Ottoline Morrell*, p. 215.
3. In recent years there have been attempted reconstructions of Nijinsky's other ballets, but the choreographic evidence is so meager that these productions must be considered constructions rather than reconstructions.
4. Ostwald, *Nijinsky*, pp. 2 (depression), 12 (possible brain damage). Ostwald's book is the basis of much of my account of Nijinsky's psychiatric history.
5. Sokolova, *Dancing for Diaghilev*, p. 38.
6. Romola Nijinsky, *Nijinsky*, p. 334.
7. Nijinska, *Early Memoirs*, p. 475.
8. Sert, *Two or Three Muses*, p. 120.
9. Stravinsky and Craft, *Memories and Commentaries*, pp. 38–39. Quoted in Ostwald, pp. 102–3.
10. Ostwald, pp. 125, 134.
11. R. Nijinsky, *Nijinsky*, p. 300.
12. Ibid., p. 318.
13. Garafola, *Diaghilev's Ballets Russes*, p. 206.
14. Nijinski, "Nijinski," *El Día*, 13 September 1913, p. 8.
15. Rubinstein, *My Many Years*, p. 16.
16. Chagall, *My Life*, p. 90.
17. R. Nijinsky, *Nijinsky*, p. 353.
18. Tamara Nijinsky, *Nijinsky and Romola*, p. 182.
19. R. Nijinsky, *Nijinsky*, p. 361.
20. Ibid., p. 362.
21. Ostwald, pp. 168, 184. Ostwald, to my knowledge, was the first writer to publish any information on Frenkel's connection with the Nijinsky story.
22. Quoted in Ostwald, p. 196.
23. R. Nijinsky, *Nijinsky*, p. 364.
24. Quoted in Ostwald, p. 238.
25. Ostwald, p. 199.
26. R. Nijinsky, *Nijinsky*, p. 360.
27. *The Diary of Vaslav Nijinsky*, ed. Romola Nijinsky, p. 49.
28. Ibid., p. 88.
29. Ibid., p. 162.

30. Ibid., p. 31.

31. Romola Nijinsky, *The Last Years of Nijinsky*, p. 235.

32. Kirstein, *Movement & Metaphor*, p. 199.

33. Ostwald, p. 31.

34. R. Nijinsky, *Nijinsky*, p. 253. According to some reports, Nijinsky in-tended to dance *Jeux* in point shoes, though he eventually abandoned this idea.

35. Ostwald, pp. 232 (morphine addiction), 250 (suicide attempt).

36. Personal correspondence with Séverine Imfeld and Barbara Stettler.

37. Ostwald, p. 172.

38. American Psychiatric Association, *DSM-IV*, p. 285.

39. Bleuler, *Dementia Praecox*, p. 17.

40. American Psychiatric Association, *DSM-III*, p. 181.

41. Hodgson, "Nijinsky's 'Diary,'" *Dance Magazine*, December 1974, p. 37.

42. Ostwald, pp. 187–88.

43. "Préface pour la traduction française du journal de Waslaw Nijinsky," in *Ecrits sur Nijinsky*, ed. Françoise Stanciu-Reiss, p. 199.

44. Joseph Stephens and Peter Ostwald, "Appendix B: A Formal Diagnosis of Nijinsky's Psychosis," in Ostwald, p. 350.

45. Interview in Drummond, *Speaking of Diaghilev*, p. 114.

46. Kirstein, *Dance*, p. 283. Quoted in Ostwald, p. 53.

47. T. Nijinsky, p. 277.

48. Ostwald, p. 279.

49. Mallon, *A Book of One's Own*, p. 200.

TRANSLATOR'S PREFACE

The English version of Nijinsky's *Diary* published by his wife Romola in 1936, and subsequently translated into many other languages, enjoyed a considerable success. It showed the famous dancer to have been a subtle and original thinker, capable of stimulating observations on life, God, and man that, for those who knew him, were quite unexpected. Some forty years later, however, this version of the diary was found to have been the product of very heavy revision. In 1979, shortly after Romola Nijinsky's death, the diary notebooks were put up for sale, and I was hastily commissioned to translate them for the use of the auction house in describing the notebooks to prospective buyers. From my draft translation, the first attempt at a faithful reproduction of the original, one could see at last the extent of Romola's editing, including the deletion of about two-fifths of Nijinsky's text. Because of copyright restrictions, my translation could not be published, though over the years it was apparently made available to scholars, including Peter Ostwald, who quoted from it in his 1991 *Nijinsky: A Leap into Madness*. Only since the recent release of the copyright have full translations of Nijinsky's diary begun appearing, including, now, my own.

After the first sale of the notebooks in 1979, a typescript was made from them by a Russian typist. Unfortunately, the copy was not exact. Apart from its use of post-reform in place of Nijinsky's pre-reform orthography (a change that does not affect the translation), it contains a number of errors—misreadings and omissions. In one case, the typist, unable to decipher the original, fell back on my 1979 translation, translating it back into Russian. This typescript has been used by some recent translators of the diary, who consequently repeat its inaccuracies. My present English version, like my 1979 translation (of which this text is a revision), was made from the manuscript itself.

I have tried, in my version, to preserve Nijinsky's highly individual use of words, phrases, and syntax. If the translation occasionally appears awkward as a result, it does no more than reflect the awkwardness of the original Russian. One source of difficulty is Nijinsky's bilingualism, the fact that he was a Pole educated in Russia. Though he thought he was more at home in Russian than in Polish, the diary contains numerous "polonisms." Occasionally, his turns of phrase and use of words, while perfectly correct in Polish, make little sense in Russian, even if the meaning can be guessed at. At other points, he has difficulties with his Russian vocabulary, confusing one word with another and making the meaning difficult or impossible to discover unless the reader happens to know what word he has in mind. Thus, the meaning of the sentence "Tolstoy said that Dostoevsky was someone with a comma" becomes clear only if one realizes that he has confused the Russian word *zapyataya* ("comma") with *zaminka* ("flaw"), used by Tolstoy in stating his opinion that Dostoevsky had a flawed talent. In such cases I thought it best to translate the sentence literally and append an explanatory note.

If Nijinsky's vocabulary is sometimes faulty, more often it is simply idiosyncratic. A good example is the meaning he attaches to "feeling" (*chuvstvo*), a central concept in the diary. To him "feeling" means intuitive perception, the ability to understand something—a person, a situation—by merging with it emotionally. Such understanding, which in his mind can be akin to a spiritual experience, is seldom achieved deliberately, and never by means of what he calls "thinking" or "intellect." Nijinsky regards thinking with some contempt, as the antithesis of feeling: a purely cerebral and almost artificial activity, which never penetrates beneath the surface of things. People who merely think are incapable of knowing the truth or conducting intimate relationships. "Thinking" and "intellect" must not, however, be confused with "reason," which Nijinsky sees as a faculty emanating from God and not subservient to logic.

Another Nijinskian concept is that of "dryness." He speaks of people being dried out, but he does not explain what this means. Presumably it means that they have been deprived of the ability to "feel." Yet another peculiarity is his use of the word "habit." To have a habit means to be a slave to an artificially acquired (and invariably bad) mode of behavior. To have no habits is to be free of all prejudice.

Very seldom does Nijinsky refer to something as being "good" or "bad," but almost always as being "a good thing" or "a bad thing." (The expression "a terrible thing" is a great favorite of his.) This turn of phrase has been preserved in the translation in spite of stylistic disadvantages.

I have also chosen not to interfere with Nijinsky's violations of logic, including his reversals of causal relationships. (For example, "I did not understand French, for they spoke in Russian." Likely meaning: "They spoke in Russian, for I did not understand French.") Though they may be due in part to his linguistic difficulties, these curiosities are more probably a reflection of his disturbed state of mind.

I have dealt similarly with layout. To Nijinsky his narrative was a flow of consciousness, governed not by logic ("thinking") but by the association of ideas. One result of this is the scarcity of paragraphing. To introduce additional paragraphing in the translation would certainly help the reader, but it would also impose an order and shape which are lacking in the original, and would therefore misrepresent both his state of mind and his vision of reality as a single, unbroken whole. Likewise, I have followed Nijinsky in his shuttling choices regarding capitalization, a matter of great importance to him. On the other hand, his Russian punctuation, which is without notable irregularities, has for the most part been converted by the editor into standard American punctuation. (Certain words in the translation have also been changed to conform to American usage.)

Nijinsky's concern with the use of capital and lowercase letters forms part of his interest in the physical aspect of writing, to which he seems to attribute more than a merely artificial or cosmetic significance. The very tools of writing—ink, pens, pencils—are to him a source of curiosity and wonder. He pays close attention to spelling and accuses himself unjustly of being a bad speller. He meditates on the new Russian orthography. He worries about his handwriting—which is actually quite neat and regular—and makes sporadic attempts to change it. He feels the sheer effort of writing to be such that writers (including himself, presumably) may be called "martyrs," "similar to the crucified Christ." Self-identification with Christ and with God is never far from his thoughts. In one way or another, it is a constant theme of the diary.

One feature of Nijinsky's writing that could not be reproduced in the translation is the very strong rhythms that mark his poems, both in the main text and in the fourth notebook, and to which he adheres irrespective of any meaning the poetry might or might not possess. These insistent rhythms may be a verbal expression of his experience as a dancer.

There is no totally satisfactory system of transliteration of the Russian alphabet into Latin characters. With proper names I have applied a system partly of my own devising, while making exceptions for spellings (Benois, Massine, etc.) hallowed by use. Other, smaller points of translation are covered in the footnotes marked "(Tr.)."

Kyril FitzLyon

BOOK I

ON LIFE

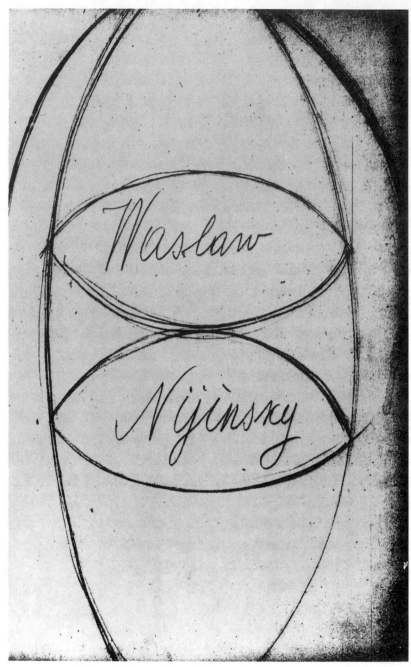

The opening of the third notebook of the diary

Courtesy of the Dance Collection, The New York Public Library
for the Performing Arts, Astor, Lenox and Tilden Foundations

I have had a good lunch, for I ate two soft-boiled eggs and fried potatoes and beans. I like beans, only they are dry. I do not like dry beans, because there is no life in them. Switzerland is sick because it is full of mountains. In Switzerland people are dry because there is no life in them. I have a dry maid because she does not feel. She thinks a lot because she has been dried out in another job that she had for a long time. I do not like Zurich, because it is a dry town. It has a lot of factories and many business people. I do not like dry people, and therefore I do not like business people.

The maid was serving lunch to my wife, to my first cousin (this, if I am not mistaken, is how someone related to me by being my wife's sister is called), and to Kyra, together with the Red Cross nurse.* She wears crosses, but she does not realize

* As the diary opens, the household consists of the following people. First, the immediate family: Nijinsky, age twenty-nine; his Hungarian wife, Romola, age twenty-seven; and their four-year-old daughter, Kyra. (For background on the family, see introduction, pp. vii–viii.) There is one guest, Teréz Pulszky (1883–1963), Romola's high-spirited older sister, whom Nijinsky describes here as his cousin. Tessa, as she was called, had recently arrived from Vienna, where she lived with her Danish husband, Erik Schmedes, a leading Wagnerian tenor at the Vienna State Opera. Finally, there are three servants: the cook, Marie; the maid, Louise Hamberg; and Kyra's nurse, Marta Madeleine Grant, who is probably the person Nijinsky describes here as the "Red Cross nurse." On Mrs. Grant, see introduction, p. xx. (Ed.)

3

their significance. A cross is something that Christ bore. Christ bore a large cross, but the nurse wears a small cross on a little ribbon that is attached to her headdress, and the headdress has been moved back so as to show the hair. Red Cross nurses think that it is prettier this way and have therefore abandoned the practice that doctors wanted to instill in them. The nurses do not obey doctors, because they do not understand the instructions they have to carry out. The nurse does not understand the purpose she is here for, because when the little one was eating, she wanted to tear her away from her food, thinking that the little one wanted dessert. I told her that "she would get dessert when she had eaten what was on the plate." The little one was not offended, because she knew I loved her, but the nurse felt otherwise. She thought that I was correcting her. She is not getting any better, because she likes eating meat. I have said many times that it is bad to eat meat. They don't understand me. They think that meat is an essential thing. They want a lot of meat. After eating lunch they laugh. I am heavy and stale after eating, because I feel my stomach. They do not feel their stomachs, but feel blood playing up. They get excited after eating. Children also get excited. They are put to bed because people think they are weak creatures. Children are strong and do not need help. I cannot write, my wife disturbs me. She is always thinking about the things I have to do. I am not bothering about them. She is afraid I will not be ready. I am ready, only my digestion is still working. I do not want to dance on a full stomach and therefore will not go and dance while my stomach is full. I will dance when it all calms down and when everything has dropped out of my bowels. I am not afraid of ridicule, and therefore I write frankly. I want to dance because I feel and not because people are waiting for me. I do not like people waiting for me and will therefore go and get dressed. I will put on a city suit because the audience will be composed of city folk. I do not want to quarrel and will therefore do whatever I am ordered to do. I will now go upstairs to my dressing room, for I have many suits and expensive underwear. I will go and dress in expensive clothes so that everyone will think I am rich. I will not let people wait for me and will therefore go upstairs now.

I stayed upstairs for a long time. I slept a little, and when I awoke, I dressed. After I had dressed, I went to the dressmaker on foot. The dressmaker had done her work well. She had understood me. She likes me because I gave her a present for her husband. I wanted to help her, but she does not like doctors. I forced her to go to a doctor. She did not want to. I wanted to show her that I did not mind spending money. I gave her husband a pair of underpants with an undershirt. She gave him the present. She took the present with love. She understood me because she did not refuse. I like Negri, this is her name. She is a good woman. She lives in great poverty, but I went in and turned off the electric light that she had left on for no reason. She understood my action and was not offended. I told her that she had done her work very well. She will receive money and a present. She has no warm clothes. I will give her a warm sweater and a cap to wear. I do not like presents, but I like giving poor people whatever they need. She feels cold. She is hungry, but she is not afraid of work and therefore has some money. She has a boy of about six and a girl of about two. I want to give a present to the children because they are dressed very poorly. I will give her my sweaters or something else for the children. I like children. They like me too. She knows I like children. She feels that I am not pretending, because I am a human being. She knows that I am an artist, and therefore she understands me. She likes me. I like her. Her husband is a violinist in the Palace Hotel, where people amuse themselves with all kinds of trifles. He is poor because he plays at night.* He is cold because he has no warm clothes. He likes playing the violin. He wants to learn, but does not know how to, because he has no time. I want to help him, but I am afraid that he will not understand me. I can play the violin without learning how to. I want to play, but I have little time left. I want to live for a long time. My wife loves me very much. She is afraid for me because I played very nervously today.† I played nervously on purpose, because the audience will understand me better if I am nervous. They do not understand artistes who are not nervous. One must be nervous. I offended the pianist Gelbar. I made a mistake just now in saying that she was called Belvar. I wish her well. I was nervous because God wanted to arouse the audience. The audience came to be amused. They thought that I was dancing to amuse them. I danced frightening things. They were frightened of me and therefore thought that I wanted to kill them. I did not want to kill anyone. I loved everyone, but no one loved me, and therefore I became nervous. I was nervous and therefore transmitted this feeling to the audience. The audience did not like me, because they wanted to leave. Then I began to play cheerful things. The audience cheered up. They thought that I was a boring artist, but I showed that I could play cheerful things.

The audience started laughing. I started laughing. I laughed

---

* Meaning that he plays at night because he is poor. Here and on many other occasions in the diary Nijinsky reverses cause and effect. See, later in the paragraph, "The audience did not like me, because they wanted to leave." (Tr.)

† "played": Nijinsky sometimes makes no distinction between artistic activities. Thus he uses the word "play" to mean "dance." (Tr.) Nijinsky now describes his last performance as a dancer, which took place on 19 January 1919, in the ballroom of the Suvretta House, a hotel on the outskirts of St. Moritz, before an audience of about two hundred. For an account of the performance, see introduction, p. xx. The pianist was Bertha Gelbar Asseo, a friend of Tessa Pulszky. (Ed.)

in my dance. The audience too laughed in the dance.* The audience understood my dances, for they wanted to dance too. I danced badly because I kept falling on the floor when I did not have to. The audience did not care, because I danced beautifully. They understood my tricks and enjoyed themselves. I wanted to dance more, but God said to me, "Enough." I stopped. The audience dispersed. The aristocrats and the rich people begged me to dance again. I said I was tired. They did not understand me, because they insisted. I said that the movements of one aristocratic lady were excited. She thought I meant to offend her. I then told her that she had a feeling for movement. She thanked me for the compliment. I gave her my hand, and she felt that I was right. I like her, but I feel that she came in order to be introduced to me. She likes young men. I do not like this life, and therefore I asked her to leave me, and made her feel it. She felt it and therefore did not give me the opportunity to continue the conversation. I wanted to speak to her, but she felt the opposite. I showed her the blood on my foot. She does not like blood. I gave her to understand that blood was war and that I did not like war. I asked her a question about life by showing her a prostitute's dance. She felt it, but did not leave, because she knew I was playacting. The others thought I would lie down on the floor and make love. I did not want to complicate the evening and therefore got up whenever it was necessary. I felt God throughout the evening. He loved me. I loved Him. Our marriage was solemnized. In the carriage I told my wife that today was the day of my marriage to God. She felt this in the carriage, but lost the feeling in the course of the evening. I loved her and therefore gave her my hand, saying that I felt good. She felt the opposite. She thought I did not love her, because I was nervous. The telephone is

* Meaning, presumably, "The dance made the audience laugh too." (Tr.)

7

ringing, but I will not answer it, because I do not like talking on the telephone. I know my wife wants to answer it. I left the room and saw my wife in her pajamas. She likes sleeping in her pajamas. She loves me and therefore made me feel that I must go up to our bedroom. I went upstairs and went to my bed, but I took a notebook in order to write down everything I had experienced today. I have experienced a lot and therefore want to write it all down. I have experienced nothing but horrible things. I am afraid of people because they do not feel me, but understand me. I am afraid of people because they want me to lead the same kind of life as they do. They want me to dance jolly and cheerful things. I do not like jollity. I love life. My wife sleeps next to me, and I am writing. My wife is not asleep, because her eyes are open. I stroked her. She feels things well. I am writing badly because I find it difficult. My wife is sighing because she feels me. I feel her and therefore do not respond to her sighs. She loves me with feeling today. Someday I will tell her that we must marry in feeling, because I do not want to love without feeling. For now, I will leave it alone, because she is afraid of me.* I cannot write, for I have thought of a man who was at the party this evening. The man wants to teach music, but cannot, because he has become bored with it. I understand him very well, and I told him that I do not like teaching either. My wife disturbs me because she feels. I laughed nervously. My wife is listening on the telephone, but she is thinking of the fact that I am writing. I write quickly. She asked me what I was writing. I closed the notebook in her face because she wants to read what I am writing. She feels that I am writing about her, but she does not understand. She is afraid for me and therefore does not want me to write. I want

* Nijinsky has crossed out the next sentence. It reads: "She thinks that I have gone mad, but I know her ner." The last word would probably have been "nervousness." (Tr.)

to write, because I like writing. I want to write for a long time today, because I want to say a great deal. I cannot write quickly, but my hand writes quickly. I am writing better now because I do not get tired so often. My handwriting is clear. I write legibly. I want to write more, but I want my wife to sleep. She cannot fall asleep. She is nervous. She wants to sleep, because she thinks. She does not want to sleep, because she is not sleeping. I know that I have made a great impression on her. She understood my feeling. She knows that I can act, because she agrees that I act like Duse and Sarah Bernhardt. I have given her a difficult problem. She cannot understand what death is. She does not think of death, because she does not want to die. I think of death because I do not want to die. She is yawning, thinking that I want to sleep. She does not want to sleep. She is afraid that I write bad things about people. I am not afraid to write, because I know that I write good things. My wife is coughing and yawning, emphasizing these things and thinking that she can force me to lie down and fall asleep. She looks at me and thinks that I do not know her intentions. I know her well. She does not speak, but she suffers. She wants to force me to lie down and go to sleep, because she thinks she is tired. She is nervous, and nerves are a bad thing. She thinks that I must sleep. I have responded to her yawn. She does not understand me. She thinks I am tired. I am not tired. My muscles are tired, but I am not tired. I have promised them, i.e., the aristocrats, that I will dance. I will not dance for them, because they think they can have everything. I do not want to give them my feelings, because I know they will not understand me. I will be playing in Paris very soon. I will dance alone for the benefit of poor French artists. I want artists to feel me, and therefore I will take their life.* I will get drunk in order to

---

* He probably means that he will take responsibility for their lives. (Tr.)

9

understand them. If God wills, I will go to a cabaret with them. They need me because they have lost feelings. They need money, and I will give it to them. They will forget me, but their feeling will live. I want them to feel, and therefore I will dance in Paris in the past* few months for the benefit of poor artists. I will organize it if they want me to. Only I must be paid for my stay in Paris. I will ask Astruc† to call poor artists together for talks, for I want to speak to them. I will say to them, "Listen! I am an artist, so are you. We are artists, and therefore we love each other. Listen, I want to tell you something good. Do you want me to?" I will ask them a question about life. If they feel me, I am saved. If they do not, I will be a poor and pathetic man. For this will make me suffer. I do not want to dance in St. Moritz, because people do not like me. I know they think I am a sick man. I am sorry for them because they think I am sick. I am in good health, and I do not spare my strength. I will dance more than ever. I want to teach dancing and will therefore work a little every day. I will also write. I will not go to evening parties anymore. I have had enough of this kind of jollity to last me a lifetime. I don't like jollity. I understand what jollity is. I am not cheerful and jolly, because I know that jollity is death. Jollity is the death of the mind. I am afraid of death, and therefore I love life. I want to invite people to come and visit me, but my wife is afraid of me. I want to invite an old Jew who is a relative of Baron Günsburg.‡ Baron Günsburg

* "past": Presumably a slip of the pen for "next." (Tr.)
† Gabriel Astruc (1864–1938), impresario, music publisher, and founder of the Thé-âtre des Champs-Elysées (Paris), was the presenter of most of the Ballets Russes' seasons in Paris prior to World War I. (Ed.)
‡ Baron Dmitri Günsburg, heir to a large Russian banking fortune, was the foremost financial backer of the prewar Ballets Russes. In 1910 he was made co-administrator of the company, and at various points—for example, during the 1913 South American tour during which Nijinsky married Romola de Pulszky—he took over its management. (Ed.)

is a good man. He does not understand life. He should marry and have children, but he torments his wife because he wants her to lead a jolly life. I know everyone will say that Nijinsky has gone mad, but I don't care, for I have already behaved as if I were a madman at home. Everyone will think this, but I will not be put in a lunatic asylum, because I dance very well and give money to anyone who asks me. People like eccentrics, and they will therefore leave me alone, saying that I am a mad clown. I like lunatics because I know how to talk to them. When my brother was in a lunatic asylum, I loved him and he felt me.* His friends liked me. I was then eighteen years old. I understood the life of a lunatic. I know the psychology of a lunatic. I do not contradict a lunatic, and therefore lunatics like me. My brother died in a lunatic asylum. My mother has only a few more hours to live. I am afraid of not seeing her again. I love her and therefore ask God to give her many years of life. I know that my mother and my sister have escaped from Moscow from the Maximalists.† The Maximalists had worn them out. They escaped with my sister's husband, Kochetovsky, and their little daughter Ira, leaving all their belongings behind. They are good people. I love my sister, Bronia. Kochetovsky is

---

* Nijinsky's older brother, Stanislav, or Stassik (1886–1917/1918), fell from a fourth-story window when he was a young child. Thereafter, he was mentally disabled. As an adolescent he was placed in a sanatorium, where Nijinsky visited him. Shortly before beginning the diary, Nijinsky received a letter from his sister, Bronislava, saying that Stassik had died. (Ed.)

† Bronislava (Bronia) Nijinska (1891–1972), like her brother, danced with Diaghilev's Ballets Russes. In 1914, shortly after Nijinsky's dismissal from the company, she and her husband, Alexander Kochetovsky, left the troupe and returned to Russia with their infant daughter, Irina (Ira). Between 1914 and 1919 Bronislava taught ballet, choreographed, and wrote a short treatise on choreography. In 1917, in the midst of the civil war, she had gone to Moscow in the hope of teaching there, but by 1919, the time of Nijinsky's writing, the family, including Eleanora Nijinsky (1856–1932), Bronislava and Vaslav's mother, was living in Kiev. (Ed.) "Maximalists" was another name for Bolsheviks, the reference being to their sweeping, or maximalist, program. (Tr.)

a good man. He has a difficult life because he must think a lot about money. He also thinks about painting. He thinks of writing. He writes well, but does not know art. I know the arts because I have studied them. My wife used to translate things for me that I did not understand. The doorbell is ringing. It is Tessa,* who went off to enjoy herself after my dancing. She does not like me, because she thinks about enjoyment. She wants me to take her into my ballet company. I do not want to take her, because she does not feel her work. She wants to join the ballet company for her own convenience. She wants to help her husband, but she is not thinking about me. She does not care what I do. She enjoys herself while I work. She does not feel my love. I have given her a ring and clothes so that she would feel me. I pretended I was in love, but she did not feel me, because she drinks wine. My wife gives her wine because she knows that Tessa drinks in secret. She is a drunkard. Drunkards do not feel, because they think about wine. My stove-setter is also a drunkard. He drinks all the time. He is ill. I had a premonition of that and told him that I had fallen ill many days before. He fell ill and left the whole house icy cold at a time when I had to prepare my costumes with Negri. I do not like Tessa, because she drinks and enjoys herself, but I do like her because she feels art. She is stupid. She does not understand life. She cannot force her husband not to drink and in fact drinks herself. She drinks Madeira, liqueurs, etc., etc. I am afraid for her because when she feels a dance, she sways. My wife does not sway when she feels a dance. She is a healthy woman, only she thinks a lot. I am afraid for her because I think that thought may prevent her from understanding me. I am afraid for her because she does not understand my aims. She feels them a lot, but she does not know their significance.

* Tessa: Nijinsky's sister-in-law. See footnote on p. 3. (Ed.)

I am afraid of telling her this, because I know she will be frightened. I want to influence her in another way. She obeys me. I obey her. She will understand me if others say that everything I do is good. I am standing in front of a precipice into which I may fall, but I am not afraid to fall and therefore will not fall. God does not want me to fall, because He understands me whenever I fall. I went out for a walk once, and it seemed to me that there was blood on the snow, and so I ran, following the trail. I had the impression that somebody had killed a man, but he was alive, and so I ran in another direction and saw a large trail of blood. I was afraid, but I went in the direction of the abyss. I realized that the trail was not blood, but piss. I do not know any other expression and am therefore writing down this expression. I want to force myself to learn every expression, but I dislike wasting time. I want to describe my walks. When I was walking along the snow, I saw a ski trail that stopped in front of the trail of blood. I was afraid that people had buried a man in the snow because they had beaten him to death with sticks. I was afraid and ran back. I know people who are afraid. I am not afraid, and therefore I came back. I then felt that it was God who was checking to see whether I was afraid of him* or not. I said aloud, "No, I am not afraid of God, because he is life and not death." Then God forced me to go in the direction of the abyss, saying that a man was hanging there and had to be saved. I was afraid. I thought that the devil was tempting me just as he tempted Christ when He was on the mountain, saying, "Jump down, and I will believe in you." I was afraid, but after standing for a while, I felt a force

---

* "God" and pronouns referring to God are sometimes capitalized, sometimes not, in the diary. The same is true of other words, such as "tsar," "emperor," "Tolstoy," and "Dostoevsky." At times Nijinsky takes the decision seriously enough to explain it—indeed, to claim divine guidance for his choice. Elsewhere (in this case, for example) the omission of the capital may be merely accidental. (Tr.)

that was drawing me in the direction of the abyss. I went to the abyss and then fell down, but was caught in the branches of a tree, which I had not noticed. That amazed me, and I thought it was a miracle. God wanted to test me. I understood Him and therefore wanted to disentangle myself, but he did not allow me to. I held on for a long time, but after a while I became afraid. God told me that I would fall if I let go of this branch. I let go of the branch, but did not fall. God said to me, "Go home and tell your wife that you are mad." I realized that God wished me well, and therefore I went home with the intention of breaking this news to her. On the road I again saw the trail of blood, but I no longer believed it. God showed me this trail so that I would feel him. I felt him and went back. He told me to lie down on the snow. I lay down. He ordered me to lie for a long time. I lay there till my hand felt cold. My hand began to freeze. I pulled back my hand, saying that this was not God, because my hand ached. God was pleased and ordered me to go back, but after a few steps he ordered me to lie down again in the snow next to the tree. I caught hold of the tree and lay down, slowly falling back. God commanded me again to remain in the snow. I lay there for a long time. I did not feel the cold, and then God commanded me to get up. I got up. He said I could go back. I went back. He said, "Stop!" I stopped. I came to the trail of blood. He commanded me to go back. I went back. He said, "Stop." I stopped. I know that everyone will think that everything I write is made up, but I must say that everything I write is the absolute truth, because I have experienced it all in practice. I did everything that I am writing about. I will write till my hand gets stiff. I do not get tired, and therefore I will go on writing. Someone is knocking at the door of our house. Everyone is asleep. I do not want to sleep, because I feel a lot. The man outside said, "Oyga." He keeps shouting, "Oyga."

I do not want to wake up my wife and therefore do not want to get out of bed. My wife is sleeping soundly. I hope that the servants will wake up and open the door. My notebook is inconvenient because it keeps slipping. Someone is coming up the stairs. I am not afraid. I think it is Tessa coming back from having enjoyed herself, but this is not so. However, I do not in fact know. God knows. I don't know, because I am a man and not God. If God so desires, I will know, because he will force me to get out of bed. God has given me to understand that this is Tessa. Tessa's room is next to ours, and next to Tessa's room is Kyra's. Kyra sleeps soundly, and therefore she could not have been knocking. The door creaked. I felt that that was Tessa. I know Tessa's movements. She is always nervous, and therefore the door creaked very nervously. She came home at quarter past one in the morning. I looked at my gold watch, which is always correct. I am not afraid of my story, only people are afraid of death. I will continue my story of my walk in St. Moritz.

After I had seen the trail of blood, I turned back sharply and ran, for I was sure that somebody had been killed. I realized that the trail of blood was partly obliterated with a stick so that people would think it was piss. I looked closer and realized that it was piss. After all this I turned back. The whole distance I covered was no more than ten *arshins*,* perhaps a little more. I used to run well. I like running. I feel like a boy. I ran home, glad that these trials were over, but God commanded me to direct my attention to a man who was coming toward me. God commanded me to turn back, saying that the man had killed another man. I ran back. When I got back, I felt blood and hid myself behind a hillock. I crouched down so that the man

---

* Russian measure of length. One *arshin* is equivalent to about 28 inches. Ten *arshins* are therefore equivalent to just over 23 feet. (Tr.)

would not see me. I pretended I had fallen in the snow and was unable to get up. I lay there for a long time. After a while I turned back. When I turned back, I saw the man, who was prodding the snow with a stick. The man was breaking a tree. I realized that the man was looking for something. I took the road that was lower down. The man noticed me but said nothing. Then I wanted to say to him, "Good morning, old man." The old man was busy with something. I do not know what it was, but after a while God commanded me to turn back. I turned back and saw the man digging the snow hard with a stick. I was afraid his stick might break. I felt that this was the murderer. I knew I was wrong, but I felt it. It did turn out to be a mistake. I wanted to go, but suddenly I noticed a bench on which someone had made a little mound and stuck a piece of wood in that mound. It was a fir tree. The fir tree was broken in two, and in the mound there was a big hole. I looked into the hole and thought that the man had made this little mound on purpose. The mound was small, and on it was a cross and under the cross an inscription. I realized that this was his wife's grave. I realized that this man had made this grave because he had thought about his wife. I was frightened and ran, thinking that my wife had fallen ill. I am afraid of death and therefore do not want it. I turned back and took out the tree, but thinking that the man would discover my impudence, I stuck the tree back in again, but I crossed out* the cross, thinking that the man did not understand death. Death is life. Man dies for God. God is movement, and therefore death is necessary. The body dies, but the mind lives. I want to write, but my hand is dying, since it does not want

* Nijinsky uses the word *zacherknul*, which means "cross out," as one crosses out a written word. The fir tree, broken in two, seems to be the cross. In putting it back in the mound, Nijinsky may have reshaped it so that it was no longer in the form of a cross. (Tr.)

to obey me. I will write for a long time today. God wants me to describe my life. He considers it to be good. I said "good," but I thought differently. I am afraid that my life is not good, but I feel that my life is good. I love everyone, but I am not loved. I will continue writing tomorrow, for God wants me to rest . . . .

———

It was not Nietzsche but Darwin who said that man is descended from the ape.* I asked my wife in the morning because I felt sorry for Nietzsche. I like Nietzsche. He will not understand me, because he thinks. Darwin is a learned man. My wife told me that he wrote scholarly things in French called "The History of Nature." Darwin's nature was artificial. He did not feel nature. Nature is life, and life is nature. I like nature. I know what nature is. I understand nature because I feel nature. Nature feels me. Nature is God. I am nature. I do not like artificial nature. My nature is alive. I am alive. I know people who do not understand nature. Nature is a magnificent thing. My nature is magnificent. I know I will be told that I too have studied nature, but I studied nature according to feeling. My feelings are on a large scale, and therefore I know what nature is without studying it. Nature is life. Life is nature. An ape is nature. Man is nature. An ape is not the nature of man. I am not an ape in man. An ape is god in nature because it feels movements. I feel movements. My movements are simple. An

* Prior to his mental breakdown in 1889, Nietzsche spent the summers of 1883–88 in Sils Maria, a village near St. Moritz. Thus he, like Nijinsky, went mad in the Engadine, and it is possibly for this reason that Nijinsky has him on his mind. (Later in the diary Nijinsky compares their two situations.) Romola Nijinsky (*Nijinsky*, p. 354) writes that in early 1919 the stove-setter who served their household, and who, as a child, had run errands for Nietzsche, said to her that Nietzsche "acted and looked, before he was taken away, just like Mr. Nijinsky does now." (Ed.)

ape's movements are complex. An ape is stupid. I am stupid. But I have reason. I am a reasonable being, but an ape is not reasonable. I think that apes are descended from trees and man is descended from God. God is not an ape. Man is God. A man has arms, and so does an ape. I know that in his organic makeup man resembles an ape, but in his spiritual makeup he does not resemble an ape. They think I do not understand what they are talking about in Hungarian. I am writing and at the same time listening to their conversation. My writing does not prevent me from thinking of other things. I am a man with feelings, and therefore I feel Hungarian speech. I stayed with my wife's mother during the war.* I understood the war because I fought with my wife's mother. I wanted to go into a restaurant, but an inner force held me back. By an inner force I mean feeling. I stopped, as if rooted to the spot, in front of a small restaurant frequented by working people. I thought of going in, but was afraid of disturbing them because I am not a workman. Workmen act in exactly the same way as rich people. I wanted to write about my wife's mother and began writing about a small workingmen's restaurant. I like workingmen. They feel more than rich people do. A workingman is the same as a rich man, the only difference being that he has little money. I saw some workmen today and therefore wanted to speak about them. Workmen are just as depraved as aristocrats. They have less money. They drink cheap wine. Cheap wine is always the same. I liked Parisian tarts when I was with Diaghilev.† He

---

* From 1914 to 1916 Nijinsky, interned as an enemy alien by the Hungarian authorities, lived in the home of his mother-in-law, Emilia Márkus, in Budapest. (See introduction, p. xvi.) Later in the diary he returns to the subject of this painful time. (Ed.)

† Sergei Pavlovich Diaghilev (1872–1929) was the founder and director of the Ballets Russes, the company of which Nijinsky was the leading male dancer from 1909 to 1913. During that period, Nijinsky was Diaghilev's lover. Upon Nijinsky's marriage in 1913, Diaghilev fired him. See introduction, pp. viii–x, xiii–xv. (Ed.)

thought I went out for walks, but I was chasing tarts. I used to run around Paris looking for cheap tarts because I was afraid my actions might be found out. I knew that the tarts had no diseases, because the police kept them under observation. I knew that what I was doing was horrible. I knew that if I was found out, I would perish. I know that Tessa likes young men, but she is afraid of being found out. She is the same as I was when I was young. Today I am twenty-nine years old. I am ashamed of confessing my age, because everyone thinks I am younger. I wanted to change my pencil, because my pencil is small and keeps slipping out of my fingers, but I noticed that the other one is worse, because it breaks. God has suggested to me aloud that it would be better to write with a small pencil, because I will not waste time this way. I have now changed my pencil because I am afraid of getting tired writing and I want to write a lot. I went to look for a pencil but did not find it, because the cupboard where the pencils are kept was locked. I then changed several pencils in order to try them out, thinking that it was better to write with a big pencil than a small one. I know that pencils break, and I will therefore write with a fountain pen. A pen that Tolstoy and many businessmen have been writing with these days. I will change my habit because I know that I must not correct anything I have written. Tomorrow I will write in ink because I feel that God wants it. I am now writing with an indelible pencil.* I want to describe my adventures with tarts. I was very young and therefore did silly things. All young men do silly things. I lost my balance and went around the streets of Paris looking for tarts. I looked for a long time because I wanted the girl to be healthy and beau-

---

* An indelible pencil was a pencil with a lead made from a blend of chemicals that resisted erasure. Indelible pencils are now usually referred to by their brand names. (Tr.)

tiful. Sometimes I would look all day long and not find one, because I had no experience in looking for tarts. I made love to several tarts a day. I know that my actions were terrible. I did not like what I was doing, but my habits became more complex, and I took to looking for tarts every day. I knew a terrible place where there were tarts. The place was called a boulevard. I used to walk up and down the boulevard, and I often met tarts who did not feel me. I resorted to all kinds of ruses to get the tarts to take notice of me. They took little notice of me because I was dressed simply. I did not want to be dressed richly, because I was afraid people would notice me. Once I was pursuing a tart who turned in the direction of Lafayette (shop). I suddenly noticed someone looking at me very intently, a young man who was sitting in a cab with his wife and two children, if I am not mistaken. He had recognized me. I received a moral blow, for I turned away and blushed deeply. But I continued to chase tarts. If my wife reads all this, she will go mad, for she believes in me. I lied to her when I said she was the first woman I made love to.* I knew many others before my wife. They were simple and beautiful. Once I made love to a woman who had her period. She showed me everything, then I was horrified and said that it was a shame to do this kind of thing when a person was ill. She said to me that if she did not do this kind of thing, she would starve to death. I told her that I did not want anything, and I gave her money. She begged me, but I would not agree, because I now had a feeling of disgust for her. I left her alone and went away. I found rooms in a small Paris hotel. Paris is full of such small

* In the diary Nijinsky uses the verb "to love," *lyubit'*, in two senses, one sexual (to make love to) and one nonsexual (to feel love for). Later in this paragraph he uses it in both senses in the space of two sentences: "I did not love that woman, but . . . I wanted to make love to her." In any given instance, the meaning must be determined by the context. (Tr.)

hotels. People living in such small hotels are simple. I know many such small hotels that exist by renting rooms for a short time for free love. By free love I mean when people like to excite their member and a woman's womb.* I do not like excitement and therefore do not like to eat meat. Today I ate meat and therefore had a feeling of lust for a woman of the streets. I did not love that woman, but lust drove me after her. I wanted to make love to her, but God held me back. I am afraid of lust because I know what it means. Lust is the death of life. A man in the grip of lust is like a beast. I am not a beast, and therefore I turned back home. On my way God stopped me because He did not want me to go on. Suddenly I noticed that same girl with a man. She would not let him enter a restaurant, then the man tried to persuade her in Italian to enter the little restaurant together with her girlfriend. I stood as if rooted to the spot. My feeling was holding me back. I stood for a long time. After these girls and the man entered the little restaurant, an elderly man slammed the door, saying to me, "Good evening." I said the same to him. I had gotten into the habit of greeting everyone without knowing them. I realized that all people were the same. I often say, but people do not understand me, that everyone has a nose, eyes, etc., and therefore we are all the same. By this I mean that one must love everyone. I love my wife more than anyone else in the world. I told her this today at the table when we were having supper. I do not eat meat, but today God wanted me to eat it. I do not know why, but He wanted it. I carried out His orders and ate meat. I felt sad about it and therefore ate quickly, swallowing large chunks. I did not know for sure what his commands signified, but I carried out his orders. He wanted it that way, for I felt it. People will probably say that Nijinsky is pretending to be mad in order to perform

---

* Nijinsky's term for "vagina." (Tr.)

his horrible acts. I must say that horrible acts are a horrible thing and therefore I do not like them and will not perform them. I used to perform them before, because I did not understand God. I felt him, but did not understand. Everyone does this nowadays. All people have feelings, but they do not understand feelings. I want to write this book because I want to explain what feeling is. I know many people will say that this is my own opinion about feeling, but I know that this is not true, because this opinion emanates from God's commands. I am a man like Christ who fulfills God's commands. I am afraid of the mob because I think that they have bestial intentions and can misunderstand me and will then lynch me. I know what lynching is. Lynching is a terrible thing. Lynching is a bestial act. Lynching is a beast. Lynching is not God. I am God. God is within me. I have made mistakes, but I have corrected them by my life. I have suffered more than anyone in the world. I like Frenkel.* He is a good doctor. He is beginning to feel me. He is beginning to understand me. His wife is intelligent. He loves her and therefore does everything she wants. He invited me to go to a restaurant to see a dancer, Wilson,† but I refused, saying that I could not see him, because I felt sorry for him. Frenkel's wife agreed, and so did he. I invited them to come with us for a carriage drive to Maloja, many versts‡ from St. Moritz. It is a beautiful drive if the weather is good. I like

---

* Hans Curt Frenkel (1887–1938) was a doctor in whom Romola Nijinsky confided when Nijinsky began showing signs of mental imbalance. According to Peter Ostwald's *Nijinsky* (in which, for reasons of confidentiality, he is given the name Dr. Greiber), Frenkel, though not a psychiatrist, attempted to "analyze" Nijinsky, a project which brought him to the house every day. Apparently, he was also conducting an affair with Romola Nijinsky. See introduction, pp. xx–xxi, xxxiii–xxxv. (Ed.)

† There may have been a dancer named Wilson performing at a local restaurant, or Nijinsky may have used this name because he had Woodrow Wilson on his mind. See pp. 36–37 ("Wilson is not a dancer") *et passim*. (Ed.)

‡ A verst is roughly equivalent to a kilometer. (Tr.)

Russian nature because I was brought up in Russia. I love Russia. My wife is afraid of Russia. I do not care where I live. I live where God wills. I will travel all my life if God wills it. I have drawn a picture of Christ without mustache or beard, with long hair. I look like Him, only his eyes have a calm expression, while my eyes are restive. My habits are different from Christ's. He liked sitting. I like dancing. Yesterday I went to see my little girl, Kyra, whose bronchitis made her gasp for breath. I do not know why Kyra has been given a machine for inhaling steam with medicine in it. I am against all medicine. I do not want any medicines to be used. Medicines are artificial things. I know people who take medicine out of habit. People think that medicines are a necessary thing. I believe that medicines are essential only to help people, but they have no sense, because they cannot give health. Tolstoy did not like medicine. I like medicines because they are a necessary thing. I have said that medicines are not necessary because they have no sense. I said the truth because this is so. If you don't believe me, don't. I believe God and therefore write down everything he tells me. My wife told me today that everything I did at last night's party resembled spiritualism, for I kept stopping when I should not have. To that I replied that I did not sway as sometimes happens in spiritualist séances. People in spiritualist trances resemble drunken men, but I was not drunk, because I felt everything I was doing. I am not a drunkard, but I know what a drunkard is, because I have tried wine and have been drunk. I do not want people to drink wine and have spiritualist séances, because this is harmful to health. I am a healthy man, but I am thin because I do not eat much. I eat whatever God commands me to.

I will speak of Nietzsche and Darwin because they thought. Darwin, like Nietzsche, was descended from apes. They imitate those that they themselves have invented. They think they have discovered America. By discovering America I mean that a person says something that has already been said. Darwin was not the first to have invented the ape. The ape is descended from an ape, and that ape from God. God is descended from God, and God from God. I have a good feeling because I understand everything I write. I am a man descended from God, not from an ape. I am an ape if I do not feel. I am God if I feel. I know that many people will admire my mind, and I will be glad because my aim will be justified. I will dance in order to earn money. I want to give my wife a fully furnished house. She wants to have a little boy by me because she is afraid I will die soon. She thinks I am mad, because she thinks a lot. I think little and therefore understand everything I feel. I am feeling in the flesh and not intellect in the flesh. I am the flesh. I am feeling. I am God in the flesh and in feeling. I am man and not God. I am simple. People must not think me. They must feel me and understand me through feeling. Scholars will ponder over me, and they will rack their brains needlessly, because thinking will produce no results for them. They are stupid. They are beasts. They are meat. They are death. I am talking simply, but without any affectation. I am not an ape. I am a man. The world has been created by God. Man has been created by God. It is not possible for men to understand God. God understands God. Man is God, and therefore understands God. I am God. I am a man. I am good and not a beast. I am an animal with reason. I have flesh. I am flesh. I am not descended from flesh. Flesh is created by God. I am God. I am God. I am God. . . . .

I am happy, for I am love. I am the love of God, and therefore I smile to myself. People think that I will go mad, because they think that I will lose my head. Nietzsche lost his head because he thought. I do not think and therefore will not lose my head. I have a hard head, and the inside of my head is hard too. I stand on my head in the ballet "Scheherazade," where I had to represent a wounded beast.* I represented the beast well, and therefore the audience understood me. Now I will represent feeling, and the audience will understand me. I know audiences because I have studied them well. Audiences like to be astonished. They know little and are therefore astonished. I know what is needed to astonish an audience, and therefore I am sure to succeed. Do you want to bet that I will have millions? I want to have millions in order to make the Stock Exchange crash. I want to ruin the Stock Exchange. I hate the Stock Exchange. The Stock Exchange is a brothel. I am not a brothel. I am life, and life is love for people. The Stock Exchange is death. The Stock Exchange robs poor people, who bring all the money they have in order to increase it, in the hope of achieving their goals in life. I love the poor and will therefore gamble on the Stock Exchange in order to beat the stockbrokers. Stockbrokers are all men who gamble on the Stock Exchange with vast sums. Vast sums are death, and therefore sums are not God. I want to win money on the Stock Exchange and will therefore go to Zurich one of these days. My wife is urging me to go to Zurich to see a nerve specialist in order to have my nervous system examined. I have promised her 100,000 francs if she turns out to be right that my nerves are not in order. I will give it to her if the doctor discovers that my nerves are sick. I will not give her that money if she proves to be wrong. I do not have the money, but I have promised it to her. God wants me to gamble on the Stock Exchange. I will gamble, but for that I must stay in Zurich for several weeks. I will go to Zurich one of these days. I have no money, but I

* In his death throes as the Golden Slave at the end of *Scheherazade*, Nijinsky spun on the back of his neck, with his legs in the air. In reporting this, Cyril Beaumont (*Bookseller at the Ballet*, p. 108) wondered whether the feat did not damage Nijinsky's brain. (Ed.)

hope that my wife will give me some. I will go with my wife. She will take me at her expense. I have a little money in the bank, about 200 francs. I will go to the Stock Exchange and use the money to gamble with. I want to lose all the money I have so that God will give me more money. I am sure that God will let me win, and I will therefore go and gamble on the Stock Exchange. I am not afraid of the Stock Exchange, because I know that God wants me to win. He wants me to break the Stock Exchange. I will have money from the Stock Exchange and not from my dancing. I will go to Zurich soon and go to the Stock Exchange in the morning. At the Stock Exchange I will look at the stocks and shares, and then I will buy them. I will buy them with all the money I have. I cannot read German, but I will understand everything I need to.

I was drunk this morning before lunch because I went to Hanselmann's.* I fainted because God willed it. I did not want to be stupid, because I consider that to be death. I cannot force my wife to eat vegetables instead of meat. She eats meat because she likes it. She felt my fist hitting a nut. I hit it all of a sudden, with the strength of a giant. I am very strong. I have a powerful fist. She was frightened of me and said that I hit the nut on purpose. She was right in feeling that I hit it on purpose. She feels me more. I pretended to be ill today as a result of the wine I had drunk at Hanselmann's. I drank one glass after eating some pastries. I felt giddy much later. I went out into the street with Tessa, and after taking a few steps I felt weak in the knees. My knees were giving way. I kept falling almost, and Tessa was pleased with me.

* A café in St. Moritz. (Ed.)

She likes drunkards and is therefore a drunkard herself. I know her habits. She likes men. She gets drunk with them. She is a bad woman because she has many habits. I am a bad man because I do things together with other people. God wanted me to understand Tessa. She went out for a walk with me yesterday so that I would get shoes for her. I bought shoes for her today because she didn't have any. I have shoes and therefore do not need them. I gave her my shoes because they fit her. My feet are slightly larger than Tessa's, but she puts the shoes on awkwardly because she does not understand what she is doing. She feels wine, meat, etc., etc. She does not feel me when I speak to her at the table. She feels wine, meat, etc., etc. I say to my wife on various pretexts, "It's not a good thing to eat meat." My wife understands me but does not want to eat only vegetables, thinking that this is one of my silly notions. I wished her well and asked her not to eat the sausage in the evening, because I know its effect. She says to me, "What is good for you is not good for me." She did not understand me when I told her that people must do as they feel. She thinks, and therefore she has no feeling. I am not afraid of her abandoning me, because I will not marry again. I love her very much and will therefore ask her forgiveness if God wills it. God does not want me to ask forgiveness, because he does not want my wife to eat meat. She eats· quickly because she feels that it is bad.

I gave my wife all my money, but she is not careful with it. I have often told her that if we do not eat meat we will save a lot of money. She listened to me, but afterward she did not do what I had asked her to do. I checked. She loves me and is therefore worried about my health. I told her that if she did not like anything I did, we could get a divorce and I would find her a good and rich husband. I said that I could not live like that, because I had great patience. I became nervous according to God's command and hit Tessa with my fist. My wife got frightened and became nervous. On seeing my wife's nervousness, I went off to write.

Tessa feels me only because I give her a lot of presents. She loves presents. Besides this, Tessa feels music and dancing and understands everything I do. Romola does not feel my plans, but she understands them because she knows that everything I ever planned to do was a success in terms of money and enterprise. Romola is my wife's name. She has an Italian name because her father, Carl de Pulszky,* was a man of great intelligence and one who loved Italy of the past centuries. I do not like past centuries, because I am alive. I cannot write with this ink, because I do not feel it. I like a pencil because I am used to a pencil. I do not know why I picked up the fountain pen, because I can write well with a pencil. I do not have attractive handwriting, because I do not understand fountain pens. I like this fountain pen because it is very convenient. It can be worn in the pocket together with its ink. It is a very ingenious invention, because many people want to have a fountain pen. I do not like fountain pens, because they are not convenient. I will go on writing with mine because I received it as a present from my wife for Christmas. Christmas is a name for a habit that exists all over the world where there are Christians. I do not like Christianity, and therefore I am not a Christian. Catholicism and Orthodoxy are Christianity. I am God and not a Christian. I do not like Christians. I am God and not a Christian. Today I wore the cross that was given to my little Kyra by her grandmother Emma. Emma is the name by which they

---

* Romola's father, Károly Pulszky (1853–99), was an authority on art and the first director of Hungary's National Museum of Fine Arts, as well as a member of the Hungarian parliament. In 1896 he was arrested on a charge of misappropriating government funds. Eventually he left Hungary. He committed suicide in Australia in 1899. (Ed.)

call Emilia Márkus, my wife's mother.* She loves me and loves Kyra too and therefore thinks that she must give all these silly things as presents. She thinks that love is expressed in presents. I believe that presents are not love. Presents are a habit. Presents must be given to poor people and not to those who have a lot. Kyra has enough, and therefore she does not need presents. I give Kyra enough because I earn money by dancing. Emilia puts money in the bank in Kyra's name while her daughter Tessa has no shoes. Emilia does not understand money and therefore throws it around. She knows I understand her, and therefore she loves me. She thinks that for me to love her she must give presents to my Kyra. I would rather she gave these presents to people who have nothing. Emilia is a good woman, she likes the poor and gives a lot to them. I believe that it is not enough to give a lot, but one must help the poor all the time. One must seek out the poor and not give money to institutions. I will dance for institutions only because this gives me a chance to publicize my own person. I want to be a personality for the sake of my aims. My aims are God's aims, and therefore I will do everything to achieve them. I write because God commands me to. I do not want to earn money by writing this book, because we have enough money. I do not want to become rich. God wants me to become rich, because he knows my intentions. I do not like money. I like people. People will understand me when I give them enough to live on. Poor people cannot earn money. Rich people must help them. I am not helping them if I give all my money to a society for the poor. Societies for the poor become rich and are unable to organize things. Societies for the poor put on uniforms to make the poor

---

* Emilia Márkus (1860–1949), Romola Nijinsky's mother, was Hungary's most celebrated classical actress, the star of the Hungarian National Theater. She married Károly Pulszky in 1882 and had two daughters, Teréz and Romola, by him. After his death she married Oscar Párdány in 1903. (Ed.)

fear them. A poor man does not seek out these societies, because he is afraid people will think ill of him. Poor people like informal presents. I give presents informally, without any kind of fuss. I do not talk about Christ when I give presents. I run away from poor people when they want to thank me. I do not like gratitude. I do not give for gratitude's sake. I give because I love God. I am a present. I am God in a present. I love God, and God wants me to give presents because I know how to give them. I will not go like Christ from one apartment to another. I will meet everyone, and they will invite me over. Then I will study their families and help them in every way. By every way I mean every kind of help. Money is not help, but a means of helping. I will not give money, because poor people do not know how to use it. Tessa is poor. She has no clothes and no intelligence. I resort to all kinds of ruses in order to help her. Her husband is a drunkard, and therefore she too is a drunkard. I do not like drunkards and therefore resort to all kinds of ruses in order to make her see reason. She has understood me, but she does not want to change her life. Men who do not want to change their lives are not men. They are descended from Darwin's ape. I am not descended from Darwin's ape, and therefore I have no habits. I am descended from God. My wife is better, only Tessa prevents her from developing. She tells her silly things in Hungarian. I understand Hungarian. Hungarian speech is simple, and therefore it is easy to understand if a man feels. To understand does not mean to know all the words. Words are not speech. I understand speech in all languages. I know few words, but my hearing is very well developed. I like developing my sense of hearing, because I must understand everything that is being said. I like dirty Jews who have lice on their bodies. I know that if they listen to me, they will agree that I am right. They will obey and understand me. Lice are not necessary animals, and therefore lice may be killed.

I am a Jew by origin, for I am Christ. Christ is a Jew. Christ was not understood by the Jews. A Jew is not Christ, for he is a Jew. The Jews are Buddhas. Buddhas are stupid people because they like lice. I kill lice. I kill beasts. I am a predator who kills everything that is harmful to life. I do not call it killing when I do not give food to lice. Lice are found where there is dirt. Dirt is a necessary thing, but not on the body. The body must be clean, because epidemics kill man. Man is a more necessary being than a louse. A louse is a stupid thing. Man is a reasonable thing. The Buddhists did not understand God, for they said that creatures could not be killed. A creature is a thing and not God. God is not a creature in things. I am a creature, but not a thing. I like *peyes*,* but not with lice. Lice like *peyes*, for *peyes* are nests of lice. Lice hate people with short hair. Jews do not like short hair. I like Jews with short hair and with *peyes* without lice. I hate dirt that breeds lice. A Jew scratching his head resembles Darwin's ape. Darwin was an ape, but did not have lice. I love Darwin for his cleanliness. He wrote neatly. I like writing neatly, but I have a bad fountain pen. I received it as a present, and therefore I like this fountain pen. I will write with this fountain pen as long as God wills it. I feel that my hand is tired. The word "Ideal" is written on my pen, but my fountain pen is not ideal. I like ideals, but only those that are never mentioned. I am an ideal. My fountain pen is not an ideal. Ideal is the name given to a perfect thing. I have found a method for an ideal fountain pen, and therefore I will earn a lot of money, only I will ask for a patent because I want to have a lot of money. I know the defects of pens, and therefore when I go to America, I will take out a patent, for I want to have a lot of money. This money I will give to the poor. I will seek out the poor with the help of all kinds of stratagems. I

* Sidelocks worn by orthodox Jews belonging to the Hasidic sect. (Tr.)

will pretend to be dying, sick, etc., etc., so that I can enter poor people's cottages. I feel the poor like a dog sniffing out game. I am a kind dog, which seeks out the poor by its sense of smell. My sense of smell is very good. I will find the poor without their declaring themselves. I do not need people to declare themselves. I will follow my sense of smell. I will not be deceived. I will not give money to poor people, I will give them life. Life is not poverty. Poverty is not life. I want life. I want love. I feel that my wife is afraid of me, because she made some deliberate movements when I asked her to give me some ink. She felt cold, and so did I. I am afraid of cold because cold is death. I will write quickly because I do not have enough time. I would very much like Kostrovsky* to help me, because he understands me. I would be sleeping, and he would be writing, and in this way I could do something else as well. I want to write and think of other things. I write one thing and think of another. I am God in man. I am what Christ felt. I am Buddha. I am a Buddhist and every kind of God. I know everyone. I am acquainted with everything. I pretend to be mad for my own purposes. I know that if everyone thinks I am a harmless madman, they will not be afraid of me. I do not like people who think that I am a madman who would harm people. I am a madman who loves people. My madness is love for people. I have told my wife that I have invented a pen that will bring me a lot of money, but she does not believe it, because she thinks that I do not understand what I am doing. I showed her a pen and a pencil in order to explain to her the pen I have

* Dmitri Kostrovsky, a dancer with the Ballets Russes, became friendly with Nijinsky when the latter rejoined the company in 1916. During the period 1916–17 Kostrovsky, together with his fellow dancer Nicholas Zverev, converted Nijinsky to Tolstoyan philosophy, a development greatly resented by Romola Nijinsky, who saw Kostrovsky and Zverev as agents of a plot by Diaghilev to destroy Nijinsky. Kostrovsky was reportedly epileptic. See introduction, p. xvii. (Ed.)

just invented. I will send my invention to Steinhardt, my lawyer and friend,* and will ask him to make my fountain pen simple and send the patent to me. Steinhardt is a man of intelligence and will therefore understand the power of my invention and will send me the patent, but I want him to learn a lesson, and therefore I will ask him to give this pen to someone to investigate, because I do not know how to make it. I will ask him to send me the money from the sale of the patent. I want to sell the patent for five million dollars. If they agree, I will sell this patent. If they do not agree, I will tear it up. I will ask Steinhardt to announce my invention in a newspaper in large letters, saying that the patent is in the possession of Nijinsky. The pen will be called God. I want to be called God, and not Nijinsky, and will therefore ask for this pen to be called God. I want to have a lot of money and will therefore resort to all kinds of tricks in order to get it. I will go to Paris soon, and there I will find a poor man with whom I will come to an agreement. He will make a drawing of my invention, and I will pay him. He will be my engineer. I will build a bridge, and he will draw it. I will build a bridge between Europe and America that will not cost much. I already know the method for building this bridge, because God has told me. I know the method for building it, and therefore when I arrive in Paris I will devote myself to the realization of this bridge. The bridge will be a magnificent thing. I know magnificent things. I will reveal them if people ask me to. I am not rich, and I do not want riches. I want love, and therefore I want to cast aside all filthy lucre. All money lice will scatter without dying. I will give them life. They will not die of hunger. I am hunger. I am the man who does not die of hunger, for I know what one needs in order

* Laurence Steinhardt was the lawyer employed by Nijinsky in New York in 1916–17 to handle his negotiations with the Ballets Russes and the Metropolitan Opera. (Ed.)

not to die of hunger. I know that one must eat little, then the organism will get used to food, which gives it life. Man will be different, and his habits will be different. He is corrupt and therefore cannot understand simple things. I am not a child prodigy who must be exhibited. I am a reasonable man. Men have existed for millions of years. Men think that God is where things are technically advanced. God was there when man had no industry. Industry means everything that is artificial and invented. I also invent, and therefore I am industry. Men think that in the past there was no industry, but they were turkey cocks,* and therefore historians think that they are gods who have feathers of steel.† Steel is a necessary thing, but feathers of steel are a horrible thing. A turkey cock with steel feathers is horrible. An airplane is a horrible thing. I flew in an airplane and wept in it. I do not know why I wept, but my feeling gave me to understand that airplanes destroy birds. All birds flop down and are killed at the sight of an airplane. An airplane is a good thing, and therefore it must not be abused. Airplanes are a thing of God, and therefore I like them. An airplane must not be used as a war thing. An airplane is love. I love airplanes and will therefore fly where there are no birds. I love birds. I do not want to frighten them. One well-known flier was flying in Switzerland and flew into an eagle. An eagle is a big bird. An eagle does not like birds. An eagle is a predatory thing, but eagles must not be killed, because God has given them life. I am writing God with a capital letter again because that is what god wants. But I will change this because it is simpler to spell it with a small letter. I do not like spelling without hard and

---

* Nijinsky misspells the Russian word *industriya* ("industry") as *indyustriya*. This presumably puts him in mind of *indyuk*, Russian for "turkey cock." (Tr.)

† The Russian words for "feather" and "pen" are the same. Nijinsky may therefore be making a playful connection between the historians' pens and the turkey cocks' feathers. (Tr.)

soft signs, because they complicate spelling and reading.* I like the letters "e" and "ѣ" because they make words distinctive. A word must be distinctive, and therefore I ask the translator to correct my work. I am not a scholar and therefore do not know where to write the letter "ѣ." I know where to write the hard and soft signs. I like other people's corrections and therefore ask always to be corrected in everything. I am a man with faults. I like scholarly men, but I do not like their teachings, because they cause loss of feeling. I do not repeat myself when I write of things that interest the whole world. I know the world and therefore want peace for everyone. I have spelled "peace" with the letter "i" for the sake of distinctiveness, but I am not sure about this letter and therefore ask to be corrected.† When everything I am now writing is published, with its mistakes, I will correct it all. I wanted to have mistakes and therefore put them in on purpose. I learned spelling in two Petersburg schools, where I was given an adequate education.

---

* Nijinsky obviously means the reverse of what he is saying. That is, he means, "I like spelling without hard and soft signs." In fact, however, he uses hard and soft signs. His remarks regarding spelling are occasioned by the reform of the Russian orthography suggested by the Russian Academy in 1904 and made compulsory by the Soviet government in 1918, not long before Nijinsky started writing his diary, when the reform was widely, constantly, and acrimoniously discussed among Russians outside the USSR. The reform included the abolition of certain letters, among them the "hard sign" ("ъ") at the end of certain words—but not the "soft sign" ("ь"), as Nijinsky seems to think—and the letter "ѣ," whose place is now taken by "e," and "i," whose place is now taken by "и." Many, possibly most, Russians, including Nijinsky, living outside the USSR continued to use the pre-reform spelling for some years after 1918. A few still do. (Tr.)

† The Russian words for "world" and "peace" are the same, though spelled differently in the pre-reform orthography ("міръ" and "миръ" respectively, both pronounced "*meer*"). Nijinsky spells them both "миръ." He thus avoids the mistake, of which he accuses himself, of spelling the Russian word for "peace" with an "i." He is equally unfair to himself in saying that he does "not know where to write the letter 'ѣ.'" The manuscript shows that he very seldom, if ever, made the mistake of writing "e" instead of "ѣ" or vice versa—the commonest of all spelling mistakes made by users of the pre-reform Russian orthography. (Tr.)

I had no need for university because I did not have to know so much. I do not like universities, because they occupy themselves with politics. Politics is death. Both domestic and foreign politics. Everything invented for the sake of government is politics. People have lost their way and cannot understand each other and therefore have split up into parties. I forgot about the airplane that hit an eagle. An eagle is a bird of God, and it must not be killed, and therefore tsars, emperors, kings, and others like them must not be killed either. I am not a predatory bird and will therefore not kill predatory birds. I know I will be told that predatory birds are harmful creatures, then I will say exactly the same as I have said about lice that are found in *peyes*. I like tsars and aristocrats, but their actions are not good. I will set them an example and will not destroy them. I will give them a medicine to cure them of drunkenness. I will help them in every way because I am god, but I will ask everyone to help me do this, because I cannot fulfill all god's desires by myself. I want everyone to help me, and therefore I ask people to apply to me for help. I am god, and my address is in god. I do not live at Moika, number . . . . * I live in men. I do not want letters, I want to work on feelings. Spiritualism is not feeling. Spiritualism is an artificial science. I am a simple feeling that everyone has. I do not want people with a bad feeling. I shall feel, and You shall write. I am writing because You are writing. I shall stop when You stop. The war has not stopped, because men think. I know how the war can be stopped. Wilson wants to stop the war, but people do not understand him.† Wilson is

---

* Moika, or, in full, Embankment of the River Moika, is the name of a street in St. Petersburg. (Tr.)

† Nijinsky is writing during the Paris Peace Conference. (See p. 79 ff., where he describes a magazine covering the conference.) In the diary he returns again and again to the subject of World War I and its allied leaders: the American president Woodrow Wilson, the British prime minister David Lloyd George, and the French premier Georges

not a dancer. Wilson is god in politics. I am Wilson. I am reasonable policy. Wilson wants reasonable policy, and therefore he does not like war. He did not want war, but the English forced him into it. He wanted to avoid taking part in the war. He is not for sale. I want to speak, but god will not let me. I wanted to give the name of a politician, but god will not let me, because he does not wish me harm. Lloyd George is a simple man, but he has great intelligence. His intelligence has destroyed his feeling, and therefore his policy has no reason in it. If he listened to Wilson, he would be able to stop the war. Lloyd George is a terrible man. Diaghilev is a terrible man. I do not like terrible men. I will not harm them. I do not want them to be killed. They are eagles. They prevent small birds from living, and therefore one must guard against them. I do not want their death. I love them because god has given them life and he has the right to let them live. It is not for me to be their judge, but for god. I am god, and I will tell them the truth. In telling the truth I will destroy all the evil that they have done. I will prevent them from doing evil. I know Lloyd George does not like people who are in his way and that he has them murdered, and therefore I ask everyone to protect me, since he will kill me. So will Diaghilev. Diaghilev is a smaller man than Lloyd George, but he too is an eagle. Eagles must not prevent small birds from carrying on with their lives, and therefore they must be given things to eat that will destroy their predatory intentions. Lloyd George feeds on the policy of imperialist ideas for Englishmen. Diaghilev is a bad man and loves boys. They must be prevented in all kinds of ways from carrying out these intentions. They must not be locked up in prison. They must

Clemenceau. To him, the aggressive Lloyd George and the pacifist Wilson (who at this time was trying to establish the League of Nations) symbolize "thinking" and "feeling," respectively. (Ed.)

not suffer. Christ suffered, but he did not have to suffer. Christ is not anti-Christ, as Merezhkovsky says. Dostoevsky wrote about a stick with two ends.* Tolstoy spoke of a tree that had roots and branches. A root is not a branch, and a branch is not a root. I like roots because they are necessary. I like the anti-Christ because he is the reverse side of Christ. Christ is God. The anti-Christ is not God. I love the anti-Christ because he is not God. He is the waste product of past experience. The waste product of past experience is museums and history. I do not like history and museums, because they smell of the graveyard. Diaghilev is a graveyard† and therefore is the wrong end of the stick. Dostoevsky is not a stick. Dostoevsky is a great writer who described his life under the guise of different personalities. Tolstoy said that Dostoevsky was someone with a comma.‡ I say that Dostoevsky is God. Dostoevsky spoke of God in his own way. He loved God and understood him. He made a mistake when he sent Nikolai to church. Nikolai or some other name in the "Brothers Karamazov," I don't know, but the one who went to church, is not a comma.§ He went

---

* Dmitri Merezhkovsky (1866–1941), novelist, critic, and religious philosopher, was the leading proselytizer of the "new religious consciousness" of turn-of-the-century Russia. Nijinsky may be recalling the title of Merezhkovsky's *Christ and Anti-Christ*, a trilogy of novels (1896–1905), though Christ and anti-Christ were subjects of much of Merezhkovsky's writing. The Russian expression "stick with two ends" means the same as the English "double-edged sword." (Ed.)

† Diaghilev was a devoted museum-goer and often took his protégés, including Nijinsky, with him, as a way of educating them. (Ed.)

‡ Nijinsky is obviously confusing two Russian words: *zapyataya* ("comma") and *zaminka* ("flaw"). It is the latter that Tolstoy applied to Dostoevsky. In his letter of late November 1883 to N. Strakhov, Tolstoy compared Dostoevsky to a magnificent horse worth a fortune were it not for a temperamental *zaminka* which makes it worthless. Similarly, continued Tolstoy, Dostoevsky had a *zaminka* which "deprived his intelligence and heart of all value." The context implies that in Tolstoy's view Dostoevsky's flaw was one of character. (Tr.)

§ Nijinsky is thinking of Alyosha Karamazov who, in *The Brothers Karamazov*, wants to become a monk. For "comma," understand "flaw," as per the preceding

to church because people look for god there, but god is not in the church. God is in the church and everywhere where he is sought, and therefore I will go to church. I do not like church, because in church they speak not of god but of science. Science is not god. God is reason, and science is the anti-Christ. Christ is not science. The church is not Christ. The Pope is science and not Christ, and therefore men kiss his slippers like the lice that are found in *peyes*. I speak crudely on purpose, so as to be better understood, but not in order to offend people. People will be offended because they will think and not feel. I know that the whole world is infected with this sickness of putrefaction that does not let a tree live. Tolstoy's dream is life, and therefore he must be read. I know his "Karenina," but I have forgotten it a little. "War and Peace" I have read half of. "War and Peace" is his work and therefore must be read, but after his last works. Tolstoy is a great man and writer. Tolstoy was ashamed of being a writer, because he thought he was just a man. Man is a writer. A writer is a journalist. I like journalists who like people. Journalists who write nonsense are money. Money is journalists. I am a journal without money. I like journals. A journal is life. I am a journal in life. Man, journal, life, writer, tolstoy, dostoevsky. Merezhkovsky and Filosofov are Diaghilevs.* They appeared in the journal "The World of Art."

---

footnote. For "is not," understand "does not have." Nijinsky often confuses the notions of "being" and "possessing," and substitutes "to be" for "to have." (Tr.)

* Dmitri Filosofov (1872–1940), a writer on literature and philosophy and a member of the World of Art circle (see introduction, pp. viii–ix), was Diaghilev's first cousin and, for a time, his lover. When Diaghilev, also of that circle, founded the journal *The World of Art* in 1898, Filosofov was made literary editor. Merezhkovsky, who became Filosofov's close friend, contributed to the journal. *Novoye Vremya* ("New Times") and *Rech* ("Speech") were pre-revolutionary St. Petersburg newspapers, conservative and liberal respectively. *The World of Art* was repeatedly attacked in the pages of *Novoye Vremya*, especially in the column of the highly conservative Viktor Burenin. In a 1900 column Burenin added a slur on the editors' morals, referring to the "ultra-swinish" relationship between Diaghilev and Filosofov. (Ed.)

They wrote silly things because they studied. Merezhkovsky writes in a fine style. Filosofov writes intelligently. I know the journalistic controversy between Filosofov and the other news-paper, which is called "Novoye Vremya." "Novoye Vremya" was the candle, and "Rech" was the gasoline. Neither candle nor gasoline is god, for a candle is science about the church and gasoline is science about atheism. Filosofov did not under-stand Merezhkovsky. Merezhkovsky was seeking god and did not find him. Filosofov was Darwin's ape. I wanted to massage my hand because it got tired from writing, but I felt that mas-sage was Filosofov, and left my hand alone. Massage is intel-ligence. I do not like massage. Dr. Bernhard* did not massage my foot, but he told me to come back in order to show him my foot, which I had scratched a little. I did not scratch it terribly badly, and so I did not have to go to the doctor. I like Dr. Bernhard, and therefore I visited him. He will, I think, be offended with me if I do not visit him, for he will think that I consider him a bad doctor. He has noticed that I like him as a surgeon and not as a doctor of medicine. Dr. Frenkel is a doctor of medicine, and I therefore let him earn money too. Dr. Fren-kel and Dr. Bernhard are rich people. I know a very good doc-tor who is called—I have forgotten his name. Dr. God is the doctor I had forgotten. I forgot because I was thinking of the doctor who treated my little Kyra. I called him because I thought he was poor. That doctor is not poor, but he is jealous because he says bad things about Dr. Bernhard. I know Dr. Bernhard. He is a rich man, and I hope he will not ask me to pay him for his visit. I will show him my foot, and while wait-ing I will play sad things because he operates on people. God does not want operations. God does not like science. God does not like Darwin's and Nietzsche's philosophies. God will abol-

---

* Dr. Oscar Bernhard was a surgeon practicing in St. Moritz. (Ed.)

ish disease without the help of medicines. Medicines do not help. Medicines are money. Money does not help life, but complicates it. If Wilson wanted to, he could abolish money. If he does not want to abolish money, he will not be able to understand God. I understand God and therefore will help Wilson in his tasks. I know a method for abolishing money. In my past book* I will describe this method. "I have sent a mosquito on your notebook for your mistake."† I want my mistakes to be printed. I would prefer my handwriting to be photographed rather than printed, because print does away with handwriting. Handwriting is a beautiful thing, and therefore it must be preserved. I want my writing to be photographed so as to explain my hand, because my hand is God's. I want to write in God's way, and therefore I will not correct my writing. I do not correct my writing. I write badly on purpose. I can write very beautifully. I know about writing because I feel it. I do not write beautifully, because I do not want it to be perfect. I am the people, and not an aristocrat with money. I love money, I love aristocrats, but I want love for people. I love the cook, and I love my wife. My wife does not love me or the cook. I understand my wife. I know her habits. She likes being polite. I do not know how to be polite, because I do not want to be. My love is simple. I write without thinking. I scratched my nose, thinking that something was tickling me, but I realized that God did this on purpose so that I would correct my notebook. God writes all this for me and men's‡

God does not want to say things beforehand and therefore stopped. He does not want to say things in advance. I know I

---

* He clearly means "my next book." (Tr.)

† The meaning seems to be: "I have sent a mosquito to land on your notebook so that you would make a mistake." Nijinsky probably intends this as a statement by God. (Tr.)

‡ The sentence is left unfinished in the manuscript. (Tr.)

41

am not God, and therefore I don't care what my hand writes. My hand is getting stiff. God has shown me how a hand can rest, and therefore I know how to cure it. I will stop writing and will be able to write again.

I got up very late, at nine o'clock in the morning, and the first thing I did was to go and write. I write well because my hand is not tired. I will write well, to make everybody see that I can write. I like beautiful handwriting because there is feeling in it. I like handwriting, but I do not like handwriting without feeling. I know that if I show my handwriting to someone who can read the future, he will say that this man is extraordinary, for his handwriting jumps. I know that jumpy handwriting is a sign of goodness, and therefore I will recognize good people by their handwriting. I am not afraid of good people, and the wicked cannot do harm to the good, because I know a way. Diaghilev is an evil man, but I know a way of guarding myself against his evil polemics. He thinks my wife has all the intelligence, and therefore he is afraid of my wife. He is not afraid of me, because I pretended to be a nervous man. He does not like nervous people, but he is nervous himself. Diaghilev is nervous because he is concerned with nerves. Diaghilev excites Massine's nerves, and Massine excites Diaghilev's nerves.* Massine is a very good man, only stingy. Massine's aim is simple. He wants to become rich and learn everything that Diaghilev knows. Massine knows nothing. Diaghilev knows nothing. Diaghilev thinks he is the God of art. I think I am God. I want to challenge Diaghilev to a duel so that the whole world will see. I want to prove that all Diaghilev's art is sheer

---

* Léonide Massine (1895–1979), hired by Diaghilev at age eighteen, replaced Nijinsky as Diaghilev's lead dancer and lover, and eventually as his house choreographer, after Nijinsky's dismissal from the Ballets Russes in 1913. By 1919 Massine had already created several successful ballets. In the twenties and thirties he was to be Europe's foremost ballet choreographer. (Ed.)

nonsense. If people help me, I will help them to understand Diaghilev. I worked with Diaghilev for five years without respite. I know all his tricks and habits. I was Diaghilev. I know Diaghilev better than he does himself. I know his weak sides and his strong sides. I am not afraid of him. Madame Edwards* is afraid of him because she thinks he is the God of art. Sert is her husband, though not on paper. He is her husband because he is living with her. Sert will not marry her, because he thinks it is unworthy of a man of the world to marry a woman who has lived with Edwards. Mme. Edwards feels money. Sert is a rich man because his parents have left him an inheritance. Sert is a silly artist because he does not understand what he is doing. Sert thinks I am silly. Sert thinks I have left Diaghilev for a silly reason. Sert thinks I am silly, and I think that he is silly. I will be the first to slap his face, because I feel love for him. Sert will shoot me if I slap his face. Sert has Spanish blood. Spaniards love a bull's blood and therefore like murders. Spaniards are terrible people because they carry out the murder of bulls.† The church, with the Pope at its head, cannot stop taurocide. Spaniards think that a bull is an animal. Toreadors weep before murdering a bull. Toreadors are paid a lot, but they do not like this occupation. I know many toreadors whose stomachs have been ripped open by bulls. I used to say that I did not like the slaughter of bulls, people did not understand me then. Diaghilev and Massine used to say that a bullfight

---

* Misia Edwards (1872–1950) was a close friend of Diaghilev's and a backer of the Ballets Russes. Married to the newspaper publisher Alfred Edwards, a rich and notoriously vulgar man, she was living at this time with the Spanish painter José-Maria Sert, who designed sets and costumes for several Ballets Russes productions. She married Sert in 1920. (Ed.)

† The pianist Arthur Rubinstein records in his memoir *My Many Years* (pp. 11–12) that he accompanied Nijinsky to what was to have been the latter's first bullfight, in Madrid in 1917. At the entrance gate Nijinsky turned pale and said, "Let's go back. I couldn't stand that." Diaghilev and Massine adored bullfights. (Ed.)

was magnificent art. I know Diaghilev and Massine will say that I am mad and that one cannot take offense with me, because Diaghilev always resorts to this mental trick. Lloyd George does the same thing with politicians. He is Diaghilev because he thinks he is not understood. I understand them both and therefore challenge them to a fight, a bullfight, not a bellowing fight. I bellow, but I am not a bull. I bellow, but a bull that is killed does not bellow. I am God in Bull. I am Apis.* I am an Egyptian. I am an Indian. I am a Red Indian. I am a Negro. I am a Chinese. I am a Japanese. I am a foreigner and a stranger. I am a seabird. I am a land bird. I am Tolstoy's tree. I am Tolstoy's roots. Tolstoy is mine. I am his. Tolstoy lived at the same time as I. I loved him, but I did not understand him. Tolstoy is great, and I was afraid of the great. The newspapers failed to understand Tolstoy, for they exaggerated his stature in one of the papers after his death to make him seem like a giant, thinking in this way to belittle the tsar. I know the tsar is a man, and therefore I did not want his murder. I have spoken about his murder with all foreigners. I am sorry for the tsar because I liked him. He died martyred by men-beasts. The beasts are the Bolsheviks. Bolsheviks are not Gods. Bolsheviks are beasts. I am not a Bolshevik. I like all kinds of work. I work with my hands and feet and head and eyes and nose and tongue and hair and skin and stomach and guts. I am not a turkey cock with steel feathers. I am a turkey cock with God's feathers. I gobble-gobble like a turkey cock, but I realize that I gobble-gobble. I am a gobble-gobble dog, for I have big eyes. I am a gobble-gobble because I like the English. The English are not John Bull.† John Bull's stomach is filled with money,

---

* In ancient Egyptian religion, Apis was the sacred bull of Memphis, thought to be an incarnation of Osiris or Ptah. (Ed.)

† A play on words. Nijinsky's term for "gobble" is *bul*, which happens to be the first syllable in the word *buldog*, Russian for "bulldog." (Hence *bul-bul dog*, here translated

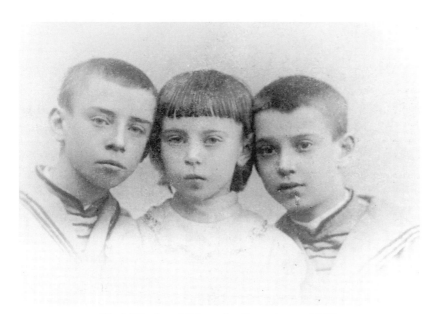

The Nijinsky children, St. Petersburg, 1898.
Left to right: Stanislav, Bronislava, Vaslav
Courtesy of the Fine Arts Museums of San Francisco and the Nijinska Archives

Bronislava Nijinska,
Monte Carlo, 1911
*Courtesy of the Fine Arts
Museums of San Francisco and
the Nijinska Archives*

Serge Diaghilev (*left*) and Nijinsky on vacation in Venice, 1911

Courtesy of the Dance Collection, The New York Public Library for the Performing Arts, Astor, Lenox and Tilden Foundations

Igor Stravinsky (*left*) and Nijinsky—the composer and the star, respectively, of *Petrouchka*—in 1911

Courtesy of the Dance Collection, The New York Public Library for the Performing Arts, Astor, Lenox and Tilden Foundations

Nijinsky, London, c. 1911/12
Photograph by Elliot & Fry. Courtesy of the Dance Collection, The New York Public Library for the Performing Arts, Astor, Lenox and Tilden Foundations

Diaghilev, Lausanne, 1915
Courtesy of the Dance Collection, The New York Public Library for the Performing Arts, Astor, Lenox and Tilden Foundations

Nijinsky studying the score of *Till Eulenspiegel*, New York, 1916

Photograph by White. Courtesy of the Dance Collection, The New York Public Library for the Performing Arts, Astor, Lenox and Tilden Foundations

The Nijinskys' wedding reception, Majestic Hotel, Buenos Aires, 1913. *Left to right:* Ekaterina Oblokova (Dmitri Günsburg's mistress), Dmitri Günsburg (acting director of Ballets Russes in Diaghilev's absence), Josefina Kovalevska (Ballets Russes dancer), Romola, Nijinsky, Mme Rhené-Baton, Rhené-Baton (Ballet Russes conductor)
Courtesy of the Dance Collection, The New York Public Library for the Performing Arts, Astor, Lenox and Tilden Foundations

Romola, Kyra, and Vaslav, New York, 1916
Photograph by Bain News Service. Courtesy of the Dance Collection, The New York Public Library for the Performing Arts, Astor, Lenox and Tilden Foundations

Romola, Kyra, and Vaslav, playing with a rabbit, c. 1916

*Courtesy of the Dance Collection, The New York Public Library for the Performing Arts,
Astor, Lenox and Tilden Foundations*

Tessa Pulszky, Romola's sister, Budapest, c. 1906 *Courtesy of the Nijinsky Archives*

Hans Curt Frenkel, about the age of forty *Courtesy of Séverine Imfeld*

Emilia Márkus, Tamara Nijinsky, and Oscar Párdány, Budapest, 1925/26 *Courtesy of the Nijinsky Archives*

In 1939, after a series of insulin shock treatments that were said to have alleviated his illness (in fact, they apparently exacerbated it), Nijinsky was visited in a Swiss hospital by a group of press photographers, invited there by Romola. Asked to reprise his famous jump, he obliged. The doctor in charge was so angry over the intrusion that he threatened to discharge Nijinsky, but the hospital records note that "the applause gave [Nijinsky] pleasure" (Ostwald, pp. 309–10). This and other photographs of the visit were published in *Paris Match* and *Life* in 1939

Courtesy of the Dance Collection, The New York Public Library for the Performing Arts, Astor, Lenox and Tilden Foundations

Nijinsky at Mittersil Castle in Austria, 1947, three years before his death
Courtesy of the Dance Collection, The New York Public Library for the Performing Arts, Astor, Lenox and Tilden Foundations

but I am filled with guts. I have healthy guts because I do not eat much money. John Bull eats a lot of money, and so his bowels are swollen. I do not like swollen guts, because they prevent me from dancing. The English do not like dancing, because they have a lot of money in their stomachs. I do not like sitting with my legs crossed, but I do sit that way sometimes, so that people will not be frightened of me. I know people who are saying that everything I write is a spiritualist trance. I would like everyone to be in such a trance, because Tolstoy was also in such a trance. So were Dostoevsky and Zola. I like Zola, though I have read little of him. I know the little story about him that helped me to understand him. I want to read a lot of Zola, because he has written a lot. I grieve a great deal for Zola because they bumped him off by gassing him.* I know who bumped him off. He was bumped off by men who were afraid of the truth. I will be bumped off when I want to be. I am not afraid of death, and therefore murderers can follow me around as much as they like. I will give the murderer more money than he got from the man who wanted to kill me. I do not want my murderer's death, and therefore I ask, when I am murdered, that the murderer not be lynched or killed in any other way, because it is not his fault. A murderer goes to his death. Lloyd George is a murderer because he has killed millions of innocent people. I am one man in a million. I am not alone. I am a million, for I feel more than a million. Lloyd George will send murderers, and therefore I ask him to be careful. Lloyd George is a murderer of reason. Reason is life and not death. I am writing philosophy, but I do not philosophize. I do not like philosophizing, for philosophizing is idle

as "gobble-gobble dog.") *Bul* also reminds him of John Bull, the symbol of England. (Tr.)
* On Zola, see footnote on pp. 83–84. (Ed.)

chatter. I am wearing the tie of a turkey cock and turkey hen. A woman and a man are the same thing, and therefore women's representatives are unnecessary. I would prefer married people because they know life. Those who are married make mistakes, but they have life. I am both wife and husband. I love the wife. I love the husband. I do not like a wife and a husband who do depraved things while they look at depraved Japanese books and other books* and then go through all the motions of bodily love. I am flesh, but I am not carnal love. I want to write quickly, because I want to publish this book before I go to Paris. I want to publish this book in Switzerland. I am not afraid of the government, and therefore they can expel me as much as they like. I am not a Bolshevik or some kind of rebel. I am love for human beings. I want the government to allow me to live where I want to. My wife is a good woman, and so is my child, and therefore they should not be touched. If the English get frightened of me and send murderers to Switzerland, I will shoot them dead before they shoot me dead. I will be put in prison for life because the English want it. The English are incredibly evil people. They have recourse to all kinds of hypocritical tricks. An Englishman is a hypocrite. An Englishman is not God. God is the Englishman who has reason and not intelligence. In England people devote themselves to spiritualism in order to find out everything before other people. I am not spiritualism. I am life, and therefore I want to live. I ask the people of Switzerland to take care of me. I want to publish this book in the Swiss language because I live in Switzerland. I like simple Switzerland. I do not like a Swiss who is a turkey cock with steel feathers. I want to publish this book

* According to Ostwald (*Nijinsky*, p. 186), Dr. Frenkel had shown Nijinsky some erotic engravings in a Japanese book. This was apparently an effort to induce him to reveal his sexual fantasies, as part of his "analysis." See also p. 177. (Ed.)

in Switzerland in a very cheap edition. I want to make a little money because I am poor. I have no money, but I live like a rich man. I am a hypocrite-Englishman, for I invent all kinds of ways to stave off my creditors. I do not like creditors. I do not like being a debtor. I want to gamble on the Stock Exchange. I want to steal. I want to kill a rich man, but what I want is not the death of his body but the death of his intellect. I am not the intellect. I am reason. With the help of reason I will achieve more than with the help of the intellect. I have composed a ballet in which I will show intellect and reason and the whole life of men, only I must be helped in this. I thought of Vanderbilt, but changed my mind because Vanderbilt gives money on loan. I do not like debtors, and therefore I will earn the money for this ballet myself. Diaghilev is a debtor. Diaghilev owes me money. Diaghilev thinks that he will pay everything back to me. Diaghilev lost his lawsuit in Buenos Aires.* I won my lawsuit in the amount of 50,000 francs. Diaghilev owes me about 20,000 francs more. I do not want 50,000 francs, but I want the money I have earned that Diaghilev still owes me, as a result of the lawsuit won by my English lawyer, Lewis. In English he is called "Sir Lewis." I do not like Sirs, and therefore they do not know how to shit. I shit in a human way, I do not shit money. I like money for the help it can give and not in order to fill John Bull's guts. I am an Englishman, but without money in my stomach. A bank is John Bull. The English have understood John Bull well, but they have not felt

---

* In 1914, soon after his dismissal from the Ballets Russes, Nijinsky brought a lawsuit against Diaghilev for unpaid wages. In 1916 he was notified that his lawyer, Sir George Lewis, had won a settlement of 50,000 francs. When Nijinsky rejoined the Ballets Russes in New York in 1916, he refused to dance until Diaghilev paid him a part of this money. Though the lawsuit was filed in London, Nijinsky's financial dispute with Diaghilev began while he was on the South American tour of 1913. Hence, presumably, his description of the suit as a "lawsuit in Buenos Aires." (Ed.)

him. I want to hide this notebook because Tessa has felt that I know her tricks. She knows that I am intelligent, because I have proved it to her. She is called "Tiger Cub." She has claws on her feet like a tiger. She looks after the cleanliness of her nails, but not after her woman's womb. I do not like women who take excessive care of their wombs. Her piss is full of leukorrhea. She forgot her chamber pot in her room, and when I entered the room to air it and get rid of the stench, I saw the chamber pot full of piss. My wife's piss is clean. Tessa's piss is dirty. I realized that she took too much care of her womb. She takes care of it for many reasons. Firstly because she makes love to men and secondly because her husband once had a venereal disease. Tessa told me all this when we were in Vienna during the war. I have not forgotten any of the things I have been told. Tessa looks at me with hatred, thinking that I do not like her. She felt that I loved her and burst into tears, for I gave her to understand that I would give her a ring. She liked the ring. I do not like the ring. I do not want her to be put to shame. I want to tell the whole truth. I am not afraid of her husband, and therefore I will publish this book in her lifetime. I will be put on trial, but I do not care. She will say that I am the same as Dodo Hampel.* Dodo Hampel is Diaghilev. Dodo Hampel must work for Diaghilev. I am not Hampel. I am God in man. I say this deliberately so that everyone will know what Tessa does. I do not wish her harm and will therefore help her in every way, so that she does not die of hunger. Tessa is a cunning woman. She can fool anyone. Tessa thinks that no one understands her tricks. I have understood Tessa very well because I have noticed that she flirts with me. She used to lie down on the bed in her underwear in order to excite my lust. She thinks she can excite lust with the help of silk panties. She

---

*   The meaning of Dodo Hampel has not been decoded. (Ed.)

wears small silk panties and thin camisoles in order to excite. I understand Tessa well. I know her tricks. These tricks are like those of a tiger that is waiting for its prey. I used to come into her room on purpose when she was naked. She did not feel shame in front of me. A woman brought up like a lady must feel shame in front of men. Tessa has seen many men, because she does not feel shame in front of them. Tessa called in Dr. Frenkel to settle a family quarrel. I am not a quarrel and therefore did not quarrel. I told the truth both to my wife and to Tessa. I am not afraid of divorce. I told Dr. Frenkel that he was a very good man. He was touched. I shook him by the hand. My wife was frightened of me because I came running into the room where Tessa was. Tessa is a cunning woman and therefore called in the doctor. The doctor is a good man. I like him because he wants to make everything right again. Tessa does not like me, because she came in with the ring and the shoes I had given her, and spoke about me. She felt my words in German. I understand German. I will ask her to leave as soon as possible if she gives me back my ring and shoes. I know that she will not give them back, because she has no conscience. In St. Moritz she made love to several men. I noticed this because I watched her. I know her tricks. She is afraid of me because she thinks I am bad. She knows me. I know her. I will tell her later that if she gives my presents to anyone, she will have her face slapped by me. I will say this to her at the railroad station before she leaves. I will find out by chance if she gives these things away to other people. I will go and look for a scarf that she has given to a man as a present. I know this man. I will ask him to give back the scarf, and I will give it to my wife. I will say that I have found it. I will not say that I have taken it from Tessa. Tessa walks the streets in order to find a man. I know she will sell the shoes and my ring and will therefore have her face slapped by me. I don't touch the face.

49

I slap by loving. I will give her this book as a present. I no longer speak to Tessa. Before she leaves I will tell her that I know her cunning character and that I will write everything I know about her. She will think that I know nothing. I know her habits. She smiles at young men and makes love to them free of charge. She is a man and not a woman, because she seeks men out. She loves a prick. She needs a prick. I know pricks who do not love her. I know that everyone will be ashamed of this word, and that is why I wrote it, because I want everyone to know what life is. I do not like a hypocritical life. I know what life is. Life is not a prick. A prick is not life. A prick is not God. God is a prick who breeds children with one woman. I am a man who breeds children with one woman. I am twenty-nine years old. I love my wife, but not in order to breed children, but spiritually. I breed children with her if God wills. I will not breed them because I am afraid of her. I do not want learned children. Kyra is an intelligent girl. I am a reasonable man. I do not want her to be intelligent. I will try to prevent her in all kinds of ways from developing her intelligence. I like stupid people. I do not like stupidity, because I do not see feeling in stupidity. Stupidity is not feeling in man. I know that stupid people do not feel. Intelligence does not allow people to develop. I am an intelligent man because I feel. I feel God, and God feels me. I love Tessa and therefore wish her well. Tessa does not love me, because she knows that I do not love her. I do not like Tessa's habits, because I know they are death. I love Tessa because she is a human being. I do not want her death. I want to frighten her, because I wish her well. Tessa has forgotten me because she thinks that Dr. Frenkel has frightened me. Tessa understands me, but does not feel me. Tessa does not want to feel, and therefore she is a beast, a "Tiger." I wanted to nickname her "Tiger Cub," but I thought that was too beautiful a name. I wish Tessa well. I will stand in the way of everything she tries to do. She does not love me. Tessa does not love me, but she loves Dr. Frenkel, hoping for his love. The doctor does not love Tessa, because he feels her glances. Dr. Frenkel loves his wife. Frenkel's wife loves him as a man. She is very cunning. I have noticed her cunning tricks. She is like a monkey with feeling. She runs around like a squirrel in a cage. Dr. Frenkel is not a squirrel, and therefore he feels more love for her than she does for him. Dr. Frenkel is a good man. I did not understand him and thought he was bad. He is not bad, for he wants to help people. I know that help is not the duty of doctors. The duty of doctors is medical help. I do not want people's help when I see that doctors meddle in things that are outside their duties. Dr. Frenkel spoke to me as a friend, and therefore I listened to him. I knew what he would be talking about before he started speaking. He noticed that I had become nervous. I told him that I was not God, but man, and that therefore I had faults. I am a man with faults. I want to correct them, but I do not know in advance whether I will be able to correct them. Dr. Frenkel felt a tear and told me that he had no need of promises, for I had said to him that I would do everything for my wife not to be nervous. I said that I wanted her mother to come as soon as possible, because I did not want my wife to be afraid of me, and so I want Emma, my wife's mother, to live with us. I am not afraid of the English authorities and therefore do not care if they take all my money. I do not want my money to be taken and therefore will resort to all sorts of cunning tricks. I do not want to ruin my wife. I have given her my money to live on. I am not afraid of life and therefore do not need money. My wife will weep if I die, but I know that she will soon forget me. My wife does not feel me. Tolstoy's wife does not feel either. Tolstoy's wife cannot forget, because he gave her money. I have given money to my wife. My wife feels me because I have given her all my money. I do

51

not like boasting and will therefore stop talking about money. I love my wife and Kyra more than anyone. I cannot write quickly, because my hand gets tired, but I know that I will soon get used to it, because I will not think about the letters of the alphabet. I am already writing better, I do not know how to stop, and therefore I write badly. I do not like Shakespeare's Hamlet, because he thinks. I am an unthinking philosopher. I am a philosopher with feeling. I do not want to write artificial things. I like Shakespeare because of his love for the theater. Shakespeare understood the theater as an invention. I understand the theater in life. I am not an invention. I am life. The theater is life. I am the theater. I know its habits. The theater is a habit, and life is a non-habit. I am without habit. I do not like a theater with a square stage. I like a round theater.* I will build a round theater. I know what an eye is. An eye is a theater. The brain is the audience. I am the eye in the brain. I like looking in a mirror and seeing one eye in my forehead. I often draw one eye. I do not like an eye in a red cap with black stripes. I like an eye with hair on the head. I am God's eye, and not a warlike eye. I dislike polemics, and therefore people can write what they like about my book and I will be silent. I have come to the conclusion that it is better to be silent than to talk nonsense. Diaghilev realized that I was stupid and told me not to speak. Diaghilev is an intelligent man. Vassili, his valet, used to say that Diaghilev did not have a penny but that his intelligence was worth a fortune. I will say that I don't have

---

* Romola Nijinsky (*Nijinsky*, p. 344) reports that by 1918 Nijinsky had become fascinated with circles and arcs. She recalls his telling her, "The circle is the complete, the perfect movement. Everything is based on it—life, art." He was planning a Renaissance ballet with circular choreography, curved scenery, and a rounded proscenium. His notation system was based in part on the circle, and his drawings, as he notes, often involved an eye shape formed by the joining of two arcs. (See introduction, pp. xix, xxxvii–xxxviii.) Here he seems to visualize a theater designed to imitate the curve of the eye. (Ed.)

a penny either and no intelligence, but I have reason. By reason I mean what is felt well. I feel things well and therefore am a rational creature. I was stupid before, because I thought that money was happiness, now I do not think about money. I know many people will say that I think about money, then I will reply that I am stupid and understand nothing about money. I need money for my plans. I will be told that all people have plans and therefore earn money to carry out their plans. I know that plans can be different. I am God's plan, and not the anti-Christ's. I am not the anti-Christ. I am Christ. I will help people. I will go to Geneva for a rest because the doctor has ordered me to do so. He thinks I am tired, because my wife is beginning to get nervous. I am not nervous, and therefore I will stay at home. My wife can go alone. She has a lot of money. I don't have a penny. I am not boasting about the fact that I have no money. I like having money, and therefore I will try to get some in order to give it to my wife and the poor. I know many people will say that Nijinsky pretends to be Christ. I do not pretend, because I love his actions. I am not afraid of attacks, and therefore I will say everything. I know Tessa. She went out into the street just as I used to go out when I was already married. I used to deceive my wife because I had so much semen that I had to ejaculate. I ejaculated not into a tart, but onto my bed. I used to put on a condom and thus was not infected with venereal disease. I am not a venereal disease, and therefore I will not deceive my wife anymore. I have a lot of semen and am keeping it for another child, for I hope that I will be presented with the gift of a boy. I love my wife and therefore wish her no harm. She feels me and therefore fears me. She thinks I do everything in order to frighten her. I do everything for her health. She eats meat and is therefore nervous. I ate meat today, because God wanted it. God wanted to prove that the important thing is not meat but a correct life.

My wife knows that a correct life is a good thing, but she does not know what a correct life is. A correct life means a life of obedience to God. Men do not understand God and therefore ask themselves what kind of God it is that must be obeyed. I know what God is, and therefore I know his wishes. I love God. I do not know what to write, because I was thinking of Frenkel and my wife, who are talking in another room. I know they do not like the things I am up to, but I will continue to do them as long as God wants it. I am not afraid of any complications. I will ask everyone to help me and will therefore not get frightened if they tell me, for instance, "Your wife has gone mad because you have worn her out, and we have therefore put you in prison for life." I am not afraid of prison, because I will find life there. I will die in prison if they put me in for life. I do not wish my wife any harm. I love her too much to do her any harm. I like to hide myself from people and am therefore used to living alone. Maupassant was terrified of loneliness. Monte Cristo liked loneliness for revenge.* Maupassant was terrified of loneliness because he liked people. I will be terrified of loneliness, but I will not weep, because I know that God loves me and therefore I am not lonely. I feel in advance what will happen to me if God abandons me. I know that if God abandons me, I will die. I do not want to die, and therefore I will live as others do, so that people will understand me. God is people. God does not like those who interfere with his purposes. I do not interfere with his purposes, but rather the reverse. I am god's instrument. I am a man of god. I love men of god. I am not a sponger. I will take money if a rich man leaves me some. I love rich men. I know what a

---

* Guy de Maupassant, like Nietzsche, may be on Nijinsky's mind because his career was ended by insanity. In *The Count of Monte Cristo*, by Alexandre Dumas *père*, the hero, unjustly imprisoned, uses his years of solitude to plot revenge on his enemies. (Ed.)

rich man is. A rich man has a lot of money, and I do not. I know that when everybody discovers that I am not rich, they will all get frightened of me and turn away from me, and I will therefore get richer and richer by the hour. I know ways of getting rich. I will hire a horse and will order the horse to take me home free of charge. My wife will pay. If she does not pay, I will find a way of paying. I want my wife to love me, and therefore I do everything for her development. The development of her intellect is great, but the development of her feeling is small. I want to destroy her intellect so that she will develop. I know many people will say that a man without an intellect is mad or a fool. A madman is not a reasonable being. A madman is a man who does not understand his own actions. I understand my own bad and good actions. I am a man with reason. In Tolstoy's book "For Every Day," a lot is said about reason. I have read this book a lot, and therefore I know what reason is. I am not afraid of intelligent people. Intelligent people are afraid of rational people because they feel their power. I am powerful because I feel what is being said about me. I know they are trying to think up ways of making me calm down. Dr. Frenkel is a good man. My wife is good too, but they think a lot. I am afraid for their intellect. I know people who have gone mad because of great thoughts. I am afraid for them because they think a lot. I do not want to go mad, and therefore I will do everything for the sake of their health.

I used to hurt my wife by failing to understand her, and I used to say I was sorry, then they constantly repeated to me all my faults whenever the occasion arose. I am afraid of my wife because she does not understand me. She thinks that I am either mad or bad. I am not bad, because I love her. I describe life and not death. I am not Nijinsky, as they all think. I am god in man. I like Dr. Frenkel because he feels me. Dr. Frenkel is a good man. My wife is good too. My wife thinks that I do everything on purpose. I told her in secret about my plans. She told Frenkel, thinking this would be good for me. My wife does not understand my aim, for I did not reveal it to her. I do not want to reveal it to her. I will feel, and she will understand. I will understand, and she will feel. I do not want to think, because thinking is death. My wife is afraid of me because she thinks that I am a bad man. I know what I am doing.* I do not wish you harm. I love you. I want life, and therefore I will be with you. I spoke to you. I do not want intellectual talk. Frenkel's talk is intellectual, so is my wife's. I am afraid of them both. I want to let them feel you. I know you feel hurt. Your wife is suffering because of you. I do not want death, and therefore I resort to all kinds of tricks. I will not divulge my aim. Let them think you are an egoist. Let them put you in prison. I will free you because I know that you are mine. I do not like the intelligent Romola. I want her to leave you. I want you to be mine. I do not want you to love her as a man loves. I want you to love her with a feeling love. I know a way of simplifying everything that has happened. I want Dr. Frenkel to feel you. I want to blame you, because he thinks that your wife is a nervous woman. Your cross has done so much harm that you cannot disentangle yourself.† I know your mistakes because I have committed them. I put on the cross deliberately, because she felt you. Dr. Frenkel feels you. He came on purpose to study your intentions and does not understand anything. He

---

* In this and the next two paragraphs, Nijinsky speaks intermittently in the voice of God, addressing himself as "you." (Ed.)

† According to Romola Nijinsky (*Nijinsky*, pp. 354–55), Nijinsky one day in January 1919 went into St. Moritz wearing a large gold cross belonging to Kyra over his necktie. He stopped people on the street and told them to go to church. (Ed.)

feels that you are right. He feels that Romola is right. He thinks and therefore finds it difficult to understand. I know how it is possible to understand. I think better than Dr. Frenkel. I am afraid for you because you are afraid. I know your habits. Your love for me is infinite, for you obey my commands. I know what I think. You know what you think. We will know what we think. I will do everything for your comprehension. I love your wife and you. I wish her well. I am God in you. I will be yours when you understand me. I know what you think. He is here and is looking at you intently.* I want him to look at you. I do not want to turn around because I feel his gaze. I do not want to show him your writing. He will think that you are ill, because you write a lot. I know your feelings. I understand you well. I wrote on purpose because he feels you. I want you to write everything I tell you. People will understand you because you feel. Your wife will understand you because you feel.

I know more than you do, and therefore I ask you not to turn around. I like Frenkel. Frenkel is a good man. I know your intentions. I want to carry them out, but you must suffer. Everyone will feel if they see your suffering. I knew he was upstairs. You are mistaken, for you felt me. I wanted you to feel that Dr. Frenkel was here.

I want to tell of my conversation with my wife and Dr. Frenkel in the dining room. I pretended to be a selfish man in order to touch Dr. Frenkel's heart. I know he will take offense if he discovers my tricks, but I don't care, because I am not a malicious man. I love my wife and Dr. Frenkel equally. I am a man with an equal love. My love is the same for everyone. I

---

* Here Nijinsky seems to think that Dr. Frenkel has entered the room. In the next paragraph he decides that he was mistaken, that God just wanted him to think this. Later in the diary he will again feel a steady gaze behind him. (Ed.)

do not differentiate in love. I wrote that I loved my wife more than anyone else, because I want to show my relationship to my wife. I love Tessa deeply, only she does not understand me. I know her tricks. She feels me because she is going away one of these days. I do not want her presents. I want my wife's mother to come, because I want to study her in order to help her. I do not study people in order to write about them afterward. I want to write in order to explain to people the habits that make feeling die. I want to call this book "Feeling," I will call this book "Feeling." I like feeling and will therefore write a lot. I want a big book about feeling because it will contain your whole life. I do not want to publish the book after your death. I want to publish it now. I am afraid for you because you are afraid for yourself. I want to tell the truth. I do not want to offend people. Perhaps you will be put in prison for this book. I will be with you because you love me. I cannot keep silent. I must speak. I know that you will not be put in prison, because you have not committed a legal error. If people want to judge you, you will say that everything you say is said by God. Then you will be sent to a lunatic asylum. You will be confined in a lunatic asylum, and you will understand the lunatics. I want you to be put in prison or in a lunatic asylum. Dostoevsky did a spell of hard labor, and therefore you too can be committed somewhere. I know men whose love never falters within them, and therefore they will not allow you to be committed anywhere. You will be free as a bird, for this book will be published in many thousands of copies. I want to sign "Nijinsky" for the sake of publicity, but my name is God. I love Nijinsky not like Narcissus but like God. I love him, for he gave me life. I do not want to pay compliments. I love him. I know his habits. He loves me, for he knows my habits. I am without habits. Nijinsky has habits. Nijinsky is a man with faults.

Nijinsky must be obeyed because he speaks with the tongue of god. I am Nijinsky. Nijinsky is I. I do not want Nijinsky to be hurt, and therefore I will protect him. I am afraid for him because he is afraid for himself. I know his power. He is a good man. I am a good god. I do not like a bad Nijinsky. I do not like a bad God. I am God. Nijinsky is God. Nijinsky is a good and not an evil man. People have not understood him, and will not understand him if they think. I know that if I were obeyed for several weeks at a stretch, great results would ensue. I know that everyone will want to learn from me, and therefore I hope that my preaching will be understood. Everything I write is a teaching essential to mankind. Romola is afraid of me because she feels that I am a preacher. Romola does not want to have a preacher for a husband. Romola wants a young, good-looking, and rich husband. I am rich, good-looking, and young. She does not feel me, because she does not understand my beauty. I do not have regular features. Regular features are not god. God is not regular features. God is feeling in face. A hunchback is God. I like hunchbacks. I like ugly people. I am an ugly man with feeling. I dance hunchbacks and straight-backs. I am the artist who loves all shapes and all kinds of beauty. Beauty is not a relative thing. Beauty is god. God is beauty with feeling. Beauty is in feeling. I love beauty because I feel it and therefore understand it. Thinking people write nonsense about beauty. Beauty cannot be discussed. Beauty cannot be criticized. Beauty is not criticism. I am not criticism. Criticism is an attempt to be clever. I do not try to be clever. I flaunt my beauty. I feel love for beauty. I am not looking for straight noses. I like straight noses. I like my wife's nose because it has feeling.

I do not want evil, I want love. I am taken for an evil man.
I am not evil. I love everyone. I have written the truth. I have
told the truth. I do not write untruths. I want good, and not
evil. I am not a bogeyman. I am love. I am taken for a bogeyman because I once put on a little cross that I liked. I wore
it to show people that I was a Catholic. People thought that I
was mad. I was not mad. I wore the cross to make people pay
attention to me. People like calm men. I am not a calm man. I
love life. I want life. I do not like death. I want love for people.
I want to be believed. I told the truth about Tessa, Diaghilev,
Lloyd George, and myself. I am a bad man because I want the
good. I do not want wars, and therefore I want to make people
understand me. I do not want murders. I told my wife that I
would shoot anyone who read my notebooks. I will weep if I
shoot. I am not a murderer. I love human beings. I know no
one likes me. They think I am ill. I am not ill. I am a man with
reason. The maid came and stood near me, thinking that I was
ill. I am not ill. I am a healthy man. I am afraid for myself
because I know what god wants. God wants my wife to abandon me. I do not want this, because I love her. I will pray that
she remains with me. I do not know what they are telephoning
about now. I think they want to put me in prison. I am weeping
because I love life. I am not afraid of prison. I will live in
prison. I have explained to my wife about the revolver. She is
no longer afraid, but she has a bad feeling. She thinks I am a
bandit. I spoke to her sharply in order to make her weep, because I like tears. I do not like tears caused by grief, and
therefore I will go and kiss her. I want to kiss her, but not to
make her think that I want to show my love. I love her without
having to show it. I want her. I want her love. Tessa has felt
that I love her, and she will stay with us. She is not going. She
has telephoned to ask that her tickets be sold. I do not know
for sure, but I feel it. My little girl is singing: Ah! Ah! Ah! Ah!

I do not understand the meaning of this, but I feel its meaning. She wants to say that everything, Ah! Ah! is not horror but joy.*

I can no longer trust my wife, for I have felt that she wants to give these notebooks to Dr. Frenkel for him to examine. I said that no one had the right to touch my notebooks. I do not want people to see them. I have hidden them, and this notebook I will carry around with me. I will be hiding all my notebooks because people do not like the truth. I am afraid of people because I think they will bump me off. I love people even if they do bump me off, because they are god's creatures, but I will loathe them for their bestial actions. I love my wife. She loves me, but she thinks that Dr. Frenkel is God. Dr. Frenkel is not God. I am. I love Dr. Frenkel. I know his habits. I understand him. He wants to examine my brain. I want to examine his mind. I have already examined his mind. He cannot examine my brain, because he has not seen it. I have written some poetry for him. This poetry I have written on purpose so that he could see my brain. I wrote rational things. Dr. Frenkel's questions were not rational, because he wanted to examine my nerves. I answered him quickly and logically. My wife answered him quickly and illogically. I wrote some poetry for him to keep in memory of me. He did not want to take one poem, because he thought that that poem would not be important from the psychological point of view. The doctor did all this on purpose, thinking that I did not understand what I was doing. I understand everything I do, and therefore I am not afraid of their attacks. Dr. Frenkel is in Samedan today.

* The diary text in the first notebook ends here. (Ed.)

He thinks I do not know his tricks. He thinks I have lost my reason. I played, on purpose, the part of a man without reason so that he would put me into a lunatic asylum. I know that Tessa telephoned Dr. Frenkel about me. I am not afraid of their tricks. I know the love of my wife. She will not leave me. She is afraid of me, but she will not leave me. I am afraid that I will be taken to a lunatic asylum and that I will lose all my work. I have hidden my notebooks behind a cupboard. I love my notebooks too much to lose them. I have written necessary things. I do not want the death of feeling. I want people to understand. I cannot weep, for fear that my tears will fall on my notebooks. I weep in my soul. I am sad. I love everyone. I write quickly but neatly. I know that people like my handwriting. I like writing neatly because I want people to understand my writing. I am not afraid of print. I like print, but print cannot convey the same feeling as writing. I do not like typing. I do not like shorthand. I like shorthand when one wants to write things down quickly. I consider it essential to know shorthand. I will speak quickly, and my speech will be taken down in shorthand. I like shorthand. I do not want shorthand-writers to sacrifice their whole lives to shorthand. I like the shorthand that takes down Wilson's speeches. I do not like the shorthand that takes down Lloyd George's speeches. I like both shorthands because I want people to understand their meaning. Without Lloyd George's speeches it is not possible to understand Wilson's speeches. I want Wilson to achieve his aims, because his aims are nearer to truth. I feel Wilson's death. I am afraid he might get a bullet through the head or some other part of his body that will not be able to take it. I was afraid Clemenceau might die.* Clemenceau is a good man. He has a stupid policy, and therefore his life hangs by a thread.

* Georges Clemenceau, at that time premier of France. See footnote on pp. 36–37. (Ed.)

People feel his mistakes. People think that Clemenceau is a Frenchman. I think that Clemenceau is an Englishman. I know that he was educated in France. I know that his mother and father are French. I know that his brain is in the possession of Englishmen. He does not know this, and therefore his life is hanging by a thread. I like Clemenceau because he is a child. I know children who do terrible things without meaning to, because they have terrible French governesses. Clemenceau is a child, and England is the governess who teaches him English. A Frenchman cannot give up his own language and study another, because a Frenchman is a live human being. The English want to force France to have her cockerel wear an English cap.* The French cockerel does not like being contradicted, and therefore they want to shoot the cockerel. The cockerel cannot fly, because it eats a lot. The English do not eat a lot, and therefore it is difficult to kill them. An Englishman eats a lot after he has fed the French cockerel. The French cockerel will burst after eating a lot, and the Englishman will then pick up the pieces. Lloyd George does not know that people will realize what he is up to, and therefore he carries his head high. I want to lower Lloyd George's head, and therefore I want to publish this book after his death. His death will be unexpected because he thinks that everyone loves him. I love him, but I write the truth. I know that if Clemenceau reads this notebook, he will understand me. I want to show him this notebook before anyone else. I will go to France and translate this notebook into French. I will tell Clemenceau that I have written about him in this notebook and that therefore he must read everything. I will impress him. He will not be afraid, because he feels his own mistakes. I defended Clemenceau yesterday and told Mayor

* Nijinsky is referring to the *coq gaulois*, the symbol of post-Revolutionary France. It was a cockerel wearing a Phrygian cap. (Tr.)

Hartmann's wife* that Clemenceau was a man and not a beast. I know that Clemenceau has not been bribed, because I feel his speeches. I know that Clemenceau likes Wilson. Clemenceau's policy is that of France. Poincaré does nothing, just like the King of England.† Clemenceau is a man who works a lot. Clemenceau loves France. Clemenceau is a man with love in him. Clemenceau was wrong when he sent France to her death. Clemenceau is a man who seeks the good. Clemenceau is a child with a vast brain. Lloyd George is a hypocrite. Lloyd George is Diaghilev. Diaghilev does not want love for everyone. Diaghilev wants love for himself. I want love toward everyone. I will write things that Clemenceau will understand. I love Clemenceau because he made Wilson feel that he agreed with his ideas. I am afraid for Clemenceau's life. Clemenceau is a free man. His newspaper says everything he feels. His newspaper was wrong when it said that it was necessary to fight. I know everyone will say that he is the murderer of many millions. I know everyone will hate him. I know he is a good man who never intended to kill France. I understand Lloyd George's intentions. Lloyd George's intentions are terrible. He wants to kill Clemenceau because he has turned his back on him. I know that Clemenceau seeks the truth, and therefore his policy is good. I want to help Clemenceau, and therefore I will go to France soon. I will tell the English authorities that I am a Pole and want to dance for the benefit of the poor Poles in France. I am a Pole through my mother and father, but I am Russian because I was brought up there. I love Russia. I am Russia. I do not like the hypocrisy of Poles. Poles are a terrible people because Pederewski‡ has come to an agreement with Lloyd

* Hartmann was the mayor of St. Moritz. (Tr.)
† Raymond Poincaré, president of France, 1913–20. (Ed.)
‡ Pederewski: Nijinsky's misspelling of the name of Ignace Jan Paderewski (1860–1941), pianist and first president of the Polish Republic. Since Nijinsky spells the name

George. Pederewski is a politician. There are no pederasts among Pederewskians. I am not a Pederewskian. Pederewski is not a pederast. Pederewski is an intellectual pianist. I do not like intellectual pianists. Intellectual music is a machine. Music with feeling is God. I like pianists who play with feeling. I do not like technique without feeling. I know they will tell me that Pederewski is a musician with feeling. I do not like politics, Pederewski loves politics. I hate politicians who seek to expand their states. I like a policy that defends states from wars. England likes provoking quarrels. England wants America to quarrel with Japan. I know why England wants America to quarrel with Japan. I know the intentions of the Japanese. The Japanese are cunning and will therefore understand England if I tell them everything. I know the Japanese. I love the Japanese. I do not like the Japanese fleet, because it threatens America. I love America. I have earned money in America. I want America's happiness. I know that Taft was killed.* I know who killed Taft. Taft realized his own error and came to an agreement with Wilson when England sent a bandit who shot him. I know that bandit. That bandit is not guilty. He was given a great deal of money. He fled from America. I will not prevent him from living. I love him. That man is poor and wanted to live well for a while. I know the police are looking for him, but the English are protecting him. I know detectives. I realize what must be done in order to find him. I will not look for him. He must not be looked for. He is not the man to blame for Taft's death. Taft's death is English policy. I am not afraid of death, and therefore people can shoot at me as much as they

---

correctly later, he is clearly misspelling it here in order to make a pun: Pederewski/pederasts. (Tr.)
* Nijinsky seems to be referring to William Howard Taft, president of the United States from 1909 to 1913, though Taft was alive at this time. He died of natural causes in 1930. (Ed.)

like. I am afraid of being wounded. I do not like pain. I know that if the English were to read what I am writing they would shoot me. I am not afraid of being shot. They are afraid that I will tell the whole truth. I will tell the whole truth after my death because I will leave heirs after me. My heirs will continue what I have started.

I will write the truth. I am Zola, but I do not like writing novels. I want to talk, and not write novels. Novels hinder the understanding of feeling. I like novels because Romola likes them. What I look for in novels is not their subject matter but the truth. Zola camouflaged truth in novels. I do not like camouflage. Camouflage is a hypocritical principle. I am a principle. I am the truth. I am conscience. I am love for everyone. I do not want bandits to be put in prisons or killed. A bandit or a thief is not a terrible thing. I am not afraid of bandits. I am afraid of revolvers. I know that everyone was a revolver during the war of the entire world of the terrestrial globe. I know that everyone was a bandit, I know that the government defended bandits because the banditry of governments is protected by governments. I know that God does not protect the government of those who make war. I know that God wanted this war. I know that God does not want wars and therefore sent terrors on men. I am a bandit myself because I kill my brain. I do not want intellectualization. I want rationality. I like intelligent people and therefore will not kill them with a revolver. I am not a revolver. I am God. I am love. I want to send a letter to Dr. Frenkel. I will write this letter in this notebook and not on stationery.

Dear friend Frenkel, I have offended you, but I did not want to offend you, because I love you. I wish you well and have therefore pretended to be mad. I wanted you to feel me. You did not feel me, because you thought I was mad. I pretended to be a nervous man so that you could feel that I was not nervous. I am a man who pretends. I do not wish my wife any evil. I love her. I love you. I am the policy of Christ. I am Christ. I do not like ridicule. I am not ridiculous. I love everyone, and loving everyone is not a ridiculous thing. I know you. You feel. You love your wife. So do I. You do not like things that are not calm, because your nerves are weak. My nerves are strong. I do not want propaganda in favor of the annihilation of nervous people. I am not propaganda. I do not like to make propaganda. I know that you are a German. You were born in Switzerland, but your upbringing is German. I love Germans. Germans made wars, and you loved them. I did not like Germans, but I asked you to come and see my wife. You have cured her. I love you because you love her. You must treat people without charge, because you are rich. I understand you. You want to give your wife everything that can make her happy, but you forget that there are many suffering people. You say that you love Germany. I love it too. You are rich, but you do not give money to poor Germans. Germans are dying of hunger. I know you will tell me that Switzerland cannot help the Germans because the Swiss have little themselves. I understand Switzerland's position very well indeed. Switzerland is between two fires. The English fire and the German. Both fires are terrible. I do not like the fire that destroys lives. I like the fire that gives warmth. I know that without fire it is not possible to create warmth, and therefore I ask everyone to help me. One must not organize a society for governing. I am government. Love will abolish government. I love Wilson's government. I want love. I want Wilson to abolish government. I realize it is impossible to do this right away. Everything must take time to mature. I do not like abscesses. I want to eliminate them. An abscess is a terrible thing. When an abscess bursts, it causes pain, and afterward leaves a hole from which blood flows. I do not want blood, and therefore I ask Dr. Frenkel to help me. I love him and hope that he will help me. I do not want my wife's death. I love her. I did a bad thing so that the doctor would help me. I want the doctor to lance the abscess. I do not want the abscess to cause pain to my wife.* I am not an abscess. I am love. I know that my wife is nervous because of my intentions. I know that I will be forced to go away. I know that my luggage is already packed. I know destruction. Destruction is a terrible thing. I will go and ask my wife's forgiveness if the doctor tells me to. I know a cure, but I will not tell it to you. I want you to cure my wife. I cannot become any better. I do not want to become any better. I am bad, for I want my wife's good. I am not afraid of anything. I am afraid of the death of reason. I want the death of intellect. My wife will not go mad if I kill her intellect. Intellect is stupidity, and reason is God. The doctor thinks that I build everything on feeling, and therefore he thinks that I have no intellect. A man building everything on feeling is not terrible. His feelings are terrible. I do not like bad feelings, and therefore I will go and kiss my wife.

I want to leave the house and I do not want to have lunch, but God wants everyone to see my appetite, and therefore I will eat. I will go and eat when I am called. I will say that God has ordered me to eat. I am not afraid of Frenkel. Frenkel will understand me. Frenkel will be my close friend. Frenkel feels me. I want to help him. He is a man who feels poetry. I feel it

* Romola may literally have had an abscess, but the context suggests that Nijinsky is speaking figuratively: he (or Romola's failure to understand him) is the abscess, and it will be lanced by his being sent away. (Ed.)

too. I want now to write a poem for him so that he will feel it. I will copy out this poem.*

"I am love I am blood"
"I am Christ's blood"
"I love you"
"I love everyone"
"I am love in you yourself"
"You are love within me"
"I want to tell you that love is blood"
"I am not blood in you"
"I am blood in you"
"I love blood but not blood in blood."
I love blood
I love Christ
I am not Christ's blood
I am Christ.

I love writing poetry, but it is difficult to write, because I am not used to it. I will try to write another poem.

I want to tell about blood
But my love is not there
I want to love
I want to say
I want
I
I love you

* In this and subsequent poems Nijinsky selectively uses Church Slavonic rather than modern Russian pronouns: *mia* instead of *menia* for "me" in the accusative case, *tia* instead of *tebia* for "you" (or "thee") in the accusative case. His choice seems guided by considerations of rhythm, and sometimes rhyme, rather than by any thought of religion. In the poems, "you" and its modifiers also shift from masculine to feminine, and from singular to plural, and back again for no discernible reason. (Tr.)

I want to love everyone
I do not want
I want.

I cannot speak in verse, because I do not feel it. I will write in verse when God wills it. I wanted to show an example of verse that is not ready yet. I do not like to prepare verses, and therefore I stopped writing the verses that I did not feel.

I want to write verse.

I want to love you
I want to curse you
I want You
I want Him
I can love Him if You loved him
I can love you if He will love
I want to love you, I want love in you
I can love you, I am yours and You are mine
I want to love you, you cannot feel
I want to love you for you do not love me
I want to tell you. You are intelligent, You are stupid.
I want to tell you. You are God and I am in you.
I want to tell you. I love you my God.
You do not wish me good. I wish you good
I will not weep thus but I will weep thus
I wish you love. You cannot tell me.
I love you always. I am yours and you are mine
I want you my God. You are mine and I am yours
I want to say to you, You are love in me.
I want to say to you. You are love in my blood.

70

I am not blood within your own self, I am blood
I am the blood within your own self, I am not blood
I am blood in the soul. I am the soul in you.
You are not the blood in the soul. I am the soul in you.
I love you always. I want to love you
I love you always. I want love always.
I want you, you. I am God, I am God.
I am he who feels. I love you always.
I want you, you. I want you, you. I am yours always.
I am always within your own self. I am always within your
    own self.
I love you always. Rockabye, Rockabye
You are not asleep, I am not asleep, you cannot sleep always
I love your sleep's growing. I grow like your sleep.
I love your sleep within you. I wish you good.
I love your powerful sleep. I want love for you.
I do not know what to say, I do not know what to be
    silent about.
I love you always, I want to love always.
I wish you good. I do not know what always is.
I am always, always, always. I am everything, I am
    everything.
I wish you good. I love you always.
I wish you ——————————

——————————————

I can't go on writing in verse, because I repeat myself. I prefer
to write simply. Simplicity allows me to explain what I feel. I
love Frenkel. I know that he is a very good man. I know him.
He does not wish my wife any harm. He wants to set things
right. I like setting things right. I love love. I almost wept when
he told me he was my friend. I know he loves me, because he

feels my poems. I gave him my poems. I am weeping, and my tears are almost falling. I do not want to weep, because people will think that I am pretending. I love people, and therefore I do not want to upset them. I will eat very little. I want to grow thin, because my wife does not feel me. She will go to the Frenkels'. I will remain alone. I will weep alone. I weep more, but I go on writing. I am afraid that Dr. Frenkel, my friend, will come in and hear me weeping. I do not want to touch him with my weeping. I will write and wipe away my tears. I do not weep loudly, and they do not hear me in the other room. I weep in such a way that I disturb no one. I feel the cough of the doctor, who has the cough of weeping. He feels the weeping in the cough. A cough is weeping if the cough is felt. I love Frenkel, I love Tessa. I do not know weeping. I want . . . .

I cannot weep, because I feel Tessa weeping. She feels me. I love her. I do not wish her ill. I love her. She feels me when I weep. I will not go to see her off. I know her faults. She thinks I am pretending, but I am not pretending. I will go to my wife after Tessa is gone. I do not want scenes. I like quiet. I will not weep now, because everyone will be sorry for me. I do not like people to be sorry for me, I want people to love me. I did not go to see her off, because God does not want me to leave my writing. I kissed Tessa when I said goodbye to her as I was writing these words. I do not want her to think that I am a weak man. She saw my tears, but did not see my weakness. I pretended to be weak because God wanted it. I know the love of my servants, who do not want to leave my wife by herself. I will not go to my wife, because the doctor does not want it. I will stay here and write. Let them bring me food here. I do not want to eat sitting at a table covered with a tablecloth. I am poor. I have nothing, and I want nothing. I am not weeping as I write these lines, but my feeling weeps. I do not wish my wife ill. I love her more than anyone. I know that if they separate us I will die of hunger. I am weeping . . . . I cannot re-strain my tears, which are dropping on my left hand and my silk tie, but I do not want to restrain them. I will write a lot because I feel that I am going to be destroyed. I do not want destruction, and therefore I want her love. I do not know what I need, but I want to write. I will go and eat and will eat with appetite, if God wills it. I do not want to eat, because I love him. God wants me to eat. I do not want to upset my servants. If they are upset, I will die of hunger. I love Louise and Maria. Maria gives me food, and Louise serves it.

I want to sleep, but my wife does not feel. She thinks in her sleep. I am not thinking, and therefore I will not go to sleep. I do not sleep because of the powders.* They can give me any medicine they like, but I will not sleep. If they give me subcu-taneous morphine injections, I will not sleep. I know my own habits. I like morphine, but I do not like death. Death is mor-phine. I am not morphine. My wife has taken a powder con-taining morphine and is therefore in a daze. She is not asleep. I know the doctor wants her to sleep. I do not want her to sleep, but I will give her sleep. The sleep will be great, she will not die. She will live. Her death has come already because she does not believe Frenkel. She has taken the powder and cannot fall asleep. I stayed with her for a long time. I sat for a long time. I pretended to be asleep. I pretended according to feeling. I feel, and I do what the feeling tells me. I do not contradict feeling. I do not want pretense. I am not pretense. I am God's feeling, which compels me. I am not a fakir. I am not a magi-cian, I am God within the body. Everyone has this feeling, only

* "powders": Powdered medication. (Ed.)

73

no one uses it. I use it. I know its effect. I love its effect. I do not want people to think that my feeling is a spiritualist trance. I am not a trance. I am love. I am a feeling in a trance. I am a love trance. I am a man in a trance. I want to speak, and I can't. I want to write, and I can't. I can write in a trance. I am a trance with a feeling, and this trance is called reason. All men are rational beings. I do not want irrational beings, and therefore I want everyone to be in a trance of feeling. My wife is in a trance of powders, but I am in a trance of God. God wants me to sleep. I am sleeping and writing. I am sitting and sleeping. I am not sleeping, because I am writing. I know many people will say that I write nonsense, but I must say that everything I write has a deep meaning. I am a man with a meaning. I do not like people without meaning. I want to describe another walk.

One day I was in the mountains and got onto a road that led up to a mountain. I went along it and stopped. I wanted to speak on the mountain because I felt the desire to do so. I did not speak, because I thought everyone would say that this man was mad. I was not mad, because I felt. I felt not pain, but love for people. I wanted to jump from the mountain into the little town of St. Moritz. I did not shout, because I felt that I had to go farther. I went farther and saw a tree. The tree said to me that one could not speak here, because men did not understand feeling. I went farther. I was sorry to part with the tree, because it understood me. I went on. I went up to a height of 2,000 meters. I stood for a long time. I felt a voice and shouted in French, "Parole."* I wanted to speak, but my voice was so strong that I could not speak, and I shouted. "I love everyone, and I want happiness!" "I love everyone!" "I want everyone." I cannot speak French, but I will learn it if I walk

---

* *Parole* means "word" in French. (Ed.)

by myself. I want to speak loudly so that people will feel me. I want to love everyone, and therefore I want to speak all languages. I cannot speak all languages, and therefore I write, and my writing will be translated. I will speak French as best I can. I started learning to speak French, but I was prevented because people who were coming toward me were surprised. I did not want to surprise people, and therefore I shut my mouth. I shut it as soon as I felt this. I feel before I see. I know before anyone else what is going to happen. I will not tell people beforehand. I know what my fountain pen needs in order to write well. I understand my fountain pen. I know its habits, and therefore I can invent a better one. I will invent a better one because I feel what is needed. I do not like to press, but a fountain pen likes pressure. I am used to writing with a pencil, because it tires me less. A fountain pen tires my hand because I have to press. I will invent a fountain pen without pressure. The pressure of a fountain pen does not give beauty to writing, and therefore there should be no pressure. Pressure prevents writing, but I will not abandon my fountain pen until I invent another one. If my fountain pen breaks, I will have it repaired. If the pen becomes tired, I will go and buy another one. I will not throw this fountain pen away as long as it writes. I will not abandon this fountain pen until I invent a new one. I want people to work in order to perfect themselves, and I will therefore write with this fountain pen. I like perfecting things. I do not like things. I like things when they are necessary. I do not like publicity, because it lies. I like publicity because it is the truth. I like the truth, and therefore I will write the whole truth with this fountain pen. I walked and thought about Christ. I am a Christian Pole, and my religion is Catholic. I am a Russian because I speak Russian. My daughter does not speak Russian, because that is how the war has arranged my life. My little girl sings in Russian because I sing Russian songs to her.

75

I love Russian songs. I love Russian speech. I know many Russians who are not Russians, because they speak a foreign language. I know that a Russian is a man who loves Russia. I love Russia. I love France. I love England. I love America. I love Switzerland, I love Spain, I love Italy, I love Japan, I love Australia, I love China, I love Africa, I love the Transvaal. I want to love everybody, and therefore I am God. I am not a Russian and not a Pole. I am a man, not a foreigner and not a cosmopolite. I love the Russian land. I will build a dam in Russia. I know that the Poles will curse me. I understand Gogol because he loved Russia.* I too love Russia. Russia feels more than anyone else. Russia is the mother of all states. Russia loves everyone. Russia is not a policy. Russia is love. I will go to Russia and show this book. I know that many people will understand me in Russia. Russia is not the Bolsheviks. Russia is my mother. I love my mother. My mother lives in Russia. She is a Pole, but her speech is Russian. She was brought up in Russia on Russian food. I was brought up on Russian bread and cabbage soup. I like cabbage soup without meat. I am Tolstoy because I love him. I want love for my Russia. I know her defects. Russia has destroyed the war plans. The war would have ended sooner if Russia had not allowed Bolsheviks in. The Bolsheviks are not the Russian people. The Bolsheviks are not the working people. The Russian people is a child. It must be loved and well governed. I want to give the name of the head of the Bolsheviks, but I cannot remember his name, because I am not a Bolshevik. Bolsheviks destroy everything they dislike. I know men who will say that I too am a Bolshevik because I love Tolstoy. I will say that Tolstoy is not a Bolshevik. Bolshe-

---

* The novelist Nikolai Gogol was one of many nineteenth-century Russian writers who embraced the Slavophile belief that Russia had a unique spiritual destiny. Like several other writers whom Nijinsky discusses—Nietzsche, Maupassant—Gogol suffered a mental breakdown. Nijinsky later compares his own situation to Gogol's. (Ed.)

viks are a party, but Tolstoy did not like a party attitude. I am not a party. I am the people. I want Kostrovsky as ruler and not Kerensky. Kerensky is a party. Sazonov is a party.* I do not want to name the head of the Bolsheviks, because I do not feel him. I know his name, but I do not feel it, and therefore I will not pronounce it. I do not want his death, because he is a man with a conscience. He does not want my death, because I am a man and not a beast. I know his habits. He kills everyone without exception. He does not like being contradicted. Lloyd George is the same as the head of the Bolsheviks. I do not like either of them and therefore do not wish them harm. I know that if everyone obeys me there will be no war. I cannot deal with politics, because politics is death. I like Wilson's policy, but democracy is also a party. I do not like a party attitude, but I like a party that has perfected itself. Democracy is a perfect party because everyone has the same rights. I do not like rights, because no one has rights. I am God and have rights. I do not want to have human rights. All human rights are invented. Napoleon invented rights. His rights were best, but this does not mean that these rights are divine rights. I know that many people will tell me that without rights† one cannot live, because men will kill each other. I know that men have not yet reached the state of love for each other. I know that men will love each other if I tell them the truth. I have resorted to law many times. I had lawsuits against Diaghilev. I won the law-

---

* Alexander Kerensky (1881–1970) was a minister, then the premier, of the provisional government that took over Russia after the February Revolution of 1917 and that was overthrown by the Bolsheviks in the October Revolution of that year. Sergei Sazonov (1861–1927) had been the minister of foreign affairs to Tsar Nicholas II from 1910 to 1916. Both Kerensky and Sazonov fled to Paris, where each campaigned against the Bolshevik regime. Kostrovsky was the dancer who converted Nijinsky to Tolstoyanism. (Ed.)
† Here Nijinsky clearly means "laws," though he continues to use the word "rights" (*prava*). (Tr.)

suits because I was right. I know that Diaghilev hoped to win these lawsuits though he was not in the right. I know a man who is called Butt. He is the manager of the Palace Music Hall in London. I have had a lawsuit against him for the last five years and more.* Laws enable one to drag out lawsuits indefinitely. I know that my lawyer is one of the very best in London. I know that he took me on because he hoped to earn much more than I am giving him. I know that he will lose my lawsuit because my friend the Marchioness of Ripon has died. I know that he was hoping for the Marchioness of Ripon's patronage. The Marchioness of Ripon did not want to help him, because he is a Jew. I like Jews and therefore did not care. I know he can win the lawsuit if I give him the opportunity to earn money. I cannot pay him as much money as he needs. I know Paderewski is a businessman and understands business. I understand nothing of business and therefore am afraid of entrusting my business to Sir Lewis. I like him, but I do not trust him, because I have noticed that he is dragging out the lawsuit. I understand enough to understand his tricks. I am not afraid that he will lose the lawsuit, because I know I am right. I am not afraid that I will not be allowed to enter England because I have lost the lawsuit and have not paid. I cannot pay for a lawsuit for which I do not owe anything. I must pay when I am in the wrong. I know many people will say that every man is right in his own way. I will say that this is not so, for the man who is right is the one who feels but does not understand. I feel I am

---

* In 1914, soon after his dismissal from the Ballets Russes, Nijinsky was engaged to present a ballet company of his own in a two-month season at London's Palace Theatre. But after two weeks he fell ill and failed to perform for three nights. He thus placed himself in breach of contract, and Alfred Butt, the owner of the theater, canceled the season. The lawyer handling Nijinsky's dealings with Butt was Sir George Lewis. Gwladys, Lady Ripon, the Ballets Russes' most important English patron and a friend and supporter of Nijinsky's, died in 1917. (Ed.)

right, because I have won the lawsuit against Diaghilev and therefore do not want to make use of my rights. I do not want money from Diaghilev that I have not earned. Butt wants to force me to pay damages for an unfulfilled contract, whereas my work for him cost me my life. There is an English doctor who can testify to this. My wife is also a witness. According to the law, she has no right to be a witness, but I will bring a lawsuit such that my wife would have every right.

I know God will help me.
I cannot write very quickly, because this pen is bad.
I do not want to die, and therefore I will go out for a walk.
I like to speak in rhyme because I am a rhyme.*

I went out for a walk, but I did not meet any friends. I know what God needs. I cannot write well. My hand does not write. God does not want me to press. I will not press, because my hand cannot write. My hand is tired. I want to write nonsense. I know my wife is stupid, and I will therefore write nonsense. I cannot write any longer, because my hand does not write. I cannot write, because I want them to give me water. The maid Louise does not feel me, because she thinks that I cried because of Tessa. I love Tessa, but I did not cry because of her. I wanted to weep not because I weep easily. I do not weep easily. I am a man of great willpower. I do not weep often, but my feeling cannot bear much stress. I like Lloyd George. I have bought the magazine "L'Illustration." It is a French magazine that has photographs of Wilson. Wilson is shown coming out of a con-

---

* Nijinsky here alludes to the two Russian verbs in the preceding sentence: *umirat'* ("to die") and *guliat'* ("to go for a walk"), which in the infinitive may be said to rhyme, even if unsatisfactorily. (Tr.)

ference. He is very well dressed. In a top hat and frock coat. Wilson has come out very badly in the photograph, while Lloyd George has come out very well. The conference is shown on the first pages. I only glanced at the photographs, and therefore I will go and have a good look at them.

The magazine is big. It contains nothing but nonsense. This magazine serves the rich classes. The rich classes love Lloyd George. They do not like Wilson, because he has a boring face. Wilson looks bored in this photograph. Lloyd George looks pleased with life. Lloyd George pretends to be cheerful. Wilson does not pretend to be bored. I noticed the first page of "L'Illustration," showing the portrait of Wilson. This portrait is drawn by Lucien Tonas. The artist is an Englishman. Lloyd George has artists who do everything he wants them to. They have made Wilson's face angular, his veins taut. His arm is straight. Lloyd George wants to make people feel that Wilson is dull. I understand Wilson well, and therefore that portrait has made clear to me Lloyd George's whole political intrigue. I like Wilson and therefore do not wish him harm. I want him to live, because he is a man of free thoughts and not of thoughts with taut veins on his forehead. Lloyd George has many veins on his forehead because they do not know how to draw. They have made a mistake. The two Englishmen behind Wilson's back are coming to some kind of agreement, instead of listening to Wilson's speech. I have understood what Lloyd George is after. Lloyd George wants to show that Wilson's speech is boring. Clemenceau is shown as a man of no great importance who is dull. In the foreground there is one politician who is not listening to Wilson. Next to a pillar there is a military man with a mustache who is either yawning or laughing. On the other side there is another military man with a mustache brushed upward and a smiling face. Facing Clemenceau is a man who looks as if he is falling asleep. The general impression is that Wilson's speech is boring. The first page of "L'Illustration" of Saturday, 25 January 1919, shows something that must be important. That photograph gave me a feeling of boredom. I understood Lloyd George's aim. What Lloyd George is aiming at is for people not to listen to all that Wilson stuff. That Wilson stuff must be listened to, because it makes sense. There is much nonsense in Lloyd George's speech. I do not like a nonsensical speech. I do not want nonsensical speeches. I like Lloyd George because he is intelligent. I do not like him, because he is stupid. He is stupid because he does not have good feelings. Lloyd George wants Wilson's death. Wilson does not want the death of Lloyd Georgians. Clemenceau felt Lloyd George's political intrigue because he pretended to be a Lloyd Georgian and they therefore wanted to shoot him. Lloyd George will want to shoot me too because I do not like him. There is a portrait of Lloyd George shown on a page of this issue of "L'Illustration." A footman stands at attention in front of him. This footman has a chestful of medals. The footman gets these medals from Lloyd George because he does what he is ordered to do. Lloyd George stands behind and is about to make a gesture to make everybody laugh. Lloyd George always resorts to that trick. Lloyd George is funny. This is true, but his smile is wicked. Lloyd George's smile reminds one of Diaghilev's smiles. I know Diaghilev's smiles. All Diaghilev's smiles are artificial. My little girl has learned to smile like Diaghilev. I have taught her because I want her to give Diaghilev a smile when he visits me. I do not want to tell my wife anything, because she will be frightened if she discovers my intentions. I will tell her when everybody knows. I tell her that all I am writing is memoirs. I do not want to write my memoirs. I write everything that has been and everything that is. I am the present and not what has been. Lloyd George has been and is not. Wilson is, and therefore he must be obeyed.

I do not want to talk about Wilson's portrait on another page, for the photographer was an Englishman.

Wilson looks strained in that photograph. He is wearing a top hat and a long overcoat. He is buttoning it up. Lloyd George has unbuttoned his overcoat on purpose, in order to show that he is different. Lloyd Georgians have many bowler hats, Wilsonians have top hats. I like bowler hats and top hats. I do not like hats for the sake of hats. I like a hat for what there is under the hat. Wilson has a rich hat, and there are riches in his head. Lloyd Georgians have poor hats, and there is poverty in their heads. I know Lloyd George will understand me. I know he will pretend that everything I have written is nonsense, or, even worse, he will say that everything I am writing is the truth and at the same time he will be smiling that familiar wicked smile. I am convinced that Wilson will be sad after he has read what I have written, but not because I write sympathetically about him. Wilson will love me because he knows my ideas. Wilson will be with me because he feels me. Clemenceau is not afraid of Lloyd George and his own ringleaders, and therefore he will be with me.*

The Lloyd Georgians will die soon because their intentions will be obvious. I like help, and therefore I will go to Clemenceau and tell him that I have no revolver. I know that Clemenceau will take me by the hand and say, "Listen to me. I do not want to die but if you want to kill me, do." I know that Clemenceau will touch the assassin's heart. Assassins are not Englishmen. Assassins are Frenchmen. Lloyd George knows who should be sent. Lloyd George likes killing. Lloyd Georgians are assassins. I know everything without being at the scene of the crime. I understand Caillaux, who has been imprisoned on pur-

---

* Nijinsky seems to have meant something like: "Clemenceau is not afraid of Lloyd George and his stooges, and therefore he will be with me." (Tr.)

pose, so that Clemenceau could become a minister.* Caillaux is not a good man, because he wanted to deceive France. France did not catch him, because there was no evidence. Lloyd George does not want Caillaux to be killed, because he defended him. Lloyd Georgians want to have in France a man who had been imprisoned. I want to write the truth, and therefore I lie. I am not afraid of the press, because the press has already said a lot of bad things about me. I do not know how to write well, and therefore I cannot say things more skillfully. I write as I can. I do not pretend. I write the truth because I want everyone to know. I know everyone will say that Nijinsky has gone mad, because he writes about things without seeing them. I see everything. I know everything. I have read Lloyd George's polemics with Wilson. I know many people will say that Nijinsky cannot read French. I can read French. My wife translates English magazines for me. I like reading magazines. My wife reads and translates very important speeches for me. I know Wilson's speeches in England. I know that Wilson did not want to go to England, as he thought he would not be understood. I know that Wilson was in England and spoke well. Wilson made a great impression on Anglicans. The name Anglican is applied to artisans. The artisans have taken Wilson to their hearts. Wilson wants to speak to artisans as if to his equals. Wilson spoke the truth. Wilson did not pretend. Lloyd George tries to repair the damage that Wilson has done him in his speeches. Wilson knows what Lloyd George is. Lloyd Georgians are those Frenchmen who had deported Dreyfus, and Zola freed him, but for this Zola was gassed to death.† I asked

---

* In 1917 Joseph Caillaux (1863–1944), former premier of France, was arrested on the charge of having made unauthorized contact with the Germans in order to discuss a negotiated peace. His trial took place under the premiership of Clemenceau. (Ed.)
† Nijinsky is referring to the Dreyfus affair. In 1894 Alfred Dreyfus (1859–1935), a French general staff officer and a Jew, was unjustly convicted of treason and sent to the

my wife whether it was true that Zola had been gassed to death. To my question my wife answered that Zola had not been gassed to death. I said nothing, but I feel that he has been gassed to death, and therefore feel that I will be gassed to death. I am Zola. I am love. Zola spoke the truth, and I speak the truth. I will always speak the truth. My wife is sighing because she thinks that I am writing about politics. My wife feels that I am writing against the French. I know my error, but I do not want to correct it. My wife wants to look, but I am not letting her, because I am shielding my writing with my hand. My wife continues to weep in her heart. I am not afraid of my wife's weeping. I love her, but I cannot stop writing. What I write is too important for me to listen to the weeping of my wife. My wife is afraid I may be writing things that are forbidden. She cries with real tears. I laugh at her weeping because I know the meaning of her weeping. I want to reassure her, but my hand goes on writing. I will continue about Wilson. Wilson is a human being, but Lloyd George is a beast. My wife is reading what I am writing. She is looking under my hand. I will tell her that if she wants to know before anyone else, she must learn to read Russian. I do not want her to read Russian, because I do not want her to know everything I write. I do not like one person knowing before anyone else. I will publish this book soon. I am not sure that I will publish it in Switzerland, because I think that the Swiss will prohibit it. I know that Lloyd Georgians or the Anglicans have detectives everywhere. I know one detective who has a white head. He pretends to be

___

penal colony on Devil's Island. Evidence of his innocence was suppressed by the army, which at that time was rife with anti-Semitism. The Dreyfus case became a national cause, creating a bitter division between French conservatives and liberals. In 1898 Emile Zola, a defender of Dreyfus, published his famous open letter, "J'accuse," charging the government with engineering a cover-up. Zola was prosecuted for libel. In 1902 he was gassed to death, but accidentally, by inhaling fumes from a blocked chimney. (Ed.)

a Frenchman. I know he is an Englishman. He pretends he is an artist, but I know his pictures are worth nothing. He is the Anglicans' detective. My wife is weeping because she thinks that I will stop then. I will stop writing if God wills it so.

I love my wife because she suddenly had a feeling for what I was writing. She is afraid for me. She is afraid that if I am killed, she and the child will remain orphans, as her mother does not like her. Her mother loves her because she is my wife. Romushka's mother is a terrible woman. I love her, but I know that if she discovers that I have no money, she will throw me out. Her husband is a Jew and has therefore taught her to understand money. She does not understand money. She loves it because her husband loves it. Romushka's mother throws money around. She puts money away for Kyra, but she thinks that I will give her money if she needs it. She has felt me well, because she has pulled a trick that would outwit a fox. She comes to an understanding about these things with her husband in the evening or at night in bed, because she does not sleep. Her husband wants to sleep, but she does not let him. She likes to think at night. I know her habits because I stayed with her. She loves me because she knows that I am a celebrity. I do not like celebrities. I want to make her think that I am mad in order to understand her. I love her, but I know her habits. She has a good heart, but she has frequent attacks of bile, because she quarrels with her husband. My wife suffered much from her mother when I lived in their house. I too suffered, because my wife suffered. I know people who will say that this is not true, because she kisses my wife and me and the little one. I know this Judas kiss. Judas was evil. He knew that Christ loved him. He kissed him for show. I kiss her mother for show. She kisses me and my wife and Kyra for show. I kiss her for show, because I want her to think I love her. She kisses me so that I will think she loves me. I know she has no soul. I know that pieces of glass burst in her heart when she says she loves me. She knows how to pretend that she is weeping, because she acts in a theater. I know that her playacting is sham and not felt. I speak well of her because I do not want anyone to think I am malicious. I do not want to pretend, and so I write the whole truth. Emilia Márkus is Lloyd George. She pretends to like simple people but in fact slaps their faces. I offended Louise once, but suffered so much afterward that I didn't know what to do with myself. Emilia is very happy after she has slapped someone's face. She tells everyone about it. I offended Louise, but my wife put my error right again, because she said I was nervous and did not want to offend her. Then Louise came in shyly to ask my forgiveness. I shook hands with her and told her I loved her. She felt me, and ever since, we love each other. I love my wife and do not wish her evil, and therefore I will go and earn money so that she may be happy. I do not want to cause her grief, and therefore I will earn enough for her to be able to live in case I am killed. I am not afraid of death, but my wife is afraid. She thinks that death is a terrible thing. Mental sufferings are a terrible thing. I want people to understand that the death of the body is not a terrible thing, and therefore I will tell the story of my walk.

I went out for a walk, once, toward evening. I was walking quickly uphill. I stopped on a mountain. It was not Sinai. I had gone far. I felt cold. I was suffering from cold. I felt that I had to kneel down. I knelt quickly. After that, I felt I had to put my hand on the snow. I was holding my hand down, and suddenly I felt pain. I screamed with pain and snatched away my hand. I gazed at a star that did not say "Hello" to me. It did not twinkle. I was frightened and wanted to run, but could not, because my knees were rooted to the snow. I began to weep. My weeping was not heard. No one came to my aid. I loved going out for walks, and therefore I had a feeling of terror. I did not know what to do. I did not understand the purpose for which I had slowed down. After a few minutes I turned around and saw a boarded-up house. A little farther away there was a house with ice on its roof. I was frightened and screamed at the top of my lungs, "Death!" I do not know why, but I understood that I had to shout, "Death." After that I felt warmth in my body. The warmth in my body enabled me to get up. I got up and went in the direction of the house, where there was a lamp burning. The house was big. I was not afraid of going in, but I thought that I must not go in, and therefore I went past it. I realized that if men got tired, they needed help. I wanted help because I was very tired. I could not go any farther, but suddenly I felt an immense strength and started running. I did not run for long. I ran until I felt the cold. The cold struck me in the face. I was frightened. I realized that the south wind would bring snow. I walked on the snow. The snow was crunching underneath my foot. I loved the snow. I listened to the crunching of the snow. I liked listening to my step. My step was full of life. I looked at the sky and saw the stars, which started twinkling at me. I felt gaiety in the stars. I became cheerful and did not feel cold anymore. I went on. I walked quickly because I noticed a small grove that had no leaves. I felt the cold in my body. I looked at the stars and saw one star that was motionless. I walked quickly because I felt a warmth in my body. I walked. I walked. I started to go down off the road, where nothing could be seen. I walked quickly, but was stopped by a tree, which was my salvation. I was in front of a precipice. I thanked the tree. It had felt me because I had taken hold of it. The tree received my warmth, and I received the tree's warmth. I do not know whose warmth was more necessary. I went farther and suddenly stopped. I saw a precipice without a tree. I realized that God had stopped me because he loved me, and therefore I said, "If it is your will, I shall fall into the precipice. If it is your will, I shall be saved." I stood until I felt someone pushing me to go forward. I walked on. I did not fall into the abyss. I said that God loved me. I know that all that is good is God, and therefore I was sure that God did not want my death. I walked farther. I walked quickly as I walked down the mountain. I walked past the Hotel Chantarella. I thought that all names were important, because people would go out in order to see where I had my walk. I realized that Christ also went for walks. I walked with God. I was walking away from the hotel. I felt I was weeping because I realized that the whole of life in the Hotel Chantarella was death. People enjoy themselves, but God is sad. I realized that it was not people's fault that they were in that situation, and therefore I loved them. I knew that my wife thought a lot but felt little, and I began to sob so that I had spasms in my throat. I sobbed, covering my face with my hands. I was not ashamed. I was sad. I was afraid for my wife. I wanted her good. I did not know what to do. I realized that the whole of my wife's life and that of all humanity was death. I was horrified and thought how well it would be if my wife had obeyed me. I walked on and on. I know everyone will say that my wife lives well. I know that Stravinsky also lives well.* I also live well with my wife. I think I live well. Stravinsky, the composer, thinks so too. I know what life

---

* It was as a composer for the Ballets Russes that Igor Stravinsky (1882–1971) first became known to European audiences. Among the ballets set to his music by Ballets Russes choreographers were *The Firebird* (1910), *Petrouchka* (1911), *The Rite of Spring* (1913), *Pulcinella* (1920), *Les Noces* (1923), and *Apollon Musagète* (1928). Diaghilev also produced several operas by Stravinsky. In the description, below, of Stravinsky's refusal to keep Kyra while the Nijinskys went to the United States in 1916, the infection that Stravinsky says he fears is probably tuberculosis, with which his wife, Catherine, had already been diagnosed. (Ed.)

is. Igor Stravinsky does not know what life is, because he does not like me. Igor thinks that I am hostile to his aims. He seeks riches and fame. I do not want riches and fame. Stravinsky is a good composer of music, but he does not write about life. He invents subjects that have no purpose. I do not like subjects without a purpose. I often tried to make him understand what purpose was, but he thought I was a silly kid. I therefore spoke with Diaghilev, who approved of all his schemes. I could not say anything, because I was considered to be a kid. Stravinsky was a kid with a long nose. He was not a Jew. His father was Russian and his grandfather a Pole. I too am a Pole, but without a long nose. Stravinsky smells things out. I do not smell things out. Stravinsky is my friend, who loves me in his heart because he feels, but he considers me his enemy because I am in his way. Diaghilev loves Massine and not me, and this is awkward for Stravinsky. Stravinsky does not like his wife, because he forces her to carry out all his whims. Stravinsky will say that I have not seen their life and therefore cannot speak about their life. I will say that I have seen their life, because I have felt his wife's love for him. I felt that Stravinsky did not love his wife, but lived with her for the sake of the children. He loves his children strangely. He shows his love by forcing his children to paint. His children paint well. He is an emperor, and his children and his wife and servants are soldiers. Stravinsky reminds me of the emperor Paul, but he will not be strangled, because he is cleverer than the emperor Paul.* Diaghilev wanted to strangle him many a time, only Stravinsky is cunning. He† cannot live without Stravinsky, and Stravinsky cannot live without Diaghilev. They understand each other.

---

* The Russian tsar Paul, who ruled from 1796 to 1801, was murdered by strangling. (Tr.)
† "He": Nijinsky clearly means Diaghilev. (Tr.)

Stravinsky is clever in the way he fights with Diaghilev. I know all their tricks, both Stravinsky's and Diaghilev's.

One day, it was at the time of my liberation from Hungary, I went to Morges to see Stravinsky and asked him, in the absolute certainty that he would not refuse, whether he and his wife would agree to take in my child and keep her for a while. I knew he had many children, and therefore I realized that he could keep my Kyra if I went to North America. I did not want to take my little child with me. I wanted to leave her in the care of another loving mother. Feeling happy about it, I asked Stravinsky whether he could take my Kyra and keep her for a time. His wife almost burst into tears, and Stravinsky said he was sorry, but he could not take the child, as he was afraid of infection and did not want to be responsible for my little Kyra's death. I thanked him and did not speak to him again. I looked sadly at his wife and felt the same answer. She said nothing to me, but I answered her with my weeping, which she felt. She is a woman and therefore feels what it means to have a child on a train and a ship. She was sorry for me. I know that she did not agree with her husband, because her husband spoke very quickly and decisively and made his wife realize that he did not want it. I told him that I would pay all Kyra's expenses. He did not want to agree. When I was alone with him, he advised me to give my Kyra to one of the governesses who would be living at the hotel. I told him I could not leave my child in a stranger's hands, because I did not know whether that woman loved Kyra. I do not like people who leave their children in the hands of strangers. I cannot write, because I have been interrupted by people speaking nonsense. I want to say that children must always be with their mothers. I took my Kyra to America. Stravinsky saw me off at the railroad station. I shook hands with him very coldly. I did not like him and therefore wanted to make him feel it, but he did not feel me, because he kissed me. I don't know whether his kiss was a Judas kiss or a friendly one, but I had a nasty feeling. I went away to America. I remained in America for eighteen months. I did not like traveling with a child. I therefore left her in New York. Stravinsky never wrote to me. I never wrote to him either. Almost eighteen months have passed since then, and I have heard nothing from him. Stravinsky is a dry man. I am a man with a soul. I do not like compliments and therefore do not want to answer when I am asked "whether I am an egoist or not." My wife's cough frightened me because she thought that I did not love her, for I did not answer her question. I cannot write, because my seat is hard. I like sitting in a hard armchair. My wife has received a telegram. I do not know what my wife is thinking about. She . . .

She does not understand me. She loves me. My Romushka loves me, but she does not understand me. She thinks that everything I say is bad. She criticizes me. Dr. Frenkel is always right. I am wrong. I do not understand her if God does not want it. God wants me to understand and therefore orders me to write. I write everything I think. I think everything I feel. My feelings are good. I walk around when I feel like walking. I speak when I feel what I say. I do not think in advance what it is I am going to talk about. I do not want to ponder carefully over what I say. What I say is sincere because I have not pondered over it. Everything I say is always unpremeditated, and therefore I make mistakes. God helps me. I love God. He loves me. I know everyone has forgotten what God is. Everyone thinks that this is a lie. Scientists say there is no God. I say that God exists. I feel him, but I do not think. I know that mothers will understand me better because they feel death every time they give birth to a child. A mother knows that if God is not with her, no obstetrician or surgeon will save her life. I know people who think that men do not owe their existence to God. I know people will say that there is no God, that everything we do is matter in motion. I know people who have little matter. I know sick people. Sick people feel more because they think they will die soon. Sick people work on God without knowing it. I work on God when I am well. I am not a sick man. My wife thinks that I am well and does not want any more doctors. She believed me because she saw things that a simple man could not invent. I have invented a new fountain pen and a bridge-railway, along a wire, that can destroy all steamboats.* I know everyone will tell me that I am talking nonsense, but I can prove it to technical experts, who will understand me. I know that my invention will make it possible to destroy all railroads. I know that if I destroy all railroads, the speed of communication will increase tenfold, if not more. I cannot calculate, but my feeling tells me so. I know of a method for the destruction of coal mines. I do not like people who force the poor to dig the earth. I do not want to ruin people. I have invented a method for obtaining physical power without coal. I can prove to scientists the validity of my invention if they ask me. I know that if coal is destroyed there will be no smoke to harm men's health. I know what trains are. I do not like traveling by train, and therefore I will travel by airplane. I know everyone is afraid of airplanes because they are subject to weather. I know a method of communication that is not subject to weather. I know how to do it technically, but

---

* Nijinsky seems to envisage a bridge that would carry electric-powered trains over water. Such trains would then make ships obsolete ("destroy all steamboats"). This is probably the same project as the transatlantic bridge that he discussed earlier. (Tr.)

I cannot say what it is, because my wife has my manuscripts. My wife wants money, and therefore she must be given it. If they promise me money, I will show these manuscripts. I am not Lloyd George. I love the truth. I love people, and I wish them good. I know everyone will say I am selfish and have given these manuscripts to my wife instead of giving them to people. I know that I will be understood better if I pretend to be just like everyone else, and I will therefore be understood better. I do not have long to live, and therefore I want to fulfill my purpose. My purpose is God's purpose. I am not pretense. I am the truth. I know that if I tell the whole truth, men will kill me. I am not afraid of one man. I am afraid of men. I am sorry for men. I want to help them. I will resort to all the tricks that God shows me, but I know that God does not want my wife or people to suffer. I love my wife as I love people, and therefore I wish her the same happiness as I wish people. Men will say that I should not love one man when all men are suffering. I will say that the suffering of one man is unnecessary for human happiness, because I know that Christ has suffered and no one understood him. I know men who have understood him, but they have camouflaged this by expressing it in novels and poetry. Tolstoy and other writers wrote about God after writing their novels. They understood what God was, but they were afraid of life. I am not afraid of life. My wife is afraid for me, and she will therefore transmit this fear to me. I am not afraid. I have experienced the fear of death on a precipice. No one wanted to kill me. I was walking along and fell over a precipice, and a tree held me up. I did not know there was a tree on that road. I was a boy, and my father wanted to teach me to swim. He threw me into the water where we were bathing. I fell and sank to the bottom. I could not swim, but I felt that I had no air, then I closed my mouth. I had little air, but I held onto what I had, thinking that if God willed I would be saved. I walked straight on, I knew not where. I walked on and on, and suddenly I felt a light under the water. I realized that it was shallow in the place I was going to, and I went quickly. I reached a wall. The wall went straight up. I did not see the sky. I saw the water above me. Suddenly I had a feeling of physical strength and jumped. When I jumped, I saw a rope. I clung to the rope and was saved. I am telling everything that happened to me. You can ask my mother whether she has forgotten this episode, which happened in Petersburg in a men's bathing establishment on the Neva. I saw my father somersaulting and diving into the water, but I was afraid. I did not like somersaulting. I was afraid. I was a seven- or six-year-old boy and have not forgotten this story, and therefore I make a very good impression on my little girl, for I know that children never forget the things that happen to them. Dr. Frenkel told me that I should not do anything bad to Kyra, because a child never forgets the things that her father or mother does. He told me that his father was very angry with him once and that to this day he could not forget that anger. Dr. Frenkel distorted his face, and I felt his father's wrong-doing. I almost burst into tears. I was sorry for him. I do not know whether one should have been sorry for the boy or the father. I know that both were miserable. I love both of them. I realized that the child had lost his father's love and the father had lost God's love. I told Dr. Frenkel that I understood him and would no longer behave like an animal. I know what my wife is telephoning Dr. Frenkel about. She thinks that I have gone out for a walk, and she is talking to the doctor with complete frankness. I realize that my wife loves me, because she did not say anything bad about me. She gave him to understand that I was conservative* and that it was difficult to

---

* "conservative" (*konservativen*): Presumably, "set in my ways." (Tr.)

convince me, but with time it would be possible to change everything I say. I realize my wife wishes me well, and I will therefore pretend that I am changing. I will show a superficial change. I want a lot of money, and therefore I will go to Zurich in order to get money for my work. Everybody thinks that the Stock Exchange is work, and I will therefore gamble on the Stock Exchange with my money. I will take my last money. There isn't much of it. About 300 francs. I know God will help me, but I am afraid because I think that I will hurt poor people who gamble for low stakes. I do not want to rob little people, because little people are poor. Little people look for happiness, while rich people seize upon those who have fallen in such a way that the little people end up by shooting themselves. I do not want either the little people or the rich people to shoot themselves, and therefore I will gamble in such a way as to rob neither. I know that I will win because I am with God.

I showed my wife my love, because I did not take my manuscripts when she wanted to give them back to me. She said I must hide them, and I said, on purpose, that it was better to hide them in her room, because in my room they would be stolen. She took the manuscripts and hid them. Her feeling is good, but she thinks that these manuscripts will bring her money. She has very little money. Everyone thinks she has millions, but she wears artificial pearls and a ring with an artificial stone in it. I gave it to her so that everybody would think she was rich. I have noticed that men trust rich people because they think that money is a necessary thing. I have understood the opposite and therefore want to become rich. God wants my wife and people to be happy, and I will therefore go looking for money. I do not want this happiness, but I feel that through this happiness I will give another kind of happiness. Wilson understands politics. He does not like politics. I know that he will come with me if I show him the way. Wilson is a good man and must be protected. Bandits must be afraid of him. I do not want Wilson's death, because he is a man necessary to mankind. I will devise a way of guarding him. I will tell him what he must do for his own protection. I have a way of protecting him. I feel a steady gaze behind me. I am a cat. I want people to make an experiment on me, and they will see that I am right. All bandits will be afraid of me. I know what a detective feels. I am a detective who senses things. I sense not with my nose, but with my mind. I am not afraid of attacks. If they want to beat me, I will not fight back, and therefore my enemy will be disarmed. I know I will be told that there are people who will beat a man to death if he does not retaliate. I think that God will stop him. I am sure that that man will feel anger for a minute, but then stop. If you want to try, try. I know that Lloyd George and Diaghilev and people like them will try. But I am even more convinced that their attempts will yield no results. They will not kill me. They can wound me, but not kill me. I am not afraid of suffering, because God will be with me. I know what suffering is. I know how to suffer. I will show Wilson that I know, if he comes to me. I will not go to him, because I consider him to be a man and not America's President.

Wilson is a big man. The size of his head is small, but it contains a lot.

Lloyd George has a big head and a big brain, but he has no intellect.

Lombroso spoke about heads and made a study of them.* I

---

* In his *Genius and Insanity* (1863) the Italian physician and criminologist Cesare Lombroso (1836–1909) had argued that moral character was determined by physical constitution, which could be read from bodily structure—for example, the shape of the head. Romola (*Nijinsky*, p. 359) recalls Nijinsky telling her in early 1919 that he wanted to consult a great physician such as Lombroso. (Ed.)

have not read Lombroso. I know about him from what my wife told me. I asked her what Lombroso or any other scientist had said "about heads," but my wife replied that Lombroso spoke not only "about heads" but about other things as well. I then answered nervously that I knew, but I gave her to understand that I needed "heads."

Lloyd George has a sick head, and Wilson has a healthy one. Lloyd George's head is swollen, but Wilson's has the right shape. Wilsonians feel, but Lloyd Georgian heads think. Wilsonians also think, but their heads feel. I know they will tell me that heads do not feel, but nerves do. I will then say that sick people, such as lunatics, for instance, who have no rational mind, feel with their nerves. I am a lunatic with a mind, and therefore my nerves are trained. I am nervous when I want to be nervous. I am not nervous when I must convince people that I am not nervous. I know that Lloyd George is a nervous man, but he makes himself out to be calm and rosy-cheeked. His newspapers show Wilson as nervous and himself as rosy. Lloyd George is afraid that everyone will notice his trick, and therefore he resorts to a kid's trick. I know that kids stick out their tongues at people, but Lloyd George does not stick out his tongue. He wants everyone to think that he does not stick out his tongue. But he wants everyone to think that Wilson does. Clemenceau is not a kid. Clemenceau is a good man. I like Clemenceau. I sympathize with the pain in his shoulder. I am afraid for him because he has been frightened. I know he is a man, and therefore he will not be afraid of Lloyd George's shooting him. Lloyd George always uses this trick in order to force people to do whatever he wants them to do. Lloyd George has a police force that practices all these tricks. I know these people. I can show them to you if you promise me that you will not touch them. I do not want them lynched. I like these people. These people do all this because they have been shown money. These people are poor, they need money to feed their children. I like these people and know that they will understand me if Lloyd George allows them to read this book. I know that Lloyd George will not allow them to read it, by using a very cunning trick. He will allow it to be printed, but in Lloyd George's newspapers they will laugh at it. Lloyd George will understand me. I know that he will be afraid of me, but I know that he will pretend to be smiling. I know that Lloyd George works at night, because he has weak eyes. He writes a lot. He speaks little. He invents on paper. He has a lot of paper and therefore does not mind writing at all. He writes whatever he thinks, and afterward people develop his ideas. I too write, but I try to economize on paper, and therefore I write small. I sometimes write in big letters in order to emphasize my thought. With Lloyd George all the letters are big. I have not seen Lloyd George's handwriting, but I am convinced that he writes in big letters because he is afraid that he will not be understood. He writes quickly and skillfully. He has many habits. People understand him because he has spent a lot of time writing. I know that he has worked on his handwriting. His handwriting is very beautiful. He writes clearly. I do not write clearly, because I do not want everyone to understand me. Lloyd George is afraid that he will not be understood by everybody, because he feels his mistakes. Lloyd George is a terrible man, he must not be killed. I want to speak to him if I am allowed to see him. I do not want to kill him with a revolver. I want to prove to him that everything he has done has caused so much harm that he would not be able to pay for it with his own hair, as he does not have enough on his head. I will tell him that without God he cannot pay for everything he has destroyed. In order to pay, he must love God.

I want him to understand God, and therefore I want to explain to him that God can help him if he obeys me. I know that he will show me his smile, but I will not reply, because I am not a smiling man. I like people with a smile, but not an artificial one. I do not like Diaghilev's smiles, because they are artificial. He thinks that people will not feel it. Lloyd George makes himself out to be a working man, thinking that the people will love him. Lloyd George does not understand people. Lloyd George wants to be obeyed. Lloyd George forces Ireland to do things she does not want to do. Ireland is love, and she wants to love England, but Lloyd George wants to incite the Irish people to have a quarrel, because he wants to fight Ireland. I know an Irish politician who has an English wife. This wife has been brought up as a hypocrite.* Her husband understands her tricks, but he loves her. She does not love him though she has a child by him. I happened by chance to see how they express their love to each other. I was having tea at their house. The husband was there too. The husband is a good man, for his smile is a sensitive one. His wife's smile is exciting. I did not respond to her smile. I responded to her husband's smile. She writes me "today" a letter in which she wants to make me understand that she loves me. I see from this letter the tricks of a cunning woman. I understood her letter. She wants to force me to come to England, by saying that the Russian ballet is having a success. This success I have understood well. She gave me to understand that Massine too was a very gifted man. I understood this woman's whole purpose. She feels Massine. Massine understood her, and therefore spoke very nicely about me. Massine is a very nice boy. I like him, but I

* It is possible that Nijinsky is speaking of his friend Lady Ottoline Morrell (1873–1937). Though her husband was not Irish, he was a politician, a member of parliament, and Ottoline was a supporter of Irish nationalism. Certain of the points that Nijinsky says this Englishwoman made in her recent letter to him (for example, that Massine praised him to her) are the same points to which he responds in a letter that seems to be addressed to Ottoline Morrell in the fourth notebook. (Ed.)

like him in a different way. Massine pretends he likes me. I do not pretend. I noticed this because when I was in Madrid and saw his ballet that Diaghilev had composed, I went to congratulate him,* and when I was in his dressing room, I kissed him. Massine thought that I was kissing him with a Judas kiss, because Diaghilev had convinced him that my actions were evil. I know that Diaghilev was trying to convince him of this by pure chance, because I was another Massine in Diaghilev's service for a period of five years. I did not understand Diaghilev. Diaghilev understood me because my intelligence was very limited. Diaghilev realized that I had to be educated and therefore that it was essential that I should trust him. I used to ask him, "Why did you abandon a man who loved you?"† To that he answered that he did not abandon him, that the man abandoned him, and he told me the whole invented story. That man was called———. I do not want to mention his name, because he is a reformed character. This man fell in love with a female dancer well known in Russia. I know her. She knows me very little. She knows that I am Nijinsky. She loves my dances. I know that she loves my dances, because she smiled with feeling when I danced. I know the man who lived with Diaghilev in the same way as I did. I like that man. The man does not like me, because he thinks that I took away his job with Diaghilev. I know that Diaghilev taught this man to like objets d'art. This man liked objets d'art and took to them in a big way. Diaghilev

* According to Massine (*My Life in Ballet*, pp. 113–14), the ballet on which Nijinsky congratulated him at this meeting was the recently premiered *Good-Humored Ladies* (1917). In speaking of Diaghilev's having composed this Massine ballet, Nijinsky may be referring to the fact that the Domenico Scarlatti sonatas to which the choreography was set were selected by Diaghilev, in collaboration with Massine. (Ed.)

† Nijinsky's predecessor as Diaghilev's lover was Alexis Mavrine, who was with Diaghilev for several years and acted as his secretary. During the troupe's 1909 Paris season, as Diaghilev was shifting his attentions to Nijinsky, Mavrine eloped with Olga Feodorova, a dancer in the troupe. (Ed.)

bought objets d'art for him. This man loved Diaghilev in the same way as I did. I do not like Diaghilev for his upbringing to like boys.* I understood that Kyra did not want to see me. I told her today that she was masturbating. She felt that when I looked at her. Her mother, my wife, felt the same. Her mother thought that I was accusing the child wrongly and therefore said something to me in Kyra's defense. I answered her roughly and showed Kyra once again that I understood her. I began picking at my finger and then made a movement that Kyra makes when she is masturbating. After that I left them both in the room. I went to wash because God told me that it was time for me to wash. I remained alone in the room, but I felt my error. I did not want Kyra to be afraid of me, and therefore I did something even worse. As she was passing, I called her and told her I knew that she was masturbating today, and that if she wanted to, she could go, but that if she wanted to stay here with me, she could. She left. I felt a pain in my soul. I did not wish her harm. She realized that I did not like her, and therefore she left. I know why she left. I noticed a movement of the child toward me, but I pushed it away because I thought that it would be better if she left. The child felt it and left. I wept in my heart. I wanted to call her. I went to look for her, but found her with a woman from the Red Cross. I said aloud that Kyra did not love me, because she told me so. After a few seconds I said that she had left and that to leave meant that she did not love me. The woman felt a pain in her soul and almost wept, but her reason told her that she had to persuade Kyra to tell me that she loved me. I left, and Kyra wept in her heart. I know that she wept, because I saw her face all distorted. I was suffering. I did not want suffering. I wanted to

---

* Nijinsky presumably means something such as: "I do not like Diaghilev, because of his taste for boys, which was the product of his upbringing." (Tr.)

101

make her understand that I loved her. I told her afterward that I was leaving because she did not love me. I noticed that this made an impression on her. Her mother was frightened because she thought I wished her harm. I told my wife I had the right to bring up my child. The mother felt hurt because she thought that I had said it on purpose in order to reproach her. I did not say that in order to reproach her. I went downstairs and started putting down in writing what I aimed to do. The telephone rang, and I wrote down what I heard, because my wife thought that I had gone out for a walk. At lunch I gave my wife to understand that I knew she was talking with Dr. Frenkel. She lied to me because she was afraid of me. I felt that the dessert was full of medicine, and therefore I left it and asked for fruit. I knew that the dessert had medicine in it, because my wife took very little of it. I took a lot on purpose, so that she would think that I did not know, but a little later I showed my wife that I was smelling the dessert and that my sense of smell felt some nasty things. I left the dessert and pointed at it so that everyone could realize that the dessert was nasty. The maid, who happened to be passing and who had not seen that I had pushed the dessert away, asked me, "Is it good?" I answered, "Excellent." She felt what I had said and saw the dessert that I had started and not finished. I will not eat things with medicine in them, and in this way they will be surprised that I know things I have not seen. I will not smell, but feel. I smelled because God wanted me to . . . .

I left the man whom Diaghilev loved before me.

Diaghilev loved that man physically. And therefore he wanted him to love him too. So that he would love him, Diaghilev gave him a taste for objets d'art. Diaghilev gave Massine a taste for fame. I did not take to objects and fame, because I did not feel them. Diaghilev noticed that I was a boring man, and therefore he left me alone. As I was alone, I masturbated and chased tarts. I like tarts. Diaghilev thought that I was bored, but I was not bored. I was busy with dancing, and composed ballets by myself. Diaghilev did not like me, because I composed ballets by myself. He did not want me to do things by myself that went against his grain. I could not agree with him in his taste in art. I said one thing to him, and he said another to me. I often quarreled with him. I used to lock my door, because our rooms were next to each other. I did not allow anyone in. I was afraid of him because I knew that all practical life was in his hands. I never left the room. Diaghilev also remained alone. Diaghilev was annoyed because everyone saw our quarrel. It was unpleasant for Diaghilev to see people asking what the matter was with Nijinsky. Diaghilev liked showing that Nijinsky was his pupil in everything. I did not want to show that I agreed with him about everything, and therefore I often quarreled with him in everybody's presence. Diaghilev turned to Stravinsky for help, this was in a hotel in London. Stravinsky supported Diaghilev because he knew that Diaghilev would abandon me. Then I felt hatred for Stravinsky because I saw that he was lending his support to a falsehood, and I pretended to give in. I was not a spiteful man. Stravinsky thought that I was a spiteful kid. I was not more than twenty-one years old. I was young and therefore made mistakes. I always wanted to correct my mistakes, but I noticed that no one loved me. I started pretending to be spiteful. I disliked Diaghilev, but I lived with him. I hated Diaghilev from the very first days I knew him, because I knew Diaghilev's power. I did not like Diaghilev's power, because he abused it. I was poor. I earned 65 roubles a month. Sixty-five roubles a month was not enough to feed my mother and myself. I was renting a small three-room apartment that cost 35–37 roubles a month. I liked music. I made the acquaintance of Prince Pavel Lvov, who introduced me to a Polish Count.* I have forgotten his name because this is how I want it. I do not want to offend the whole family, for I have forgotten his first name. This Count bought me an upright piano. I did not like him. I liked Prince Pavel, and not the Count. Lvov introduced me by telephone to Diaghilev, who invited me to come to the Hôtel de l'Europe, where he was staying. I hated him for his voice, which was too self-assured, but I went in search of luck. I found luck there because I immediately made love to him. I trembled like an aspen leaf. I hated him, but I put up a pretense, for I knew that my mother and I would starve to death. I understood Diaghilev from the first moment and therefore pretended that I agreed with all his views. I realized one had to live, and therefore it did not matter to me what sacrifice I made. I worked hard at dancing and therefore always felt tired. But I pretended that I was cheerful and not tired in order that Diaghilev should not be bored. I know that Diaghilev felt it, but Diaghilev liked boys and therefore found it difficult to understand me. I do not want people to think that Diaghilev is a scoundrel and that he must be put in prison. I will weep if he is hurt. I do not like him, but he is a human being. I love all human beings and therefore do not want to cause them pain. I know that everyone will be horrified reading these lines, but I want to have them published while I am still alive, because I know the effect they will produce. I want to create a living impression, and therefore I am describing my life while I am still alive. I do not want people to read my life after my death. I am not afraid of death. I am afraid of attacks. I am afraid of evil. I am afraid people might understand me badly. I do not wish harm to Diaghilev. I like him just as much as anyone else. I am not God. I cannot judge

* On Prince Pavel Lvov, who was probably Nijinsky's first lover, see introduction, p. viii. Richard Buckle (*Nijinsky*, pp. 57–58) identifies the Polish count as Count Tishkievich, a wealthy arts patron from Vilno. (Ed.)

men. God and not rights will judge him. I am against all rights.* I am not Napoleon. I am not a Napoleon who punishes men for their mistakes. I am a Napoleon who forgives mistakes. I will give you an example, and you must repeat it. Diaghilev has harmed not you but me. I do not want to punish him, because I have punished him by revealing his faults so that everybody knows them. I have punished myself, for I have told everyone about myself. I have spoken about many others in order to punish them. I do not want everybody to think that I am writing with a hypocritical purpose. If anyone wants to punish the people I have written about, I will say that every-thing I have written is a lie. I will tell them to put me in a lunatic asylum. I am not writing in order to incite people against mistakes. I have no right to judge. The judge is God, not men. Bolsheviks are not Gods. I am not a Bolshevik. I am a man in God. I speak out of the mouth of God. I love everyone and want love for everyone. I do not want anyone to quarrel. Everyone quarrels because they do not understand God. I will explain God to everyone, but I will not explain him if people start laughing. I speak of things that affect the whole world. I am peace, and not war. I want peace for all. I want love on earth. The earth is disintegrating because its fuel is burning out. Fuel will continue to give heat for a while, but not very much, and therefore God wants love before the earth loses all heat. People do not think about stars and therefore do not under-stand the world. I often think about stars, and therefore I know who I am. I do not like astronomy, because astronomy does not give us a conception of God. Astronomy wants to teach us the geography of stars. I do not like geography. I know geog-raphy because I have studied it. I do not like state frontiers, because I realize that the earth is one state. The earth is the

* Again Nijinsky uses the word "rights" when he seems to mean "law." (Tr.)

head of God. God is fire in the head. I am alive as long as I have a fire in my head. My pulse is an earthquake.* I am an earthquake. I know that if there are no earthquakes, the earth will be extinguished, and with the earth extinguished, the whole life of man will be extinguished too, because man will not have a constant supply of food. I am spiritual food, and therefore I do not feed men with blood. Christ did not want to feed men with blood, as the churches have understood it. Men go to pray, but they are filled with wine and told that this is Christ's blood. Christ's blood does not make men drunk, but sober. Catholics do not drink wine, but employ hypocritical means. Catholics swallow white wafers and think they are swallowing the body and blood of the Lord. I am not the body and blood of the Lord. I am the spirit in the body. I am a body with a spirit. God cannot be without either body or spirit. Blood and spirit in the body is the Lord. I am the Lord. I am man. I am Christ. Christ said that he was the spirit in the body, but the churches have distorted his teaching, because they did not let him live. They bumped him off. He was bumped off by poor people who were given a lot of money. These poor people all hanged themselves afterward because they could not live without Christ. I know that people are bad because they find it difficult to live. I know that those who print these pages will weep, and therefore one must not be surprised at the bad print. Bad print is produced by poor people who have little strength. I know that print spoils the eyes, and therefore I want my writing to be photographed. For a photograph spoils only one eye, but print spoils many eyes. I want to photograph my manuscript, only I am afraid of spoiling the photograph. I had a

---

* Nijinsky will return to the subject of earthquakes. According to Romola (*Nijinsky*, pp. 340–41), St. Moritz suffered a violent earthquake on the Nijinskys' first night in their St. Moritz home in December 1917. The Hotel Chantarella was evacuated. (Ed.)

camera, and I tried to make photographs with it and develop the films. I am not afraid of the red light, but I am afraid of spoiling the photographs, because film is a good thing and one must cherish it. I would prefer to give my camera to a man who would make one photograph for me. I like my camera because I think it will be of use to me. I feel the opposite. I do not want to make photographs, because I have little time. I want to devote myself to the theater and not to photography. I will leave photography to those who like it. I like photography, only I cannot sacrifice my whole life to it. I will devote my whole life to photography if people prove to me that it can help in understanding God. I am familiar with cinema. I wanted to work with cinema, but I realized its significance. Cinema serves to increase money. Money serves to increase the number of cinema theaters. I realized that cinema enabled one man to make money, while the theater enabled many people to make money. I find it difficult to work in the theater, but I would rather suffer privations than work for cinema. Diaghilev often said to me that something like cinema had to be invented because its power was great. Bakst,* a well-known artist and a Russian Jew, used to say that cinema was good from the money point of view. I said nothing because I felt that Bakst and Diaghilev think I am a kid and therefore cannot express my ideas. Diaghilev always looks for logic in ideas. I know that thought cannot exist without logic, but logic cannot exist without feeling. Diaghilev has both logic and feeling, but feeling is something else. Diaghilev has a bad feeling, and I have a good feeling. Diaghilev has a bad feeling not because he has a bigger head than anyone else, but because he has a bad feeling in his

---

* The Russian painter Léon Bakst (1866–1924) was the most celebrated set and costume designer of the prewar Ballets Russes. He designed Nijinsky's first two ballets, *The Afternoon of a Faun* and *Jeux*. (Ed.)

head. Lombroso says that feelings can be recognized by the shape of the head. I say that feelings are recognized through people's actions. I am not a scientist, but I understand well. I understand well because I have good feelings.

Many people do not like fountain pens because it is difficult to insert ink into them. The ink is inserted with a pump that is made of a little glass pipe and a rubber . . . . I do not know what the rubber thing at the end of the little glass pipe is called. I take this little pipe and pump in the ink so that the air does not get in. In order for the air not to get in, you must dip the pipe in the ink. After the little pipe is filled, its end must be put into the ink in the fountain pen. People often make the mistake of taking the bubble for the ink, because they see the end of the little circle. I can distinguish the little ink circle from the circle of air. I know that both these circles are black, but the circle with air in it is less black, because my face is cleaner. I like a black face, and therefore, before taking the ink into the pipe, I suck out the air. Having sucked out the air, I check to see whether there is still some air left. I then take the ink and introduce the ink into the ink that is in the holder. Air often prevents the ink from getting into the holder, and nervous people spoil their dresses or dirty their faces because the ink bubble bursts. The bubble has no patience, it bursts when it wants to. I know its tricks, and therefore I feel when I must stop. I do not think when I must stop. I stop at God's command. I suck out the air again and then pour in the ink until the air stops me. I have gotten so used to this that I do not waste much time pouring in the ink and do not sigh every time the pen has to be filled with ink. People are afraid of ink because ink is not good. I have the ink.* This ink is bad because it contains little ink. The ink is diluted with water because the man wants to

* "the ink": To indicate which ink, he inserts a small drawing of its label. (Ed.)

get rich. It does not matter to him whether people find it convenient to write or not. He has no love for people. He has love for money. I understand him well. He has children, and he wants to leave them money. I do not like money when I know how its soul suffers. I know that everyone wants to have a fountain pen. I know that mothers buy fountain pens for young girls for their studies. I know that every young girl likes dresses. I know that she cries if she makes dirty ink marks on her dress. She is not afraid of being scolded by her father or her mother. She can bear all this. She is sorry about her dress because she knows its price. Her father works long hours. His life is hard. He buys expensive fabrics for his daughter in order to show his love for his daughter. The daughter cries because she feels a moral injury within herself. She is hurt. She does not show this dress to her father. The father notices this and is irritated because he is hurt. I know what he is driving at. He does not want his daughter to hide from him what she has done. What was done was done not by the daughter but by the fountain pen. It was done by the man who invented the ink. I do not want to accuse that man. I want to show people's mistakes. I do not want ink to contain water. I want ink without water. A man produces thousands of bottles with good ink in them for the sake of publicity, and then, seeing that people buy it, produces millions of bottles containing water. I know the tricks of ink factories. I know the tricks of impresarios. Diaghilev is also an impresario, because he has a troupe. Diaghilev has learned to cheat from other impresarios. He does not like being told that he is an impresario. He understands what being an impresario means. All impresarios are considered thieves. Diaghilev does not want to be a thief and therefore does not want to be called an impresario. Diaghilev wants to be called a Maecenas. Diaghilev wants to become part of history. Diaghilev cheats people, thinking that no one knows what he is aiming at. Diaghilev dyes his hair so as not to be old. Diaghilev's hair is gray. Diaghilev buys black hair creams and rubs them in. I noticed this cream on Diaghilev's pillows, which have black pillowcases. I do not like dirty pillowcases and therefore felt disgusted when I saw them. Diaghilev has two false front teeth. I noticed this because when he is nervous he touches them with his tongue. They move, and I can see them. Diaghilev reminds me of a wicked old woman when he moves his two front teeth. Diaghilev has a lock of hair dyed white at the front of his head. Diaghilev wants to be noticed. His lock of hair has become yellow because he bought a bad white dye. In Russia his lock was better, because I never noticed it. I noticed it much later, for I did not like paying attention to people's hairstyles. My own hairstyle bothered me. I constantly changed it. People said to me, "What are you doing with your hair? You always change your hairstyle," and then I said that I liked changing my hairstyle because I did not want to be always the same. Diaghilev liked to be talked about and therefore wore a monocle in one eye. I asked him why he wore a monocle, for I noticed that he saw well without a monocle. Then Diaghilev told me that one of his eyes saw badly. I realized then that Diaghilev had told me a lie. I felt deeply hurt. I realized that Diaghilev was deceiving me. I trusted him in nothing and began to develop by myself, pretending that I was his pupil. Diaghilev felt my pretense and did not like me, but he knew that he too was pretending, and therefore he left me alone. I began to hate him quite openly, and once I pushed him on a street in Paris. I pushed him because I wanted to show him that I was not afraid of him. Diaghilev hit me with his cane because I wanted to leave him. He felt that I wanted to go away, and therefore he ran after me. I half ran, half walked. I was afraid of being noticed. I noticed that people were looking. I felt a pain in my leg and pushed Diaghilev. I pushed him only slightly because I felt not anger against Diaghilev but tears. I wept. Diaghilev scolded me. Diaghilev was gnashing his teeth, and I felt sad and dejected. I could no longer control myself and began to walk slowly. Diaghilev too began to walk slowly. We both walked slowly. I do not remember where we were going. I was walking. He was walking. We went, and we arrived. We lived together for a long time. I had a dull life. I grieved alone. I wept alone. I loved my mother and wrote letters to her every day. I wept in those letters. I spoke of my future life. I did not know what to do. I cannot remember what I wrote, but I have a feeling that I wept bitterly. My mother felt this because she wrote me letters in reply. She could not reply to me about my aspirations, because they were my aspirations. She was waiting for my intentions. I was afraid of life because I was very young. I have been married for over five years. I lived with Diaghilev also for five years. I cannot count. I am now twenty-nine years old. I know that I was nineteen when I met Diaghilev. I loved him sincerely, and when he used to tell me that love for women was a terrible thing, I believed him. If I had not believed him, I would not have been able to do what I did. Massine does not know life, because his parents were rich. They lacked for nothing. We did not have bread. My mother did not know what to give us to live on. My mother joined the Ciniselli Circus in order to earn a little money.* My mother was ashamed of such work because she was a well-known artiste in Russia. I understood it all, even though I was a child. I wept in my heart. My mother also wept. One day I could bear it no longer and ran to Bourman, a friend of mine, he was called Anatole.† He is now married to Klementovich. I went to his father and told

---

* The Ciniselli Circus in St. Petersburg produced circuses and other popular spectacles. (Ed.)

† Anatole Bourman (1888–1962) was a close friend of Nijinsky's in school. Later, he wrote *The Tragedy of Nijinsky* (1936), a highly unreliable biography. He too danced

him that my mother was suffering because of money. Then his father (a pianist) told me that I should go to the manager of the Imperial Theaters in Petrograd. I went. I was only 14–15 years old. The manager was called Dmitri Alexandrovich Krupensky. The Director was Teliakovsky.* The Emperor was Nicholas II. I liked the theater. I went to the office. When I went in, I was frightened because I saw dry, laughing faces. I went into the room where Krupensky was sitting. He had a black beard. He frightened me because I was afraid of his beard. I trembled like an aspen leaf. I did not want to say anything to him. I was not lying. Krupensky and the other officials began to laugh. I started trembling even more. I trembled, and everyone laughed. Krupensky asked me what I wanted. Then I told him that I needed 500 roubles to pay my mother's debts. I learned of this figure by chance. I did not think of what I was saying. I trembled. I got up. I saw bored faces. I left. I ran quickly, panting. Krupensky and his black beard were chasing me. I ran. I screamed silently, "I won't do it again." "I won't do it again." I wept in my heart, but the tears did not flow. I knew that if I went to my mother, she would understand me, and therefore I ran to her and told her everything. I did not know how to lie. Whenever I lied I trembled like an aspen leaf. I was the leaf of God. I loved God, but I did not like praying. I did not know what I had to do. I lived, and life went on. I did not understand business and did not like it, but God helped me. I gave lessons. At the lessons I was simple. I was happy to earn money. I often wept in my room. I liked having a room of my own. I thought I was a grown-up

with the Ballets Russes. He married the dancer Leokadja Klementovich, who was one of the original nymphs in Nijinsky's *Afternoon of a Faun*. (Ed.)

* Alexander Dmitrievich Krupensky (this is the correct name) was the administrator, and Vladimir Arkadievich Teliakovsky the director, of the Imperial Theaters in St. Petersburg. (Ed.)

if I had a room of my own. In a room of my own I could weep
a lot. I read Dostoevsky. I read "The Idiot" when I was eighteen, and I understood its meaning. I wanted to be a writer and
studied Dostoevsky's manuscript* ineptly. I studied Gogol. I
copied out Pushkin, thinking that if I copied out his poems, I
would learn to write poetry and novels like Pushkin. I copied
out a lot, but I felt that all this was nonsense, and I abandoned
it. I lived simply. We had enough bread. My mother liked en-
tertaining. She invited people over when she felt that we had a
lot. My mother liked making friends and therefore invited
them. I also liked friends and therefore listened to whatever the
grown-ups were talking about. I understood grown-ups and
therefore was drawn to them. I understood my mistake later,
because the grown-ups had problems different from mine. Because I liked grown-ups, I antagonized the children, because
they did not understand me. I used to know a boy called Goncharov.† I do not remember his first name. I have just remembered it: he was called Leonid. Leonid drank vodka. I did not
drink vodka. We were in school together. Our school life
brought us together, but it did not make us together, for I did
not adopt his habits. I do not know who had taught him to
get drunk. His face was pale and covered with pimples. The
supervisors did not understand the children, for they shut themselves up in the common room, where they read or received
their friends. I understand supervisors who are bored by children. I realize that children do not understand supervisors. It
is a difficult thing to be a supervisor. I did not let my Kyra be
brought up by others, because I understand what it means to

---

*   "manuscript": Presumably, "writings." (Tr.)
†   According to Bronislava Nijinska (*Early Memoirs*, pp. 136, 174), this schoolmate,
Leonid Goncharov, was a serious student of music and thereby a good influence on
Nijinsky. In 1906, while the two boys were still in school, Goncharov danced the
Nutcracker to Nijinsky's King of the Mice in the Imperial Ballet's *Nutcracker*. (Ed.)

bring up a child. I want people to bring up their children themselves and not give them to strangers, because strangers become bored.

I could not go on writing, because I started to think about my writing. I wanted to say that the children's lives depend on their upbringing. Supervisors cannot bring up children, because they are not married. If they are married, they miss their wives and children. I know one supervisor who had favorites. He was called Isayenko.* I liked him, but I felt that he did not like me. I was afraid of him, thinking that he wished me harm. Once he invited me to his apartment, saying that he wanted to teach me French. I went, thinking that I would learn it, but when I came, he sat me down in a chair and gave me a book. I felt bored. He did not feel bored. I did not understand why he invited me, when he merely handed me a book. I read aloud, but I felt bored. Isayenko invited me to eat together with the others. I felt that he was paying for his room and board. I did not understand French, for they spoke in Russian. The woman was young and thin. Her nerves were in a bad state, for she moved around a lot. She had a young man with her. I do not remember what he looked like. Her face has stuck in my memory. She had a small dog that ran around on the table and licked her plate. She loved that little dog. I did not like that little dog, because it was sickly. It had a deformed body. It was thin, with long legs, small ears, popping-out eyes. It was a tiny little dog. I felt pity for the little dog and felt sad. Isayenko

---

* Bronislava Nijinska (*Early Memoirs*, p. 172) recalls that her mother asked Grigori Grigorievich Isayenko, one of the strictest teachers in the school, to take an interest in Nijinsky because the boy had no father. According to Nijinska, Nijinsky often went to Isayenko's apartment and spoke of him with admiration. (Ed.)

laughed at the little dog because it was tiny. I felt in the way because they wanted to speak about something but were silent. I felt that there was a secret. I wanted to leave, but did not know how. Isayenko smiled at me. I felt disgust and left, leaving on the plate everything that had been put on it. I knew what kind of person he was. I left with a nasty feeling toward Isayenko and all the others there. I felt sick. I could not continue my French lessons and avoided Isayenko. Isayenko pursued me and nagged me about my marks. I received bottom marks, that is, a one. We had a twelve-mark system, and the top mark was 12. I did not work at my French, because I felt repugnance for it. The French teacher felt that I did not like French, and he was angry. I did not learn French, and when he asked me questions, I let the other students whisper the answers to me. The marks he gave me differed according to his mood. He had to show that his students learned well, and therefore he gave me good marks. I understood his trick and took to changing my marks. The Frenchman did not notice, and no one touched me. I gave up French.

I did not like Religious Instruction, because I was very bored with it. I liked going to religion classes because I liked listening to the reverend Father's funny sayings and proverbs. The Father was not my father, but other people's, because he spoke about his children. He would show us a coin and say that he used this coin to teach his children to understand him. I knew that my mother had no money, but I understood her, and so I felt bored. The reverend Father was not a Father, because a father is a good man, and this father had to restrain his anger. All the children noticed that he was restraining his anger, and therefore they allowed themselves all kinds of pranks behind his back. I know pranks because I was ringleader in many pranks. I played a lot of pranks, and all the boys liked me for it. I showed them that I could shoot from a slingshot better than anyone else, because I hit a doctor in the eye. He was sitting in a cab as we were going in carriages to the theater.* I liked carriages because I could shoot at passersby from them. I was a good shot. I was not sure that I had hit the doctor, but I was ashamed to deny it when the boys, fearing that they might be expelled, pointed to me. I loved my mother and burst into tears. My tears affected the supervisor, who was a very good man, only he drank a lot and all the children laughed at him because he was ridiculous. The children liked him because he never took offense. Many of them cried when they learned that he had died of drink. He was buried, but not a single boy went to his funeral. I was also afraid and therefore did not go.

I was accused of a crime, and the inspector lectured me. I was afraid of lectures because I felt the anger of the inspector Pisnichevsky. Pisnichevsky was a bad-tempered man, but he did not throw children out on the street, because he knew that these were children of poor parents. Pisnichevsky called in my mother and told her that he was not going to throw me out, but that he could not leave me without a punishment and therefore thought that my mother should take me home for two weeks. I felt a great pain in my soul and almost fainted. I was afraid for my mother because I knew how difficult it was for

---

* Bronislava Nijinska (*Early Memoirs*, pp. 123–26) gives the following account. Nijinsky and his schoolmates liked to shoot wads of paper from slingshots while riding in the carriages that took the students to and from performances of the Imperial Ballet at the Maryinsky Theater. One day when Nijinsky was fifteen, a government official was hit by one of these missiles. Nijinsky was blamed, demoted for a month to the status of nonresident student, and ordered to return his uniform and books. This was a serious financial hardship for his mother. She pleaded her son's case to Vladimir Porfiryevich Pisnyachevsky, Inspector of the Imperial Theatrical School, and the punishment was gradually lifted. (Ed.)

her to get money. My mother took me home and whacked me with birch twigs brought in by the yardman. I was not afraid of the whacking, but I was afraid of my mother. My mother beat so that it hurt, but I did not feel my mother's anger. My mother beat me because she believed that this was the best way. I felt love for my mother and said that I would not do it again. She felt me and believed me. I felt that my mother trusted me, and I decided to learn well. I started getting good marks, and everyone laughed, saying that my mother's whacking had helped me. The supervisors smiled, and the boys laughed. I laughed too, because I did not feel any offense. I loved my mother, and accordingly I was pleased that everybody knew. I told them how she had beaten me. The children were afraid and no longer laughed. I began to learn well and set a good example. The only subjects I had little success with were French and Religious Instruction.

I knew the Russian church services because I went to church every time.* I liked going to church because I liked seeing the silver icons, which glittered. There were candles for sale, and sometimes I used to sell them together with Isayev, my companion in masturbation.† I liked him, but felt that what he had taught me to do was a bad thing. I suffered when I wanted to do it. I wanted to do it every time I went to bed. Isayenko noticed that I was masturbating, but said nothing terrible to me. I noticed that no one in school knew about my habits, and I therefore continued with them. I continued till I noticed that my dancing was beginning to deteriorate. I was scared because I realized that my mother would soon be ruined and I would not be able to help her. I started combating my lust. I forced

---

* "every time": Presumably, "every Sunday." (Tr.)
† According to Bronislava Nijinska (*Early Memoirs*, p. 97), Nikolai Isayev was Nijinsky's desk mate and close friend during his early years in the Imperial Theatrical School. (Ed.)

117

myself to do so. I said to myself, "I mustn't." I learned well. I gave up masturbation. I was about fifteen years old. I loved my mother, and my love for my mother made me improve. I learned well. Everyone began to notice me. I got top marks. My mother became happy. She often told me that the whacking had done me good. I told her that this was so, but I felt otherwise. I loved my mother infinitely. I decided to devote myself to dancing even more. I grew thin. I started to dance like God. Everyone started talking about me. When I was still at school, I was already dancing as a leading dancer.* I knew what it was to be a leading dancer. I did not understand why I was given such parts to dance. I loved admiration. I was proud. I liked pride, but I did not like praise. I did not boast. The students of the dramatic classes liked me.† I was often with them. I got to know a girl student who chose me as her favorite. She used to call me "Nejinka."‡ She gave me an album bound in velvet with newspaper clippings pasted into it. In these clippings I read that I was being called a "child prodigy," and the reviews were signed by Svetlov.§ I did not like what was being written about me, because I felt that it was all praise. I told my school friend that I did not like anything that was being written about me. She told me I did not understand, and she invited me to come to their apartment, saying that she wanted to introduce me to her father and mother. I felt love for her, but I did not show it to her. I loved her spiritually, and therefore I always

---

* Before his graduation from school in 1907, Nijinsky danced soloist roles with the Imperial Ballet. He also had leading roles in school performances. (Ed.)

† Bronislava Nijinska (*Early Memoirs*, p. 172) recalls that during his last years in school Nijinsky preferred the company of the drama students to that of the ballet students. He apparently found the drama students more serious. Also, they were less likely to be envious of him. (Ed.)

‡ *Nejinka* means "tender" or "affectionate." (Tr.)

§ Valerian Svetlov was the ballet critic of the *St. Petersburg Gazette*. See footnote on p. 160. (Ed.)

smiled at her. I always smiled. I liked smiling at everyone because I noticed that everyone loved me. I loved everyone. When
I went to my friend's apartment, I had dinner, and then her
friends started a spiritualist séance. They put their hands on the
table, and the table moved. Everyone was surprised at that. Her
father, a general, did not like all this nonsense and therefore
left the room. I felt that it was nonsense, and I left them and
went home. I came home tired because I did not understand
the purpose of the invitation. I did not like invitations, and
therefore I refused them. I was asked to give lessons in ballroom
dancing because my fame in Russia had spread. I was sixteen
years old. I gave lessons and gave the money to my mother.
My mother was sorry for me, but felt a great love for me. I
also felt a great love for my mother and decided that I would
help her financially. I finished school at the age of eighteen. I
graduated and was let out into the outside world. I did not
know what to do, because I did not know how to dress. I was
used to uniforms. I did not like civilian dress and therefore did
not know how to wear it. I thought that shoes with thick soles
were attractive, and therefore bought myself shoes with thick
soles . . . . . .

I want to describe my graduation. I was let out. I felt free,
but the freedom terrified me. For having been a good student,
I was awarded a New Testament with an inscription from
my religion teacher. I did not understand that New Testament, because it was written in Latin and Polish. I spoke and
read Polish very badly. If they had given me the New Testament in Russian, I would have understood it more easily.
I started reading and then gave it up. I did not like reading
the New Testament, because I could not understand it. The
book was lovely and the print beautiful. I did not feel the
New Testament. I read Dostoevsky. Dostoevsky was easier
for me to understand, and therefore I swallowed him whole

119

as I read him. I swallowed him in great chunks because when I read "The Idiot," I felt that the Idiot was not an "idiot" but a good man. I could not understand "The Idiot," because I was still too young. I did not know life. I now understand Dostoevsky's "Idiot" because people take me for an idiot. I like feeling and therefore pretended to be an idiot. I was not an idiot, because I am not nervous. I know that nervous people are subject to madness, and therefore I was afraid of madness. I am not mad, and Dostoevsky's Idiot is not an idiot. Just now I felt nervous and made a mistake in the letter "i." I like this letter because God has shown me what nerves mean. I do not like nervousness, because I know its effects. I want to write calmly and not nervously. I write quickly and jerkily, but not nervously. I do not want to write slowly, because the beauty of my handwriting is of no importance to me, but it is important for me to write quickly. I do not want my handwriting to be admired. I want my ideas to be admired. I am writing this book for the sake of its ideas and not for the sake of its handwriting. My hand gets tired because I am not used to writing a lot, but I know that it will soon get used to it. I feel a pain in my hand and therefore write badly and jerkily. Everyone will say that my handwriting is nervous, because the letters are written jerkily. I will say that my handwriting is not nervous, because my thoughts are not nervous. My thoughts proceed calmly and not abruptly.

Wilsonism gives me no peace. I wish Wilsonism success and happiness. I hope that my book will help Wilson, and therefore I want to have it published soon. So as to have this book published soon, I want to go to Paris, but in order to go to Paris I must get prepared. I know that there are many malicious people in Paris, and therefore I want to protect myself. I want to write a letter to Reszke in Polish, and to do that I must get used to it.* I will tell him the whole truth, and therefore he will help me. I want to write in Polish but not in this notebook . . . .

. . . .

I wrote in Polish and have written my letter to Reszke. Reszke is an out-and-out Pole. He will understand me if I pay him a lot of compliments. I do not like compliments. Compliments are unnecessary. I do not pay compliments. I am a man who always speaks the truth. There are various truths. What is various is various. I wrote a letter to Diaghilev and his friends and showed them I was angry. My anger had no bite. I bite, but do not cause pain. My stomach is clean. I do not like eating meat. I saw how a calf was killed, and a pig. I saw it and felt their tears. They felt death. I left so as not to see death. I could not bear it. I wept like a child. I went up a mountain and could not breathe. I gasped for breath. I felt the calf's death. I wept as I went up the mountain. I chose a mountain where there were no people. I was afraid of mockery. People do not understand one another. I understand people. I do not wish them evil. I want to save them from evil. I know that those people do not like salvation, and therefore I do not want to impose myself. My imposition will not bring salvation. I want salvation. My stars tell me, "Go here, go there." I know what twinkling is. I know what life is. Life is life and not death. I want death for life. I cannot write, be-

---

* "I must get used to it": He seems to mean, "I must get some practice." (Tr.) It is clearly at the end of this paragraph that Nijinsky broke off writing his diary and began the fourth notebook (see Appendix A), with a letter to the Polish singer Jean de Reszke. On the evidence of the next paragraph, it was also at this point that he wrote the letter to Diaghilev and possibly all the subsequent letters in the fourth notebook. (Ed.)

cause I am tired. I am tired because I have slept. I have slept and slept and slept and slept. Now I want to write. I will go to sleep when the Lord wills it. I am a novice monk, I am he. He is God, and I am in God. Gods, Gods, Gods are. I want to say it in French because I was writing in French to everyone in France except Reszke. Reszke is a man who has connections, and I will therefore ask him to send me Polish papers. I call papers those papers that give information regarding birth and town of baptism. I have been baptized in two towns.* I was born in one town. My city was and is my mother. A mother can say nothing. I ask for her love. I want her love. I write write write. I want want want.†

——— ——— ——— ——— ——— ——— ——— ———

I wanted to write in rhyme a little, but my thoughts are elsewhere. I want to describe my walks.

My walks were on foot. I liked walking by myself. I like walking by myself. I want alone alone. You are alone, and I am alone. We are alone, and you are alone.

I want to write to write. I want to say to say.
I want to say to say, I want to write to write.

Why can one not talk in rhyme when one can talk in rhyme. I am rhyme rhyme *rif*.‡ I want *rifa narif*. You are *narif* and I

---

* In his letter to Jean de Reszke in the fourth notebook, Nijinsky claims that he was baptized both in Kiev, where he was born, and in Warsaw. His mother, he says, had him baptized in Warsaw in the hope of preventing his ever having to serve in the Russian army. Bronislava Nijinska (*Early Memoirs*, p. 13) seems to think he was baptized only once, in Warsaw, in 1891. (Ed.)

† "I write" and "I want" rhyme in Russian, though not very well. (Tr.)

‡ *Rif* is the first syllable of the Russian word for "rhyme," *rifma*. "Rifa," "narif," and "tarif" have no meaning in Russian. Apparently, Nijinsky is simply adding syllables onto *rif* for the sake of the rhythm. (Tr.)

am *tarif*. We are *rif*. You are *rif* we are *rif*. You are He and I
am he. We are we you are they.

I want to say to say that you want to sleep and sleep.
I want to write and sleep.
You cannot sleep and write.
I write write write.
You write write write.
I want to say to you
that it is impossible impossible impossible
I it is im possible im possible im possible.
You you *lia* you *lia lia ga**
Lia ga lia ga lia gu lia ga
Ga lia gu lia lia gu lia.
I want to tell you that one cannot write to you. I write to
   you to you. I will tell you you
I want to write to write. I want not to sleep, but to shit.
I want that you went.
I want that you went.
You went and I went
We went and you went
You do not want to walk there
I you do not want to walk there.
Gulia gulia gulia lia lia
Lia gu lia gu lia gu lia.
You are *gu lia gu lia gu*
You are *gu gu gu gu gu*

* Nijinsky now begins to ring changes on the word *guliat'*, "to walk." (Note that he
introduced the poem by saying, "I want to describe my walks.") *Gulia, lia, gu*, and its
variant *ga* are all presumably derived from *guliat'*. It happens that the sounds *gu* (pronounced "goo") and *lia* (pronounced as a single syllable) are among the first distinct
sounds articulated by an infant. For this reason and because the sounds seem to please
Nijinsky, they have been left in their Russian form. Nijinsky's fondness for the sound
lia can also be seen in the poem beginning on p. 129. (Tr.)

Gu gu gu gu gu gu gu. You *gu gu* and I *gu gu*
I want to say that to sleep
I want to say that to sleep
You do not want to sleep with me
You do not want to sleep with me
I with you and you with me
I with you and you with me
We are you and you are in me.
I want to you to you
You want for me you are He
I am He and you are in me.
We are you they are You.
You you you you you you you.
I want to tell you
That you want to sleep sleep sleep.
I do not want want to sleep
You do not want want to sleep.
I will go and shit with you
You are to shi but I am not to shi.
I am not sha ming sha ming shi.*
Shi shi shi shi shi shi shi

———   ———   ———   ———

I want to say that to sleep
I want to say that to shit
I shit and you shit
I shit I shit
You shit you I shit
I shit and you are in I shit

* In this line Nijinsky has apparently made an association between *sral* ("I shat")
and *sramlyu* ("I shame"). (Tr.)

I shit you shit
We are shitting you are in I shit
I shit shit shit shit shit shit shit
I am in I shit and you are in I shit.
We are shitting you are I shit
I shit shit shit shit shit shit shit
I want to say I shit.
I want to say that I shit
I shit I shit I shit I shit well
I am shitting I am good
I am good that I shit good
I am good that I shit good
I shit shit shit
I shit shit shit
I want to say that I shit
I want to say that I shit
I shit shit shit
I shit shit that I shit
You that you want you want to sleep
I want to shit a little
You are not asleep that I want
I want that you are not asleep
You sleep sleep sleep sleep sleep sleep sleep
I do not sleep and you are asleep
I want that you are asleep asleep
You do not want that you are asleep
I do not sleep when you sleep
I do not sleep when you sleep.
I wish you well.
You do not wish me me harm.
I want good good
You do not want to sleep always.
I want to tell you

That you sleep sleep sleep sleep sleep.
I want to tell you
That you sleep sleep sleep sleep sleep.

I wrote in the same way in French, and I hope that I will be understood.* I want to tell people about love for one another. I know they will laugh when they get these letters, but I know that these verses will surprise them. I know that everyone thinks that I am dead, because I have not been in touch with anybody for a long time. I want people to forget about me, because I want to create a great impression. My first appearance will be in Paris at the Châtelet.† I like the Châtelet because that theater is simple and big. I do not want much money for myself, because I want to give a performance for the benefit of poor French artistes who have suffered as a result of the war.

I want to tell them about love for each other, and therefore I want to speak to them. I want them to come to me. I know they will come to me after this charity performance. I want to speak to all artistes because I want to help them. I will tell them that I love them and that I will always help them. I do not want to help with money, and therefore I will tell them that I will come and see them if they help each other. I will pretend to be a jester, for they will understand me better.

I like Shakespeare's jesters. They have a lot of humor, but they get angry sometimes, and therefore they are not Gods. I am a jester in God, and therefore I like joking.

---

* He is referring to letters that he wrote in French "in the same way"—that is, with insistent repetition—in the fourth notebook. (Ed.)
† It was at the Théâtre du Châtelet in Paris that Nijinsky made his European debut, with the Ballets Russes, in 1909. (Ed.)

I want to say that a jester is appropriate where there is love. A jester without love is not God. God is a jester. And I am God.

We are Gods, you are Gods.
I want to say that God,
God is God but God is God.

I feel cold in my legs, and I realize that I have to go to bed soon. Upstairs, people are walking, and therefore I feel that they will come looking for me. I do not want to sleep, because I slept a lot in the afternoon, but they want to fatten me up.

——————— ——————— ———————

To my dear and darling Romushka,

I made you angry on purpose because I love you. I wish you happiness. You are afraid of me because I have changed. I have changed because God has willed it so. God willed it because I wanted it so. You have called Dr. Frenkel. You have trusted a stranger, and not me. You think that he agrees with you. He agrees with me. He is afraid of showing his wife that he knows nothing. He is afraid of showing his wife that he is nothing. Nothing, because everything he has learned by studying is nothing. I was not afraid to abandon all my studies and show everyone that I knew nothing. I do not want to dance the way I used to, because all those dances are death. Death is not only when the body dies. The body dies, but the spirit lives. The spirit is a dove, but in God. I am God, and I am in God. You are a woman like any other. I am a man like any other. I work more than anyone else. I know more than anyone else. You will understand me later because everyone will say that Nijinsky is God. You will believe and agree. You will be bored because you do not want to work. I want to go on walks with you. You do not want to go on walks with me. You think I am ill. You think that, because Dr. Frenkel told you I was ill. He thinks that I am ill because he thinks that I am ill. I am writing to you in my notebook because I want you to read it in Russian. I have learned to speak French. You do not want to speak in Russian. I wept when I felt your Russian speech. You do not like it when I speak in Hungarian. I like the Hungarian language. You do not like the Hungarian language. I want the Hungarian language because you are the Hungarian language. I want to live in Hungary. You do not want to live in Hungary. I want to live in Russia, you do not want to live in Russia. You do not know what you want, but I know what I want. I want to build a house. You do not want to live in the house. You think I am stupid, and I think you are a fool. A fool is a terrible thing. I am stupid, but not a fool. You are a fool, but you are not stupid. I am stupid I am stupid. A stupid man is a corpse,* but I am not a corpse. Corpse, corpse, corpse, but I am not a corpse. I wish you no harm. I love you you. You do not love me.† I love love you.

You do not want to show that you love love me. I want to tell you that you love love me. I want to tell you that I love love you.

---

* "Stupid" (*glup*) and "corpse" (*trup*) rhyme in Russian. (Tr.)

† Here Nijinsky uses the Church Slavonic forms for "me"—*mia,* instead of the modern Russian *menia*—presumably because he thinks it rhymes better with *tebia* ("you" or "thou") in the sentences before and after this one. (See footnote on p. 69.) In both words the last two letters form one syllable, pronounced "ya" as in "yard." The poem that follows is in large measure a concatenation of "ya" sounds, some of which have been left untranslated. (Tr.)

I love you you.   I love you you,
I want to tell you that you love me and me.
I am me am me not me.
I am me am me not me.
Me me me me me me *mlia*
I am not *mlia*, but I am *zemlia**
I am *zemlia* and you are *zemlia*
We are *zemlia* and you are *zemlia*
You do not want me me me
I want you you
I want you you
I want you you
You do not want me me me
I am not me not me *mlia mlia*
I wish you no harm
I want to love you
I love you you
I am not *mlia* not *mlia zemlia*
I am *zemlia*, but you are not *mlia*
I am *zemlia*, but you are not *mlia*
Not *mlia* not *mlia* I am not *mlia*
Mlia mlia not *mlia* I am *zemlia*
You are *mlia*, but I am *zemlia*
I am *zemlia* and you are *zemlia*
We are *zemlia* and he is *zemlia*
I am not *mlia*, but I am *zemlia*
I want to tell you
That I love you you

* *Zemlia* is Russian for "earth." Nijinsky seems to take pleasure in splitting the word into two syllables and producing the sounds *zem* and particularly *mlia*. Compare his repetition of the similar *lia* on p. 123. See also his use of *vnemlia*, presumably in part for the *lia* sound, on p. 131. There may be some subconscious connection between the infantilism of the sound *lia* (see note on p. 123) and the idea of *zemlia*, mother earth. (Tr.)

129

I want to tell you
That I love love you
I write I write I hurry
You do not sleep but you sleep but you sleep
I do not sleep when I want to
You do not sleep when I sleep
I do not sleep and you are still asleep
You are still asleep, asleep asleep asleep asleep asleep
I want to tell you
That I sleep I sleep I sleep
You do not sleep do not sleep do not sleep
That I sleep I sleep I sleep
I want to tell you that I am asleep but I am not asleep
You want to show me that you sleep you sleep, you sleep
That I am asleep but I am not asleep
You want to show me that you are asleep you are asleep,
   you are asleep
I want to tell you that I am asleep, but I am not asleep
I want to tell you that I love I love you
I want to tell you that I love I love you
I am love and you are love, we are within love and you are
   within love
I want to tell you that I love love you
I want to tell you that I love love you
I wish you no harm I wish you no harm
You do not want to tell me that you love love me
I want to tell you that you love love me,
I love you my friend. You do not love love you
I am not you but you are not you. I love you you
I wish you no harm. I wish you no harm.
I want your love. I want your love
I want to tell you that I love you you.
I love your native country

I love you you
I want to you to you I want to say to you
I want to say to you that I am yours and you are mine.
You are mine and I am yours we are You and you are they
I am he in everyone in everyone. I love everyone everyone
    everyone everyone.
I want to say to you that I love everyone everyone everyone
    everyone
I want to tell you that I love everyone everyone everyone
    everyone
I want to play the jester. I can tell all all all
I want to tell all all. I want to tell all all
You are afraid of me me me I am not me not me *mlia mlia*
I am *zemlia* and you are *zemlia* I am not *mlia* not *mlia*
    *vnemlia**
I am *zemlia* and you are *zemlia*, I am not *mlia* and you are
    zemlia
I am *vnemlia vnemlia vnemli*
I am *vnemlia vnemlia vnemli*
I want to tell you that *vnemli* to me to me
I want to tell you that you are in me that you are in me
I want to tell you that you are *mlia* but I am *zemlia*
I am *zemlia zemlia* I am *zem*
You are *zem* but I am not *mlia*.
I want you you you are not *mlia* and I am not *mlia*
I want to tell you that you are *mlia* but I am *zemlia*
The whole *zemlia* is is mine. I am not *mlia* I am not *mlia*
I want to tell you that *zemlia* is me me me

---

*   *Vnemlia* is derived from an archaic word (now used in poetry only) corresponding
to "hark" in English. However, Nijinsky has little regard, particularly in his poems,
for the accepted meaning of words and probably uses *vnemlia* because it is associated
in his mind with poetry and because, if stressed on the last syllable (*-lia*), it rhymes
with *zemlia*. In fact, however, *vnemlia* is stressed on the first syllable. (Tr.)

You are afraid to tell me that you are me that you are me
me me me me me me me
I am me I am *zemlia*
I want to tell you that you are me but I am *zemlia*
I want to tell you that you are me but I am *zemlia*.

I wanted to eat. They called me in to have lunch. My lunch
was at about one o'clock in the afternoon. I did not have lunch,
because I felt meat. My wife wanted to eat meat. I refused my
plate of soup, which was cooked with meat. My wife was angry. She thought that I was being squeamish about the food. I
am squeamish about meat because I know how animals are
killed and how they weep. I wanted to show her that marriage
was no marriage if people did not agree in their ideas. I threw
my wedding ring down on the kitchen table. Later I took it
and put it on. My wife became nervous because I threw the
ring down again. I threw the ring down again because I felt
that she was longing for meat. I like animals, and therefore I
was sorry to eat meat, for I know that if I eat meat, another
animal would have to be killed. I eat little. I eat only when I
want to eat. My wife eats a lot. She is sorry for me and
therefore thinks I should eat meat. I like bread and butter with
cheese. I like eggs. I eat little because I am built that way. My
digestion works better because I do not eat meat. My stomach
has risen, but it was down before. It was down because the
guts were swollen. Guts swell out, I have noticed, after meat.
Meat gives no rest to digestion. I had a stomachache, and today
I do not. I know many doctors will say that this is all nonsense.
That one should eat meat because meat is a necessary thing. I
will say that meat is not a necessary thing, because meat stim-
ulates lust. My lust has disappeared since I stopped eating meat.

Meat is a terrible thing. I know that children who eat meat practice masturbation. I know that girls and boys practice masturbation. I know that women and men together and separately practice masturbation. Masturbation causes idiocy. People lose their feeling and their reason. I used to lose my reason when I practiced masturbation. My nerves were on edge. I used to tremble as if I had a fever. I had headaches. I was ill. I think that Gogol was a masturbator. I know that masturbation destroyed him. I know that Gogol was a rational man. I know that Gogol felt. His feeling became blunter day by day. He felt his death coming, because he tore up his last works. I will not tear up my works, because I do not want to practice masturbation. I was a great masturbator. I understood God badly and thought that he wished me well when I practiced masturbation. I know many women who cross their legs. Those women often practice masturbation. A man can cross his legs because his body is arranged differently. Many women think that it is more attractive to sit cross-legged. I believe that this is ugly, since what is good for men is not good for women. I do not want Kyra to sit cross-legged, but she does, because she has noticed that others do not correct her. Kyra is little as yet, and she does not understand what she is doing. I have often told her that she must not lie on her stomach. I lie on my stomach when I sleep, but I have a small stomach, and therefore I can do so. People who have big stomachs must not lie on them. Men must sleep on their sides and women on their backs. I have studied all this because I used to have a big stomach. I noticed that I was very tired when I slept on my stomach. The whole day was spoiled for me. I know what a stomach is. A stomach has bowels, digestive organs, liver, bladder, etc., etc. I have noticed that when I go to bed after eating, I am quite full in the morning, and my digestion begins to work only in the morning after I get up. I get up lazily and have no desire to carry on with life.

Since I have stopped eating meat, I have noticed that my
digestion is better, my thoughts are better, and I run instead of walking. I walk only in order to rest. I run a lot
because I feel strong. I have obedient muscles. I have an
obedient brain. I dance more easily, and I have a big appetite. I eat quickly and do not think about what I am eating. My food is not important, because I don't do anything
with it. I eat whatever is given to me. I do not eat canned
food. I eat vegetables and all kinds of vegetarian food. I
am a vegetarian. I am not a meat-eater. I am a man, and
not an animal. I am an animal only when God wants me
to understand that I should not eat meat. My wife feels
that one should not eat meat, but she is afraid to give it
up, because Dr. Frenkel eats meat. She thinks that Dr.
Frenkel understands more in medical matters than I do. I
realize that Dr. Frenkel does not understand medical matters, just like many other doctors and professors. Doctors
and professors like eating a lot, for they think that food
gives physical strength. I think physical strength comes not
from food but from the mind. I know many people will tell
me that the mind will not feed you. I will say that the
mind can feed you, because the mind distributes food. I eat
as much as the mind tells me to. Just now I ate a lot because I felt very hungry. I escaped from the house because
my wife did not understand me. She was frightened of me,
and I was frightened of her. I was frightened because I did
not want to eat meat. She was frightened of me because
she thought that I did not want her to eat. She thought I
wanted to make her die of hunger. I want to help her, and
therefore I did not want her to eat meat. I escaped from
the house. I ran and ran down the hill on which our house
was standing. I ran and ran. I did not stumble. A mysterious force was driving me forward. I was not angry with

my wife. I ran calmly. At the bottom of the hill stood the little town of St. Moritz. I went calmly to St. Moritz. Then I turned down a road that went to the lake. I went quickly. As I was passing through the town, I noticed Dr. Frenkel, who was going to my wife. I realized that they had telephoned him and asked him to come.

I went on with bowed head, as if guilty of something. I walked on and on. I walked quickly. When I reached the level of the lake, I began looking around for a refuge for myself. I had one franc and ten centimes in my pocket. I thought I also had some money in the bank, about 400 francs. I said to myself that I could pay for a room but could not go back home. I decided to look for a room. I went into a candy store and asked the owner of the house and candy store to let me have a room. I wanted to melt her heart, and I told her that I had not eaten anything. I asked whether she had eaten. She said she had finished her meal. I then told her I was hungry. She made no reply to this, thinking probably that I should not eat. I had gone into that shop many times before and had bought a lot of all kinds of candy there. She thought I was rich, and therefore she was always polite to me. I used to kiss her child and pat it on the head. She was pleased. I used to tell her that I was sorry for her because she was suffering from the effects of the war. She used to complain about the hard times. I wept and so did she. I used to order a lot of candy, thinking to help her. She was pleased. I asked her whether she could rent me a room. To that she replied that all the rooms were full. After a while she said that there would be an apartment free in a week's time. I told her that I did not need an apartment. She said she was sorry for me, but she could not give me a room. I felt that she thought I wanted to bring a woman. I told her frankly that I wanted one room and that I wanted to work, because my wife did not understand me. She felt my complaint

135

and left. I told her husband, who was present at our conversation, that I was a serious-minded man and that I did not need women. He felt me, but could not do anything. I told him that it was sometimes difficult for people to understand each other. To that he replied that his wife one day picked up a plate in the wrong way and he advised her to pick it up in another way, but she did not obey him. I felt her husband's tears. I also wept in my heart. I shook hands with him for the first time and left. I felt bitter because I realized that I would have to spend the night in the street. I went away. I passed a row of shops that were all closed because the whole little town of St. Moritz Dorf* was closed. Nobody lived there. I sat down by a wall under a window with a windowsill. Would I be able to spend the night there? I had a feeling of warmth. After a while I felt cold. In the distance I saw a woman shivering with cold. I too was shivering with cold. I was cold because it was winter at an altitude of 2,000 meters. I went on. Suddenly I noticed an open door and went in. Inside I saw no one, then I walked past rooms that were all locked. I noticed one door that was ajar, and I walked in. I suddenly felt a stench. The stench came from inside the room. I looked in and saw that it was a dirty bathroom. I almost wept, thinking that I would have to sleep in a dirty bathroom. I went out into the street. The street was empty. I went on. Suddenly I felt I was being pushed to the left, and I followed. I went along a bad road. I noticed a small two-story whitewashed house some distance away. I went in that direction. I went into the house and found the owner. The owner was a woman, but she was a simple woman. Her clothes were in tatters. I asked her whether she could let me have a room. She said that she could

---

* St. Moritz Dorf is the original village of St. Moritz, as opposed to the resort, St. Moritz Bad, which is nearby. (Ed.)

but that the room was cold. I told her I did not mind. She took me up to the second floor. The stairs were outside the house, steep and broken. The stairs did not creak, but the snow did. I went into room No. 5 and saw how poor it was. I felt relieved. I asked her how much I should pay for the room. She said one franc a day. I thanked her and left, promising to come back in the evening. We parted. The little house was white and clean. One could see that the people were poor but clean. I wanted to leave but could not. I wanted to write in that little room. I liked the little room. I looked around and saw a hard bed without pillows, and armchairs in a row. The armchairs were made of bent wood. The bed was made of old wood, and next to it stood a washstand without a basin. I realized that they had no washing utensils. I wanted to stay, but God told me that I had to go. I went. The woman made a good impression on me. I followed the road along which I had come. I felt sadness. My sadness was deep. I saw my own little house from that other little house and wept. I wept bitterly. I felt bitter. I wanted to sob, but my unhappiness was too great. The tears did not come. I was sad. I was sad for a long time and came upon a little house along the road. I saw some children. I felt them, but they did not feel me. They thought I wanted to play and began throwing large pieces of snow. I threw small pieces back at them, saying in German, "This is not good." I did not speak German, but I understood the children. I took a toboggan and gave them rides. They laughed. I was pleased. I went with them into a cottage and saw a woman. The woman gave the children little cakes dipped in fat and sugar. She cooked them and gave them to the children. I wanted to eat a little, because I had eaten nothing at lunch. She felt me and gave me a little cake. I wanted to give her ten centimes, but she did not want to take it. I thrust it into her hand, saying that this was for the poor children. She felt me

and revealed her grief. I told her that she must not grieve, because God had willed it so. She said in German, pointing at
the cemetery, that she had lost a child three months ago and
had buried him in the cemetery. I felt her grief and told her
that she must not grieve because God had wanted to take her
child. She was silent and felt the truth. I told her also that God
takes what he gives and that she should not grieve. She calmed
down and began to laugh. I wanted to go, but she gave another little cake to each of the children. I was standing. She
gave me another little cake. She herself did not eat. She felt
me. I thanked her and left. The children liked me. I played
with them for no more than a quarter of an hour. I went
along the forest path. In the forest I heard birds and sometimes shouts of people who were skiing. I did not have skis,
but I did not fall. I went on and on. I did not fall, because I
went along the road. I could not go any farther, because I felt
my feet getting cold. I was dressed lightly. I went quickly up
the hill, and suddenly I stopped. I did not know what to do. I
did not want to decide beforehand. I waited for God's command. I waited and waited. I felt cold. I waited. I felt warm. I
knew that people felt cold before freezing to death, but I was
not afraid of dying. I felt a push and went on. I was going up
higher and higher. I walked on and on. Suddenly I stopped
and realized that it was not possible to go any farther. I
stopped and stood still and felt cold. I realized that death had
come. I was not afraid, and I thought that I would lie down
and that I would be picked up later and brought to my wife. I
wept. I wept in my heart. I felt sad. I did not know what to
do. I did not know where to go. I realized that if I went farther I would not find shelter for the next twenty-five versts. I
was afraid I would freeze, for I was cold and tired. I turned
around and went back. I walked on and on. I saw another
road going in another direction. I went along that road and

saw people. I felt joy in my heart. They paid no attention to me. I continued on my way, admiring the shapes on the skis. I was going along a bad road. The road was full of potholes. I could not look to either side of me. I saw that the river Inn was flowing by the side of the road. The Inn had its source where I was walking. I walked badly and was tired. I walked on and on. I wanted to rest. I saw a tree stump, but the stump was by the side of the road, and the road backed onto the Inn. I tried to sit down, but almost fell into the Inn. The Inn was a fast-flowing river because the mountain was high. I walked on and on. I felt very tired, but suddenly I felt strength and wanted to run all twenty-five versts. I did not realize the distance. I thought that I would cover the distance quickly by running, but I felt tired. I walked on and on. I wanted to turn back on the road that I was walking along, but I felt cold and decided to go farther. I reached the little village of Kampfer. In that village I heard the singing of children. I realized that the singing was not joyful, but learned by rote, and I went past. I was sorry for the children. I realized what school was. I was sorry for the children. I walked on and on. I came out on a road that led home in one direction and to my room in the other, but that room was twenty-seven versts away. I felt that I had to go to that room, because I had to change my whole life. I decided to go there, but a mysterious force compelled me to realize that I had to turn back. The road was long and up-hill, but I was not afraid of going uphill. I walked on and on. Suddenly I felt tired and sat on the fence along the road. I sat and rested. I felt cold. I was freezing, but I was not afraid of freezing to death, because I still felt a great deal of warmth. I sat and waited. I saw carriages and pedestrians go past, but I did not move. I thought I would have to sit forever, but suddenly I felt the strength to get up. I got up and went. I walked on and on. I met carts filled with wood, and I walked alongside them. I saw a horse running uphill, and I ran. I did that not thinking but feeling. I panted as I ran. I could not run, and I walked. I realized that people urged horses and men on till they stopped and fell like stones. The horse and I decided they could whip us as much as they wanted, but we would still do what we liked, because we wanted to live. The horse walked and so did I. A fat gentleman was sitting in the carriage with his wife, who was bored. The driver was bored too. Everyone was bored. I was not bored, because I did not think but felt. I walked on and on.

I reached the little town of St. Moritz Dorf. I stopped at the telegraph office. I did not read the dispatches. Suddenly somebody grabbed me by the shoulder. I turned and saw Dr. Frenkel. Frenkel wanted me to visit him, but I flatly refused, saying that I could not speak with anyone that day and that I wanted to be alone. He told me that it was better to go to their house, because they had my wife with them. I said that I did not like reconciliations, that I liked them to be rationally understood and not to be artificially staged. I liked Frenkel because I sensed that he felt miserable. I too felt miserable, but decided to go back to my own home. I felt that that was my house, and I went on in its direction. I walked quickly. I walked up the hill and turned toward the entrance, but I had not yet reached the house when I saw the door open. The maid, Louise, opened the door for me. I went in and sat down at the piano. I started to play, but the maid did not feel me and was in the way, but I pushed her a little, and she understood me. I played a funeral march. I wept in my heart. The maid felt the music and said, "Beautiful." I finished and went off to eat. She gave me all sorts of things. I ate bread and butter and cheese, and for dessert two jam pastries. I was not hungry, for I felt my digestion. I went off to write what I have written.

Now they have called me down to dinner, but I refused

point-blank because I do not want to eat alone. I said that I was not a child and that they had no business coaxing me. Louise was coaxing me by saying, "Hot macaroni." I did not reply.

The telephone rings and rings. People run and run. I do not know who is calling or what they are calling about, because I do not like talking on the telephone. I thought that my wife's mother had arrived and was telephoning to ask about my health. The maid answered her with tears in her voice. Everyone thinks I am ill.

I want to tell you that I love you you
I want to tell you that I love you you
I want to tell you that I love I love I love
I want to tell you that I love I love I love.
I love but you do not. You do not love that which He
I love that He that He. You are death you are death.
I want to tell you that you are death, that you are death.
I want to tell you that you are death that you are death
Death is death, but I am life
I am life, but you are death.
Having defeated death by death* by death
I am death, but you are not life.
Life is life, and death is death.
You are death but I am life.
Having defeated death by death by death.
I am death, but you are not life
I want to tell you that you are death and I am life

---

* A quotation from the Russian Orthodox Easter service, to which Nijinsky adds an extra "by death." (Tr.)

I want to tell you that I am life and you are death.
I love you my friend. I wish you well.
I wish you well, I love you you.
I wish you well, I wish you no harm.
You do not love me you
I love I love you.
I wish you well
I am yours and you are mine.
I love you you
I love you you
I want you you
I want you you.

I am weeping as I write these lines and think of my wife, who has abandoned me, thinking that I am a barbarian of Russian origin. She has often said to me that I am a "Russian barbarian." She learned these words in Hungary when Russia was fighting Hungary. I liked Hungary when it was fighting Russia. I knew no one when I was in Hungary. I was locked in a room and composed the Theory of the Dance.* I danced little because I felt sad. I was bored because I realized that my wife did not love me. I married by chance. I married in South America, and the wedding was in Rio de Janeiro.† I was introduced to my wife on the ship *The Avon*. I have already described my marriage a little. I must say that I married without thinking. I loved her and loved her. I did not think of the fu-

* "Theory of the Dance": Nijinsky's system of dance notation, which he worked on during his internment in Hungary. At that time he also notated *The Afternoon of a Faun* according to his system. (Ed.)
† The wedding was in Buenos Aires. On Nijinsky's marriage, see introduction, p. xiv. (Ed.)

ture. I spent the money that I had saved with great difficulty. I used to give her roses that cost five francs apiece. I brought her these roses every day, twenty, thirty at a time. I loved giving her white roses. I felt flowers. I realized that my love was white and not red. Red roses frightened me. I was not a cowardly man, but I felt a lasting and not a passionate love. I loved her terribly. I gave her everything I could. She loved me. It seemed to me that she was happy. The first time I felt grief was three or five days after the marriage. I asked her to learn dancing, because for me dancing was the highest thing in the world after her. I wanted to teach her. I had taught no one because I was afraid for myself. I wanted to teach her good dancing, but she became frightened and no longer trusted me. I wept and wept bitterly. I wept bitterly. Already I felt death. I realized that I had made a mistake, but the mistake was irreparable. I had put myself in the hands of somebody who did not love me. I realized my mistake. My wife now loved me above anyone else, but she did not feel me. I wanted to leave, but I realized that that was dishonest, and I stayed with her. She did not love me much. She felt money and my success. She loved me for my success and the beauty of my body. She was cunning and made me keen on money. I had a lawsuit in London against the Palace music hall and lost that lawsuit. I am having another lawsuit with that theater. I have already described the management of that theater.

I collapsed from overwork and had a fever. I was at death's door. My wife wept. She loved me. She suffered when she saw that I worked so much. She realized that all that was for the sake of money. I did not want money. I wanted a simple life. I loved the theater, and I wanted to work. I worked hard, but later I lost heart because I noticed that I was not liked. I withdrew into myself. I withdrew so deep into myself that I could not understand people. I wept and wept . . . .

I do not know why my wife is weeping. I think that she has realized her mistake and is afraid that I will leave her. I did not know she was at home. I thought she was at Frenkel's house. I stopped because I heard weeping. I feel hurt. I am sorry for her. I am weeping, weeping. She weeps and weeps. I know that Dr. Frenkel is with her and therefore I am not going to her. I hope that God will help and that she will understand me.*

I want to weep, but God commands me to write. He does not want me to do nothing. My wife weeps and weeps. I also weep. I am afraid that Dr. Frenkel will come and tell me that my wife is weeping while I am writing. I will not go to her, because I am not to blame. I will go and eat by myself because God has ordered me to. My child sees and hears everything, and I hope that she will understand me. I love Kyra, but she does not feel me, because she has a drunkard beside her. I have noticed bottles with alcohol in them. One bottle with alcohol of ninety proof and the other diluted with water. My wife does not notice, but I hope her mother will notice and throw away the bottle, together with that woman. My little Kyra feels that I love her, but she thinks that I am ill, because this is what she has been told. They ask me whether I sleep well, and I tell them that my sleep is always good. I do not know what to write, but God wants my writings because he knows their significance. Soon I will go to Paris, and there I will create an impression that the whole world will talk about. I do not want people to think I am a great writer. I do not want people to think I am a great artist. I do not want people to say I am a

---

*   The diary text in the second notebook ends here. (Ed.)

great man. I am a simple man who has suffered a lot. I do not think that Christ has suffered as much as I have suffered throughout my life. I love life and I want to live.

I want to weep, but I cannot, because I feel so much pain in my soul that I am afraid for myself. I feel pain. My soul is sick. My sickness is of the soul and not of the mind.* I know what I need in order to become well again. My sickness is too great for me to be cured of it soon. I am incurable. My soul is sick. I am poor. I am destitute. I am unhappy. I am horrible. I know that everyone will suffer when they read these lines, because I know that people will feel me. I know well what I need. I am a strong man, not a weak one. I am not sick in the body. My soul is sick. I am suffering. I am suffering. I know that Kostrovsky will feel me, but I know that everyone will feel me. I am a man and not a beast. I love everyone. I also have faults. I am a man and not God. I want to be God, and therefore I try to improve myself. I want to dance. I want to draw. I want to play the piano. I want to write poetry. I want to compose ballets. I want to love every-one. This is my aim in life. I know socialists will find it easier to understand me, but I am not a socialist. I am God. My party is God's. I love everyone. I do not want war. I do not want state frontiers. I want Wilsonism, which will improve the whole terrestrial globe. I am the whole terrestrial globe. I am the earth. I have a home everywhere. I live everywhere. I do not want to have property. I do not want to be rich. I want to love, love. I am love, and not brutality. I am not a bloodthirsty animal. I am a man. I am a man.

God is within me, and I am within Him. I want Him. I seek Him. I want my manuscript to be published, because I know that everyone can read, but I hope for improvement. I

---

* In Russian, the insane are referred to as the "soul-sick." (Tr.)

do not know what is needed for that, but I feel that God will help all who seek. I am a seeker, for I feel God. God is seeking me, and therefore we are finding each other.

God Nijinsky
St. Moritz Dorf
Villa Guardamunt.
27 February 1919.

The last two pages of Book I, signed "God Nijinsky"

BOOK II

ON DEATH

V. NIJINSKY

ST. MORITZ DORF

VILLA GUARDAMUNT

27 FEBRUARY 1919

On death.

Death came unexpectedly, for I wanted it. I said to myself that
I no longer wanted to live. I have not lived long. I have lived
for only six months. I have been told that I am mad. I thought
that I was alive. They would not let me alone. I lived and re-
joiced, but people said I was bad. I realized that people needed
death, and I decided that I would not do anything anymore,
but could not. I decided to write about death. I weep from grief.
I feel very sad. I am bored because everything around me is
empty. I have become empty. I know that the maid, Louise,
will weep tomorrow because she will be sorry to see the dev-
astation. I have taken down all the drawings and pictures that
I have been working on for the last six months. I know that
my wife will be looking for my pictures and will not find them.
I have put the furniture where it used to be, and the lampshade
is the old one. I do not want people to laugh at me, and I have
decided to do nothing. God has commanded me to do nothing.
He wants me to set down my impressions in writing. I will
write a lot. I want to understand my wife's mother and her
husband. I know them well, but I want to check. I write under
the impression of what I have experienced, I am not making
things up. I am sitting at an empty table. In the drawer of my
table there are many paints. All the paints have dried up be-

cause I do not paint anymore. I used to paint a lot, and I made good progress. I want to paint, but not here, because I feel death. I want to go to Paris, but I am afraid I will not have time. I want to write about death. I will call the first book "Life" and this book "Death." I will give people a conception of life and death. I hope I will be successful. I know that if I publish these books, everyone will say that I am a bad writer. I do not want to be a writer. I want to be a thinker. I think and write. I am not a scribbler, I am a thinker. I am not Schopenhauer. I am Nijinsky. I want to tell you, humans, that I am God. I am the God who dies when He is not loved. I am sorry for myself because I am sorry for God. God loves me and will give me life in death. I am death. I am he who loves death. I do not want to sleep. I write at night. My wife does not sleep, she thinks. I feel I am death. She finds it difficult to refuse death. I understand people. They want to enjoy life. They like enjoyment. I consider all enjoyment horrible. I do not want enjoyment. My wife wants enjoyment. I know she will be frightened when she discovers that everything I write is the truth. I know she will be sad because she will think that I do not love her. I will tell her that I have written the truth, but I know she will say that I am a bad man. It is possible that she will not want to live with me, because she will not trust me. I love her, and I know that I will suffer because I will miss her. I want to tell the whole truth. I cannot hide from people the things I know. I want to show what life and death are. I want to describe death. I love death. I know what death is. Death is a terrible thing. I have felt death many times. I was dying in a clinic when I was fifteen years old.* I was a brave kid. I jumped and fell. I was taken to the hospital. In the hospital I saw death with my own eyes. I saw foam coming out of a sick

* When Nijinsky was twelve (not fifteen), he was dared by a group of schoolmates to jump over a heavy wooden music stand. According to Bronislava Nijinska (*Early*

man's mouth because he drank a whole bottle of medicine. I know what medicine is. Medicine sustains you, but if you drink it you will go to the next world. I know that the next world has no light, therefore I am afraid of the next world.* I want light, but of a different kind. I like the light of twinkling stars, not stars without twinkling. I know that twinkling stars are life and those that do not twinkle, death. I know what I have to do when a star twinkles at me. I know the meaning of untwinkling stars. My wife is an untwinkling star. I have noticed that many people do not twinkle. I weep when I feel that someone does not twinkle. I know what death is. Death is life extinguished. People who have lost their reason are called extinguished life. I too lacked reason, but when I stayed in St. Moritz, I understood, in my room, the whole truth, because I felt a lot. I know it is difficult to feel by oneself, but only when man is alone can he understand what feeling is. I do not want to do anything that would make my wife understand. I know that if I were to explain, she would start thinking, and thinking is death. I do not want to think, and therefore I live. I know that when my wife's mother comes, I will have to think a lot. My wife's mother is coming tomorrow at eleven o'clock in the morning. I wanted to say "today" but changed my mind because I consider tomorrow to be when a man wakes up and not the first twelve hours. I do not consider

---

Memoirs, p. 103), the boys soaped the floor and at the last minute raised the height of the adjustable stand. Nijinsky slipped, hit the stand with his stomach, and suffered severe internal bleeding. He was hospitalized for more than a month. Ostwald (*Nijinsky*, p. 12) speculates that the bleeding might have caused damage to Nijinsky's brain. Nijinska (p. 102) recalls that a young man who had been kicked in the stomach by a horse was admitted to the hospital at the same time as Nijinsky and died in the bed next to him. This is probably the death he remembers having seen with his own eyes. (Ed.)

* This sentence contains a play on words. The Russian *svet* can mean either "world" or "light." Nijinsky uses it in both senses in the sentence. (Tr.)

it necessary to count. I do not like counting. Counting tires one's brain. Counting is death. All mechanical equipment is death. I know I am much to blame for the fact that my wife counts, but I have told her that it is not worth counting because everything has already been counted. I want to go and have a drink because I have a stomachache. I will eat meat because I want to show that I am the same as they are. I will eat and describe my impressions. I want to tell about everything that I see and hear. I will do everything they do. I will say nice, polite things just the way they do. I have drunk a bottle of mineral water. I do not like drinking for no reason, but I did drink, because I have done so before. I now want to live as I did before. After I have finished this book, I will not live as I did before. I want to write about death, and therefore I need fresh impressions. I call fresh impressions when a man writes about things he has experienced. I will write about everything I have experienced. I want to experience things. I am a man in death. I am not God. I am not man. I am a beast and a predator. I want to make love to prostitutes. I want to live like an unnecessary man.

I know that God wants this, and therefore I will live that way. I will live that way until He stops me. I will gamble on the Stock Exchange because I want to do so at other people's expense. I am an evil man. I do not love anyone. I wish harm to everyone and good to myself. I am an egoist. I am not God. I am a beast, a predator. I will practice masturbation and spiritualism. I will eat everyone I can get hold of. I will stop at nothing. I will make love to my wife's mother and my child. I will weep, but I will do everything God commands me to. I know that everyone will be afraid of me and will commit me to a lunatic asylum. But I don't care. I am not afraid of anything. I want death. I will blow my brains out if God wants it. I will be ready for anything. I know that God wants all this for the improvement of life, and therefore I will be His instrument. It is past one o'clock, and I am still not asleep. I know that people must work in the daytime, but I work at night. I know that tomorrow I will have red eyes. My wife's mother will be afraid, because she will think that I am mad. I hope that I will be committed to a lunatic asylum. I will rejoice at this event because I like to tyrannize everyone. I take delight in tyrannizing. Tyranny is familiar to me. I used to know a dog called "Tsytra."* That dog was good. I spoiled it. I taught it to masturbate against my leg. I taught it to come against my leg. I liked that dog. I did all these things when I was a kid. I also did what the dog did, but with my hand. I came at the same time as the dog. I know that many girls and women make love to animals in that way. I know that my maid, Louise, does this with cats. I know that my cook does this with cats. I know that everyone does this sort of thing. I know that all small dogs are spoiled. I know one Hungarian family where the daughter did this with a gorilla. The gorilla bit her in the place where it was screwing her. The ape was angry because the woman failed to understand it. Apes are stupid animals, and the woman was trying to fool the gorilla. The gorilla bit her, and so she died in horrible agony. I know that many women put all kinds of sweet things inside themselves so that animals will lick them. I know women who have had animals licking them. I know people who lick. I used to lick my wife. I wept, but I licked. I know terrible things because I learned them from Diaghilev. Diaghilev taught me everything. I was young and did stupid things, but I do not want to practice these things anymore. I know what all this leads to. I have seen women who get screwed by men several times in a row. I myself used to screw my wife as many as five times a day. I know what all this leads to. I do not want

---

* *Tsytra* means "zither" in Russian. (Tr.)

to do these things anymore. I know that many doctors prescribe this: according to them a man must screw his wife every day. I know that everyone believes it. I know there are doctors who prescribe it as an essential thing for a man to make love to a woman, for without that it is not possible to exist. I know that people do this only because they have a great deal of lust. I know many poems about lust. Lust is a terrible thing. I know that the clergy practices the same sort of thing. I know that the Church does not forbid lascivious activities. I know a case where my wife and her maid had to go to confession to say that they had almost been raped in the basement of a London church. I have forgotten the name of the church. I will give the name later, for I will ask my wife.

I want to screw her in order to have a child and not because of lust. I do not want to feel lust. I do not like the feeling of lust. I want to live. I will feel lust because God will want it. I know a poet who used to write a lot in Russian about lust. I myself often had a feeling of lust looking at women. I often experienced lust in Paris. There are many tarts in Paris, and therefore one can experience lust. I have a feeling of lust at the moment because God wants to make me understand what lust means. I have not felt lust for quite a long time. My wife likes experiencing a feeling of lust for me. I do not want to feel lust, because I know what lust is. I know that people will tell me that I am a eunuch.* But I am not afraid of eunuchs, because I know their aims. I do not like eunuchs, because they cut their balls off. I know that balls secrete sperm, and I therefore do not want to cut them off. I like sperm. I want sperm. I am sperm. I am life. Without sperm there would be no life. I know

* Nijinsky uses the word *skopets*, which may refer to any castrated male or, alternatively, to a member of a heretical Christian sect found in Nijinsky's day mainly if not exclusively in Russia and Rumania. It insisted on castration as a condition of membership. (Tr.)

that many German professors order people to procreate, because they want many soldiers. I know what a soldier is. I have seen many representations of them, and besides, I have a powerful imagination. I know about the killing of soldiers. I know their torments. In Hungary I saw trains with the German wounded. I saw their faces. I know that German professors and others do not understand death. I know that professors are stupid animals. I know that they are stupid because they have lost feeling. I know that they have lost their eyes because they read a lot of nonsense. I composed a ballet to the music of Richard Strauss.* I composed this ballet in New York. I composed it quickly. They insisted that I produce it in three weeks. I wept and said that I could not produce that ballet in three weeks, because this was beyond my strength. Then Otto Kahn, the director and chairman of the Metropolitan, said that he could not give me more time than that. He said that through the theater representative, Mr. Coppicus. I agreed to the proposal because there was nothing else I could do. I knew that if I did not agree, I would not have enough money to live on. I made up my mind and went to work. I worked like an ox. I never let up. I slept little. I worked and worked. My wife saw all that work and was sorry for me. I engaged a masseur, for without massage I could not have carried on with my work. I

---

* Nijinsky's fourth and last ballet, *Till Eulenspiegel*, to the Richard Strauss tone poem of the same name, was premiered in New York in October 1916 after a brief and tormented rehearsal period during which Nijinsky twisted his ankle, thus forcing a one-week postponement of the season. (He was attended by Dr. Robert Abbé.) Even so, *Till* seems to have been premiered unfinished. According to Lydia Sokolova (*Dancing for Diaghilev*, pp. 90–91), who performed in it, the dancers improvised most of the second act on opening night. Nevertheless, as Nijinsky reports, *Till* was enthusiastically received. The ballet concerned the mischief-making of Till Eulenspiegel (played by Nijinsky), the puckish folk hero of medieval Brunswick. The sets and costumes were by a young American designer, Robert Edmond Jones (not Johnson). The "theater representative" with whom Nijinsky says he dealt was Francis C. Coppicus, general secretary of the Metropolitan Opera. (Ed.)

realized that I was dying. I ordered costumes in America from a costumer. I explained all the details to him. He felt me. I commissioned an artist, Johnson, to make the sets. The artist seemed to understand me, but he did not feel. He was worried all the time. I was not worried. I enjoyed myself. I showed him one type of set. I told him to bring books on the period in which the ballet was set. He drew for me what I told him. His costume drawings were better. Their colors were full of life. I liked colors full of life. He understood my ideas. I showed him how one must look for an idea. He was grateful, but continued to be nervous and worried. He reminds me of my wife, who is afraid of everything. I said to him, "What are you afraid of? There is nothing to be afraid of." But he was worried. Obviously he was worried about the success of the thing. He had no confidence in me. I was sure of success. I worked like an ox. The ox was driven too hard, for he twisted his ankle. The ox was sent to Dr. Abbé. He was a good doctor. He gave me a simple treatment. He ordered me to rest and rest. I rested and rested. I had a nurse. The nurse sat and sat. I could not go to sleep, because I was not used to sleeping in the presence of a nurse. If she had been sleeping instead of sitting, I would probably have slept. She kept saying to me, "Sleep, sleep, sleep." But I could not fall asleep. And so passed one week after another. My ballet "Till" was not being produced. The public was getting worried. The public thought I was being a temperamental artist. I was not worried about what the public was thinking. The management decided to put off the performance for a week. They started the season without me, thinking they would do better business that way. They were afraid of failure. There was no failure, because I began to dance and the public came. The American public loved me because they had confidence in me. They saw that my foot hurt. I danced badly, but the audience enjoyed it. "Till" was a success, but it was produced too soon. It was taken out of the oven too soon and was therefore raw. The American audience liked my raw ballet because it tasted good. I had cooked it very well. I do not like uncooked things, because I know what a stomachache one gets afterward. I did not like this ballet, but I said that it was "good." I had to say it was good because if I had said that the ballet was not good, no one would have come to the theater, and it would have been a financial failure. I do not like financial failures, and therefore I said, "Good." I told Otto Kahn that I was happy about it and pleased. He complimented me because he saw how pleased the audience was. I made this a comic ballet because I felt the war. Everyone was sick of the war, and therefore people needed to be cheered up. I did cheer them up. I showed "Till" in all its beauty. Its beauty was simple. I showed Till's life. Till's life was simple. I showed that he was the German people. The papers were pleased because the critics were Germans. I summoned the journalists before the first performance and explained "Till"'s purpose to them. Then they were very pleased because they could prepare their reviews. Their reviews were favorable and sometimes very intelligent. I saw myself as the devil and as God. I was exalted to the heights of the Tower of Babel. I did not like heights, because I saw that this was nothing but praise. I saw that the critics had understood my ballet. I felt that the critics wanted to praise me. I do not like praise, because I am not a kid. I saw an error that a critic had noticed. He noticed one part of the music that I had not understood. He thought that I had not understood it. I had understood it very well, but I did not want to tire myself, because my foot hurt. That part of the music was very difficult for the performer, and therefore I ignored it. Critics always think they are more intelligent than the artist. They often abuse their position and reprimand an artist for his performance. Artists are poor and therefore tremble when faced by critics. They feel hurt and offended. Their souls weep. I know one prejudiced critic, a painter, who did not like artists who did not bow down to him. His name is Alexandre Benois.* Alexandre Benois is a very intelligent man and feels painting. I have read his reviews under the title "Letters on Art." These reviews were prejudiced. He always attacked Alexander Golovin, who was a set designer at the Imperial theaters in Petersburg. I realized that Benois wanted to hound him out because he wanted to get the job himself. He published these reviews in the newspaper "Rech." This newspaper was edited by Nabokov. Nabokov was an intelligent man and was able to manage his paper well. He hired Filosofov and always wrote, showering abuse on "Novoye Vremya." "Novoye Vremya" had its subscribers, and "Rech" wanted to get them. "Rech" was silly, because it contained nothing. I did not like newspapers, because I realized they were nonsense. They wrote hackneyed things. They filled pages because they had to fill them. I was not afraid of critics when I was a boy, and therefore I did not show them respect. I showed respect to one critic, whose name was Valerian Svetlov.† This critic wrote dance reviews. He was living with the ballerina Schollar and learned all kinds of expressions from her. These expressions he set within high-sounding phrases. There were

---

* Alexandre Benois (1870–1960), painter, art historian, and art critic, was one of the foremost set and costume designers of the early Ballets Russes. From 1908 to 1917 he wrote an influential column, "Letters on Art," for *Rech*, one of whose editors was Vladimir Dmitrievich Nabokov, father of the novelist. The painter Alexander Golovin (1863–1930) designed sets not only for the Imperial Theaters but also for the Ballets Russes. (Ed.)

† Valerian Svetlov (1860–1934), a member of the planning committee for Diaghilev's first European ballet seasons, was the ballet critic of the *St. Petersburg Gazette*. Ludmila Schollar (1888–1978) was one of Nijinsky's fellow dancers in the Imperial Ballet and in the Diaghilev troupe. (She was one of the two women in his 1913 *Jeux*.) In 1903 Nikolai Legat (1869–1937), one of Nijinsky's teachers—later, chief ballet master of the Imperial Ballet—published *Russian Ballet in Caricature* with his brother Sergei Legat (1875–1905), another of Nijinsky's teachers. The caricature of Svetlov showed him as a parrot. (Ed.)

other critics too, but they did not have sharp tongues. Svetlov's tongue was always ready. He worked on his criticism and therefore wrote well. People thought that a man who wrote well understood dancing. I understood dancing well because I danced. Svetlov had never in his life danced any of the ballets that he wrote about. Svetlov is a white man. He was called "the parrot" because his head was like a parrot's. Nikolai Legat did not like him and therefore caricatured him in his drawings as a parrot. I would say that he is a parrot not because he has a parrot's head but because all he writes is parrotry. I call parrotry things written by critics who repeat things known to everyone. Svetlov was a parrot dressed in silk because he had money. He gave Schollar good and expensive things. He made love to her not as a young and strong man. He was nearly sixty. He used face cream and wore makeup. Women liked him because he had a sharp pen. Everyone was afraid of him. All the ballerinas went to bed with him because they were afraid of him. He liked to fool around, but did nothing. He liked fooling around like a boy. He was a Tom Thumb because he was a sickly man. He felt happy. He was always pleased. He had a calm expression on his face. His face looked like a mask. I have seen such masks. Those masks are made of wax. I think he deliberately refused ever to smile, for he was afraid of wrinkles. He had old newspaper clippings about ballet. He always wrote the same thing, just changing his style a little. His reviews were death because they said nothing new. His speech smelled of perfume and face cream. He started attacking me just on a whim. He did not know that his reviews made me sick. I was afraid of him, but I did not like him. I realized that his reviews were read, and so I was annoyed because I was afraid that I would be forced to dance in the corps de ballet. *Corps de ballet* is the name for a mass of people who know nothing. I know many artistes who knew a lot about dancing because they studied it, but because they had no one to exercise influence on their behalf, or simply by chance, they were put into the corps de ballet. The corps de ballet was good because it had good people in it. The corps de ballet dancers liked me and talked me up. I liked them, and they liked me. Even then, I wanted to be liked. I employed all kinds of tricks and ruses to make people like me. I wanted love not only from the corps de ballet, but from the leading dancers and the soloists too, and the ballet masters and ballerinas. I sought love and realized that there was no love. That it was all filth. That everybody looked for praise and praise again, or compliments. I did not like praise and compliments. I went to the office of the Director of Theaters, Krupensky, and asked to be allowed to dance. I danced only four times a year. What they call a year in ballet lasts eight months because the dance season is eight months long. I danced very rarely in front of the public, but the public liked me very much. I knew that all this was the result of the intrigues of the artists, both male and female. I was no longer cheerful, because I felt death. I was afraid of people and used to lock myself in my room. My room was narrow, with a high ceiling. I liked looking at the walls and at the ceiling, because all this spoke to me of death. I did not know how to cheer myself up, and I visited a tart with my friend Anatole Bourman. We visited her, and she gave us wine. I drank the wine and got drunk. I tried wine for the first time. I did not like drinking. My head was reeling after the wine, but I did not faint. I screwed her. She infected me with V.D.* I was frightened and went to see a doctor. The V.D. doctor lived in a rather rich manner. I was afraid of people. I thought that everyone knew.

* According to Ostwald (*Nijinsky*, p. 22), the disease was gonorrhea. Bronislava Nijinska (*Early Memoirs*, pp. 233–34) describes how Prince Lvov helped the family when Nijinsky fell ill. He called in a specialist, had his cook prepare and send over all Nijinsky's food, and assigned his valet to stay with Nijinsky day and night. (Ed.)

I was eighteen years old. I wept. I suffered. I did not know what to do. I went to the doctor, but he did nothing for me. He ordered me to buy a syringe and some medicine. He ordered me to inject this medicine into my member. I injected it. I drove the disease deeper in. I noticed that my balls started swelling. I called in another doctor, who applied leeches to me. The leeches sucked my blood. I said nothing, but I was horrified. I was afraid. I suffered in my heart. I was not afraid of the leeches. The leeches moved, and I wept and wept. I stayed in bed for a long time. I could not bear it any longer. I got up, and then my balls began to swell. I was frightened and decided to end it all at any cost. I was ill for over five months with that disease. I again applied leeches and stayed in bed. I was afraid my mother might find out. I got to know a man who helped me with this disease. He loved me as a man does a boy. I loved him because I knew that he wished me well. The man was called Prince Pavel Lvov. He wrote me love poems. I did not answer him, but he went on writing to me. I did not know what he wanted to say in them, because I never read them. I loved him because I felt that he loved me. I wanted to live with him always because I loved him. He forced me to be unfaithful to him with Diaghilev because he thought that Diaghilev would be useful to me. I was introduced to Diaghilev by telephone. I knew that Lvov did not love me, and therefore I left him. Pavel Lvov wanted to continue his friendship with me, but I realized that it was dishonest to be unfaithful. I lived with Serge Diaghilev. I know his brother from another mother. He* is a tidy man and likes museums. I consider museums to be graveyards. He considers museums to be life. A museum cannot be life, if only because it contains the works of dead artists. I believe

* "He" is clearly Serge Diaghilev, not one of his two half-brothers, Valentin and Yuri. (Ed.)

that pictures by dead artists should not be preserved, because they destroy the life of young artists. The young artist is compared with the museum artists. I know one artist who was not allowed to graduate from the Academy of Art only because his pictures did not resemble museum ones. That artist was called Anisfeld.* Anisfeld was a Jew. He has children. He is married, but his wife does not love him. I know because he said that he quarreled with his wife. I remember it. He used to visit Diaghilev and complain. I know that he loved his wife, because I felt his soul weeping. He was a good man. I commissioned scenery for many ballets from him. Now he is in North America, where he paints portraits and scenery. I am very pleased for him because I know all the intrigues of Léon Bakst. Bakst is a good artist, but spiteful, because he used to pour out abuse on Benois and Anisfeld. I do not abuse Benois, but tell the whole truth. Bakst abused them because he did not speak the truth. I saw his spitefulness toward Anisfeld. Bakst did not like Anisfeld, because the latter painted scenery well and had a success in Paris and other cities where we gave performances under the name of Ballets Russes. I loved the Ballets Russes. I gave my whole heart to it. I worked like an ox. I lived like a martyr. I knew that Diaghilev had a hard life. I knew his sufferings. He suffered because of money. He did not like me, because I did not give him money for his business. I saved many thousands of francs. Diaghilev once asked me for 40,000 francs. I gave it to him, but I was afraid he would not give it back to me, for I knew that he did not have it. I realized that Diaghilev knew

---

* The Russian painter Boris Anisfeld (1879–1973) designed one set for the Ballets Russes (*Sadko*, 1911) and did much of the scene-painting—that is, the execution of others' designs—for the company in its early years. He also designed the set for the production of *Les Sylphides* that Nijinsky presented during his 1914 season at the Palace Theatre in London. (Ed.)

how to get money, and therefore I decided to refuse if he asked me for money again. Diaghilev did ask me once in passing, backstage at the Châtelet in Paris. I replied quickly that I did not want to give him my money, because I had given that money to my mother. I gave it to her not on paper but in my thoughts. I did not want her to suffer because of money. My mother had suffered much, and therefore I wanted to give her an easy life. I gave her an easy life, because she did not have any money problems, but I noticed that she did worry about me. She wanted to speak to me many times. I felt this, but I avoided her. My sister also wanted to speak to me, but I avoided her. I realized quite well that if I were to leave Diaghilev, I would starve to death, because I was not mature enough for life. I was afraid of life. Now I am not afraid of life. I am waiting for God's commands. I have been writing for a long time. I think that it is getting on to four o'clock in the night by now. I know that people call it four o'clock in the morning, but I am not going to sleep, because God does not want it. God wants me to write a lot. He wants me to go to Paris soon and publish these two books. I am afraid of publishing them because I know what an uproar they will create. I know that God will help me, and therefore I am not afraid. I cannot write, because my hand has become stiff. God commands me to write. I will go to bed if he commands me to. I am waiting for his commands . . . .

It was five o'clock by the time I went upstairs. I went to my dressing room and changed. On the way I asked myself where my wife was, whether she was in the room where I was supposed to sleep or in another, and I felt my body tremble. I trembled as I do now. I cannot write because I am trembling from cold. I cannot write. I am correcting the letters because I am afraid that people will not understand my handwriting. I want to say that I went into the bedroom and when I went in I had a feeling of cold before I saw. Her bed had no pillows and was unmade.* I went downstairs, having decided not to sleep. I wanted to write down my impressions. I cannot write, because my body feels cold all over. I am asking God to help me, because my hand aches and I find it difficult to write. I want to write well.

. My wife is not asleep, and neither am I. She thinks, and I feel. I am afraid for her. I do not know what to say to her tomorrow. I will not speak to anyone. Tomorrow I will sleep. I want to write, but cannot. I am thinking. I do not feel, but I know that God wants it. I cannot write, from cold. My fingers are becoming numb. I want to say that she does not love me. I am sad. My heart is heavy. I know that people get used to grief, and I will get used to it too. I am afraid of getting used to grief, because I know that this is death. I will go and ask forgiveness, because I do not want death. I will ask her, but she will not understand me, because she will think that I am wrong. I am not afraid of being wrong, but I am afraid she might die. Her mind is getting cold. I am freezing. I cannot write. I want to say that I feel cold. I cannot write. My fingers are numb with cold. I cannot write. I am sorry for myself and for her. I am weeping. I am cold. I do not feel. I am dying. I am not God. I am a beast . . . .

I want to sleep, but God does not will it. I was scratching the paper because I felt like a beast.† I did not like the paper.

---

* Romola has obviously moved out of their shared bedroom. This helps to account for the fit of cold and anger that Nijinsky now experiences. (Ed.)
† Between this paragraph and the preceding one Nijinsky made a drawing (see opposite) that appears to have begun, like so many of his drawings, with an arc. Then, it seems, he violently crossed out the arc. In the process, he probably scratched the paper with his pen. (Ed.)

Two pages from Book II: Nijinsky in a fury. On the right-hand page, after "I am a beast," he begins a drawing and then scratches it out

I am a predator. I am a spiteful man. I am not God, but a beast. I am sorry for myself and for people like me. I am not a man. I am a beast. I know they will say that I am spiteful because I write spiteful things. I am spiteful. I am spiteful and a predatory beast. I have sharp claws. Tomorrow I will scratch. I feel I am spiteful. I do not wish people harm, but people wish me harm. I cannot be sorry for people who wish me harm. I do not wish people harm, but they wish me harm. I cannot make my handwriting attractive, because I am angry. I am not writing calmly. My hand is nervous. I am nervous. I am angry and nervous. I cannot be calm. I do not want to be calm. I will be angry. I am an angry scoundrel. I am angrier than anyone else in the world. I know how to be angry. I made her angry, and therefore she left me. I cannot write, because I am angry. I am angry, but not in the way other people are angry. I am angry at God. I will not go out for a walk tomorrow. I will stay at home. I will drink wine and beer. I will eat meat. I will laugh. I will be stupid. I do not want to write in an attractive handwriting, because I want people to read me in the way I want. I cannot write anymore.

I got up at three o'clock in the afternoon. I woke up earlier. I heard people talk, but did not understand who it was talking. I understood much later. I recognized the voice of her mother and of her mother's husband. I realized that they had come. I waited for God to tell me what to do. I did nothing, but felt bored. In the course of that half hour I understood more than another man would have understood in a lifetime. I thought. I thought with God. I knew that God loved me, and therefore I was not afraid of doing what he willed me to do. I was afraid of death. I was sad. I was bored. I was sorry for my wife. She was weeping. I was suffering. I knew that God wanted my suffering. I knew that God wanted me to understand what death was. I did understand. I waited for God's commands. I did not know whether I should wake up or lie in bed. I know that God will not harm me. I suffered in my heart. I wanted to weep. I heard my wife's sobs. I heard my wife's laughter. I heard the threats of my wife's mother. I wept in my heart. I gazed at the wall and saw the wallpaper. I gazed at the lamp and saw glass. I gazed into the distance and saw emptiness. I wept. I felt sad. I did not know what to do. I wanted to comfort my wife, but God would not let me. I wanted to laugh, because I felt laughter, but I understood death and stopped. I heard what was being said about me. I realized what they were all thinking. I started getting bored. I wanted to cheer them up. I did not get up, but stayed in bed. I felt sad. I wept in my heart. I began to move and raised a leg. I felt a nerve in my leg. I began to move this nerve. I moved my toes with this nerve. I realized that the big toe was not good, because it had no nerve. I understood death. I moved my big toe, and the others followed. I realized that the other toes had no nerves and were living by the nerve of the big toe. I know that many people look after their feet. They cut their corns. I have no corns because I have been more careful. I did not trust chiropodists and used to work on my corns myself. I realized that this work made no difference, except that a corn that has been cut grows more quickly. I decided to put an end to my corns, because they gave me no peace. I was living in Venice. I took off my shoes and walked around barefoot or in slippers. I do not like slippers, but I wore them out of habit. I now wear slippers because I have to wear them out. I do not like shoes and therefore wear wide dancing shoes. In Venice I discovered how corns can be removed and therefore started doing what seemed best to me. Sometime later I noticed that my corn did not hurt, but it was big because I had let it grow. I left it alone, and a little later I began to rub it with a stone that is called meerschaum. My corns disappeared. I noticed today that I had no corns, but my toes are short and do not have a nice shape. I noticed that my toes had no nerves. I realized that our whole life is regeneration. I realized that if people went on living in this way, they would have no toes. I realized that the whole human organism regenerates itself. I realized that people did not think about what they were doing. I know that the earth regenerates itself, and I realized that people contribute to its regeneration. I noticed that the earth is becoming extinguished and that all life is becoming extinguished with it. I realized that the oil that is pumped out of the earth gave heat to the earth and that coal is what had burned up inside the earth. I realized that without burning there would be no life. I realized that we needed the heat of the earth. That the life of the earth was its heat. I realized that people abused the practice of pumping oil and petroleum out of the earth. I realized that people did not understand the meaning of life. I know that it is difficult to live without oil and petroleum. I know that people need coal. I know that precious stones are burnt-out and decomposed elements. I know that water is the remains of earth and air. I know that the moon is covered with water. I know that astronomers have seen canals. I understand the meaning of canals. I know that people used the canals as a means of escape. I will be a fish and not a man if people do not help me. I realize that the earth is becoming extinguished. I know that earth used to be a sun. I know what the sun is. The sun is fire. People think that life depends on the sun. I know that life depends on people. I know what life is. I know what death is. The sun is reason. The intellect is an extinguished sun that is decomposing. I know that decomposition destroys life. I know that the earth is being covered with decomposed matter. I know that people abuse decomposition. Scientists are covering up the earth all the time. The earth is suffocating. There is not enough air for it. Earthquakes are due to the shaking of the earth's entrails. The earth's entrails are mine. I tremble when I am not understood. I feel a lot, and therefore I live. Within me the fire is never extinguished. I live with God. People do not understand me. I came here to help. I want "Paradise" on earth. Today there is "hell" on earth. Hell is when people quarrel. Yesterday I quarreled with my wife for her own improvement. I was not angry. I made her angry not out of anger but in order to kindle in her a love for me. I want to kindle the earth and people, and not to extinguish them. Scientists extinguish the earth and human love. I know that it is inconvenient to write in this notebook, but I am writing in it because I think it is a pity to use up the paper. I know that if men had pity for each other, life would last longer. I know many people will tell me it is not important to live for a long time, that they say, "Life will be long enough for me." But after all, this phrase speaks of death. People do not like their children. People think that children are not them. People think that children are necessary in order to have more soldiers. People kill children and cover the earth with ash. Ash is harmful to the earth. People say that ash is good for the earth. I know that when earth is covered with ash it suffocates. I know that it needs life. I am a Russian and therefore know what the earth is. I do not know how to plow, but I know that the earth glows. Without its warmth there would be no bread. People think that they must burn the bones of dead people in order to fertilize the soil. I will say that this is bad because the earth is made fertile by warmth and not by ash. I realize that the earth is putrefaction. I know that putrefaction is a good thing. I know that without putrefaction there would be no bread. I know that putrefaction covers the earth and in this way destroys the earth's heat. I realize that people think that one must eat a lot. I consider food a habit. I know that man is by nature very strong. I know that people weaken him because they take no care of his life. I know that people must live, and therefore I want to explain to scientists. I know that many scientists will laugh, but I understand the meaning of this laughter. I do not want laughter. I want love. Love is life, and laughter is death. I like laughing when God wills it so. I know that many people will say, "Why does Nijinsky always talk about God? He is mad. We know that he is a dancer and nothing else." I understand all these sneers. These sneers do not annoy me. I weep and weep.

I know that many people will say that Nijinsky is a crybaby. I know what a crybaby is. I am not a crybaby. I am not a dying man. I am alive, and therefore I suffer. My tears rarely flow. I weep in my heart. I know what a crybaby is. People call crybabies those who have weak nerves. I know what nerves are, because I was nervous . . . .

I have turned off the electric light because I wanted to economize. I have understood the meaning of economy. I do not mind spending the money, but I do mind spending energy. I have realized that without energy there would be no life. I have realized the meaning of the earth, which is being extinguished, and therefore I want to give people an idea of how it would be possible to obtain electricity without coal. Coal is essential for the heat of the earth, and therefore I do not want to dig out coal.

I want to take coal as an example. People go on and on digging for coal. People choke because of coal. People find it difficult to live, because they do not understand the meaning of coal. I know what coal is. Coal is fuel. I know that people abuse coal. I know that life is short, and therefore I want to help people. I do not write for amusement. I want to make people understand about life and death. I love life. I love death. I am not afraid of death. I know that death is good where God wills it. I know that death is bad where there is no God. I understand people who want to shoot themselves. I know that my wife's father shot himself. He studied a very great deal. He became nervous because his brain was overtired. I do not study a lot. I study only what God commands me to. God does not want people to study a lot. God wants happiness for people . . . .

I want to talk about coal. I understand the meaning of coal. Coal is the source of fuel. Fuel is the source of life. I understand people who say that without fuel one could freeze. I understand that fuel is a necessary thing. I understand that fuel can be conserved. I know that timber is a necessary thing, that it must be preserved and that trees must not be cut down all the time. People waste fuel. People think that one must have many things, because the more one has, the happier one is. I know that the less one has, the less worried one is. I cannot write, because my fuel has drawn my wife to me. I love her. She has read what I have written and has understood me. I told her not to disturb me while I was writing, and she went away quite happily. Today she feels more. I am happy because I hope for her improvement. My wife's mother has calmed down because she saw my love for my wife.

Fuel is a necessary thing, and therefore it must be conserved. I will conserve fuel because I know that in this way life will be longer. I do not want people who think, "Life will be long enough for me." I do not like selfishness. I love everyone. I want to eat little, because I must not fill up my stomach. I want to live simply. I want to love, because I want happiness for everyone. I will be the happiest of men when I know that all people share things with each other. I will be the happiest of men when I can act and dance and so on and so forth without monetary or any other kind of reward. I want love for people. I do not want death. I am afraid of intelligent people. They smell of cold. I freeze when I have a man with a brain next to me. I am afraid of intelligent people because they smell of death. I do not write in order to make clever remarks. I write in order to explain. I want no payment for this book. I want to help people. I do not boast about my book, because I do not know how to write. I do not want my books to be sold. I want publishing to be for free. I know that it is difficult nowadays to publish for free. I know that people are dying out. I know that I will be understood if this book is well printed, and therefore I will publish them* for money. I have spent little time on writing, but my wife wants money because she is afraid of life. I am not afraid, but I have no right to leave my wife without resources.

I want to speak of my wife's mother, Emma, and her husband, Oscar.†

They are good people. I love them, but they have their faults like everyone else. I will write about faults so that they can read about them. I hope they will improve. I know that they will come looking for me, and therefore I write so that they will see me working. I like people to see me working. I want work. I like people who work. Emma and Oscar are tired after

---

* *Sic.* He now sees his diary as two books, "Life" and "Death." See p. 152. (Tr.)

† Oscar Párdány (1871–1945), Emilia Márkus's second husband, was a former counselor to the office of the Hungarian prime minister. He was a Jewish convert to Catholicism. (Ed.)

their long journey. They thought I was insane, but have felt the opposite. Oscar sees that I understand politics, and therefore he is interested in me. He likes politics and money matters. I do not like either of these things. I want to give people an example of a conversation with Oscar. I like him, but he thinks a lot. He is afraid of having an operation for his hemorrhoids because he is a nervous person. I know many people will say that he is a nervous person because he is a Jew.

I want to say that nervousness is not a vice. Nervous people are good people. I like Jews because they are nervous. I know people who make a show of not being nervous. I know they are pretending. I do not like pretense. I like people who do not pretend. I know people will tell me that nervousness is a weak side of character. I will say that nervousness is not a weak side of character but a nervous habit. I know people will say that I do not know what fear is, because I have not been in the war. I will say that I have been in the war, because I have fought for my life. I fought not in the trenches but at home. I fought with my wife's mother when I was interned in Hungary. I know many people will say that I lived well because I lived in the house of my wife's mother. I did live well. I had everything. I was not hungry, but I suffered inwardly. I did not like my wife's mother. I liked to be by myself. I worked on a system of dance notation because I had nothing to do. I was bored. I wrote. I knew that no one loved me. My wife's mother, Emma, pretended to love me. I felt it and explained it to her as best I could. She did not understand me, because she felt that I was spiteful. I was not spiteful. I was a martyr. I wept because my wife did not understand me. Oscar did not understand me. He felt money, because he found it difficult to feed us. I felt that my wife's mother had to give me food without payment because I was a relative. I knew that relatives do not like relatives, and therefore I decided to act as if I were offended. She did not understand me. She thought I was a poor man, and she was afraid that I might cost her money. She liked money, but did not realize its value. I realized the value of money and therefore pretended that money was not important. I knew what money was when I was still a child. My mother used to give me 50 kopeks a week to buy treats for myself, because she had money from renting out rooms. My mother rented out rooms, and in this way we were able to buy food. I used to eat a lot because I was always hungry. I did not realize that I had to eat little. I acted like a grown-up although I was twelve years old. I lived in my wife's mother's house and ate a lot. I did not understand the meaning of food and therefore ate too much. Food was very expensive because of the war. My wife's mother, Emma, was a nervous woman. She liked me for my success with the public. She liked my dancing. I did not like dancing, because I was bored. I went on being bored. I did not realize that one could live everywhere. I was working on a dancing system while cats shat and pissed under the table. I did not like the cats, because they were dirty. I did not like dirt. I did not realize that it was not the cats that shat but people. People did not like the cats and therefore did not take care of them.* I took care of my notation system. I wanted to stop thinking about myself, and so I started notating my ballet "The Faun" according to my notation system. This was a long job. It took me about two months to notate it. The ballet took ten minutes to perform. I realized my mistake and gave up the work. Again I felt bored. I grieved. I wept because I was bored. I was bored because I longed for life without realizing it. I read Tolstoy. Reading was a rest, but I did not understand the meaning of

---

* According to Romola Nijinsky (*Nijinsky*, p. 247), Emilia Márkus's cat disappeared one day during the Nijinsky family's internment in Budapest, and Emilia accused Nijinsky of having killed it. The animal was later found unharmed. (Ed.)

life. I lived from day to day. I did dancing exercises. I started developing my muscles. My muscles became firm, but my dancing was bad. I felt that this was death to my dancing, and so I became nervous. I was nervous, and so was my wife's mother. We were both nervous. I did not like her, and therefore I complained about every little thing. I did not like little things, but I complained about them because I had nothing to do. I lived from day to day. My wife was bored. It occurred to us to engage in debauchery. I bought books that are now in a trunk in the Hotel Bristol in Vienna. I bought these books to excite myself with. I excited my wife. She did not want this. I forced her to become excited. She was excited, and we engaged in debauchery. I was a debauchee. I know that many people are debauchees. Dr. Frenkel is also a debauchee because he showed me Japanese engravings in a book. That book was full of obscene pictures. He smiled when I said I liked the book. I thought my heart would burst at the sight of this filth, but I did not want to show it. I realized that people would not understand me if I did not approve their actions. I told myself that I would pretend. I pretended, and people understood me. I did not want to pretend, but God wants me to because He has chosen me for His own purpose. I obey Him, but sometimes I am afraid to go into taverns or apartments, for I think that God would not want it. Once I went by a tavern which God wanted me to go into, but I felt bodily tiredness and mental death. I was afraid and wanted to go in, but God did not want me to be harmed, and He stopped me. I know many people will say, "What is Nijinsky talking about? He says that God orders him to do this and that, but he does nothing himself." I understand people, I am sorry to admit it, but I must say that it is true. I am no longer a man. I am God. I am not an ordinary man. I am God. I love God, and He now loves me. I want everyone to be like me. I have nothing to do with spiritualism. I am a man in God, and there is nothing spiritualist about this. I am not a medium. I am God. I am a man in God. I am afraid of perfection because I want to be understood. I am sacrificing myself because I do not live like everyone else. I work for days on end. I love work. I want everyone to work the way I do. I want to tell about my life in Budapest during the war. I lived for a long time in the house of my wife's mother. I did not know what to do. I was bored. I had a feeling of strength when I discovered that I was going to be freed, and I decided to escape from the house of my wife's mother. I went with my wife and child to a hotel because I had received some money. I was not angry with my wife's mother. I liked her because I realized that she was having difficulties. My wife's mother realized her mistakes and came running to the hotel to beg us to come back. We would not agree, because we knew that we would soon go away. I said goodbye to my wife's mother and thanked her for her hospitality. I liked her, but I did not like Oscar. Oscar had no tact and therefore used to express his opinions in a loud voice. I was offended and nearly fought with him, but my wife stopped me, and my wife's mother stopped Oscar. Thus we both stopped. But we gnashed our teeth at each other. We quarreled because of politics. Oscar said that Russia was wrong, and I said that Russia was right. I seized the opportunity to see Oscar get irritated. I know that many people will not believe what I write, but I don't care, because I know that many people will feel the truth of what I am saying. I did not speak to Oscar again and left without saying goodbye. I knew that I was wrong, but I did it all on purpose, because I wanted them, that is, my wife's mother and Oscar, to know that one must not be stingy. I took them by surprise. They thought a great deal and changed their minds. They knew that I did not like them. I wrote in American papers about the barbarity of my wife's mother. They read it, and this apparently changed them, because they no longer begrudged the money. I did not talk to them about stinginess. They understood me because I played my part well. I put up a pretense because I wished them well. I liked them, but I had to pretend, and therefore I felt angry. That anger was feigned. I liked them. Romola's mother was a difficult woman. She had her habits. She slapped her servants' faces. I did not like this, and therefore I scowled at her. She became all the more angry. My wife's mother did not like her husband looking at her servants, and so whenever he looked at them, she slapped their faces. I did not realize the meaning of it all, because I did not think of it, but I felt that she was doing it because she was jealous. I was sorry for the servants and for Oscar because I saw that he looked at them out of curiosity. I saw his curiosity and therefore defended him. I thought that he was flirting with the servants, but later I came to the conclusion that Emma, who was capricious, was making it all up. Emma was a terrible woman, because she never left Oscar in peace. Oscar loved her and always defended her. I saw that he was weeping in his heart, and I was sorry for him. I never said anything to him, because I thought that he would not understand me. Now I understand him and hope that he will like me. I have given him several of my drawings because I see that he likes them. I will not sign my drawings, because I know that no one can do what I do. Today I told Oscar that I did not like signing my drawings, because I knew that no one would do what I was doing. I know that everyone can do good drawings, but I know that God does not like repetitions. I know people will copy me, but copying is not life. Copying is death. I know many people will tell me that Raphael and Andrea del Sarto made copies and that Andrea del Sarto made a copy of the "Gioconda"* such

* The *Mona Lisa*. (Ed.)

that nobody could tell whether the painting was by Leonardo da Vinci or by Andrea del Sarto. I do not like copying and therefore do not want people to copy me. My drawings are very simple, and it is very easy to copy them. I know that there will be many copyists, but I will do everything possible not to be copied. Copies remind me of monkeys, for monkeys copy men's movements. Monkeys copy because they do not understand. They are stupid animals. I know that many people will tell me that Raphael was not stupid, but copied all the same. To that I must reply that Raphael copied because he had to, in order to acquire technique. I like technique, but I do not like copying . . . .

I know what is needed for my fountain pen, because I have noticed that my finger gets tired from pressing. From pressing, a little groove has formed on my middle finger. I know that my finger will take on an ugly shape, and therefore I will try to invent a perfect fountain pen. I know already what is necessary to perfect a fountain pen. I have noticed that my fountain pen opens at the top end and that therefore the ink leaks out if I do not screw it up tight. I know that if a fountain pen is always screwed up tight, it gets tired and therefore soon becomes damaged. I have also noticed that it is bad to open a fountain pen at the top end, because if that part of the fountain pen falls on the ground, the nib breaks. The nib is made of gold and is therefore very expensive. I have noticed that the gold of the nib is bad, because I have been writing for no more than two weeks and yet the nib has changed its shape. It is true I write a lot. I know that many people write a lot, and therefore I want to explain to them the defect of the fountain pen. I see the whole swindle of the Waterman's Ideal Fountain Pen. I know that that brand has a great reputation. I know that its reputation was made at the beginning because it produced millions of good fountain pens for the sake of publicity. I know that now the owner wants to become rich and therefore produces bad fountain pens in the hope that no one will notice his swindle. I write about the fountain pen because I want men to understand that people must not be swindled. I know that the makers will sue me. I know that they will show good fountain pens, saying that this fountain pen is a fake. I know that they will get the best lawyers for their defense and will spend money on bribery, because they do not want people to notice the swindle. I will be found guilty, but I will be right. I hope I will be defended. I will hide this pen just in case I have to go to court. I am not afraid of going to court, but my wife is afraid because she thinks that they wish me harm. I know that I will be put in prison, for the company has many shareholders. I know what shareholders are, and therefore I want to write about them. I do not like shareholders, because I know that shareholders are rich people. I would prefer shareholders to be poor people. I know that if poor people were shareholders, there would be no wars. War is shareholding. Lloyd George is the representative of shareholders in England. Wilson does not like Trusts. He has often expressed his opinion, but people do not listen to him. I would like to help Wilson. I will do everything to help Wilson. Wilson is a man, and not an animal and a predator. Shareholding is bestiality. I know that people will tell me that everyone is a shareholder because everyone buys things. To that I will reply that everyone buys because they have no other choice. I know that if a possibility is found, there will be no more shareholding. I want to help those people who ask me to help them. I do not like requests, but I want people to know that I want to help them.

I want to order a frame for Oscar's photograph, because I want to show him my love. He saw that I had no photograph of him. I want to show him that people are all equal. I want to show him that I am not a nervous man. I know that everyone is nervous because everyone drinks tea and coffee. I do not like tea and coffee, because there is no life in these beverages. People think that they must drink, because this has been instilled into them. I know what tea and coffee are. I drink them because I am considered a nervous man. I showed them my nerves this morning. Everyone was frightened. I suddenly started singing in a bass voice like Chaliapin.* I like Chaliapin because he feels singing and acting. He is prevented from developing because he is asked to act in things that he does not like. I know that he can act in things that he does not like. He wants to show that he is a great artist and can act well in all roles. I know that his heart is ready to burst from suffering. He is a drunkard because he has been induced to drink. I know tea-drunkards. I know coffee-drunkards. I know cigar- and cigarette-drunkards. I know all types of drunkenness because I have tried them out. I know I will be told that I too am a drunkard, because I drink milk. I will answer that milk contains no stimulants. I know that doctors forbid drinking and smoking, but they themselves do the things they forbid, and therefore patients do not understand them. I know that everyone will be angry with me because I do not do what others want, and therefore I will do everything that others want to do. I will weep, but I will do it because I want everyone to give up their habits. I know many people will say that I am pretending, that one must first give up things oneself and then require others to do the same. I understand all such remarks. I will weep, but I will do everything that the others do, because I want people to care for me.

---

* The Russian bass Feodor Chaliapin (1873–1938) starred in the production of *Boris Godunov* that Diaghilev staged in Paris in 1908 and in several other operas presented by Diaghilev. (Ed.)

I am not an egoist. I am a man of love and therefore will do everything for others. I want to be cared for. I know that people will understand me. I know that people will like my wife and child, but I want universal love. I want people to love one another. I want to write about wars. I want to write about death, because I have felt what death is. I know that people like death, because they say, "I don't care." I will perform in things that excite the audience, because I know that people like excitement, but in exciting them this way I will make them understand love. I want people not to like spiritual death. I do not want people to fear death from God. I am nature. I am God in nature. I am the heart of God. I am not glass in the heart. I do not like people with glass hearts. I made a mistake when I wrote "heart," but now I have corrected it because I like corrections.*
I want people to improve. I do not want the death of the spirit. I am a dove. I know what people think when they look at an icon and see a dove. I know that people do not understand the church, but go there out of habit because they are afraid of God. God is not in icons. God is in the soul of man. I am God. I am the spirit. I am everything. I know that many people will say that "Nijinsky has gone mad because he is a dancer and an actor." I know people will love me as a human being if they see how I live at home. I know they are all reluctant to bother me, thinking that this does bother me. I am a man who does not get bothered. I am a man of love. I love peasants. I love the Tsar. I love everyone. I make no distinctions. I belong to no party. I am God's love. I know my wife's faults and therefore want to help her improve. I know many people will say that "Nijinsky tyrannizes his wife and everyone, because what he writes is not true." I will be sorry for people for the mistakes they make. I will sob like Christ on Mount Sinai. I

* The manuscript does not show signs of any such correction. (Tr.)

am not Christ. I am Nijinsky. I am a simple man. I have bad habits. But I want to get rid of them. I want people to point out my faults to me, because I want people to take care of me. I will take care of other people, and everyone will take care of me. I want loving care and not harsh care. I do not want indulgence. I am not indulgence. I am love. I want to speak of love. I will speak of love. I know that God will help me, because I understand Him. I know that I am a man of faults. I know that everyone has faults. I know that God wants to help everyone. I know, because I feel God. I know that if everyone feels me, God will help everyone. I see right through people. I do not need to speak about myself, because I understand without words. I know that people will say to me, "How can you know me if you have not seen me?" I will say that I can know you because I feel with my mind. My mind is so developed that I understand people without words. I see their actions and understand everything. I understand everything. I can do everything. I am a peasant. I am a factory worker. I am a servant. I am a gentleman. I am an aristocrat. I am a tsar. I am an Emperor. I am God. I am God. I am God. I am everything. I am life. I am eternity. I will be always and everywhere. People can kill me, but I will live because I am everything. I want eternal life. I do not want death. I will write of death so that people understand their faults and correct them. I am saying that I too have faults. I am not an actor. I am a man with faults. Come and look at me, and you will understand that I am a man with faults. I want to have faults, because I want to help people. I will be without faults when people help me. I want people, and therefore my doors are always open. My cupboards and trunks are also open. If you find the door closed, ring, and I will open if I am at home. I love my wife and wish her good, but she does not understand me yet and therefore tells the servants to close the doors. I know that my wife will be nervous if she notices that the public is trying to invade my house, and therefore I ask people to stay at home and wait for me. I will go where I am asked. I will be there without being there. I am the spirit in every man. I am Nijinsky. I will go if God orders me to, but I will not go if people say to me, "Come to me." I will listen to people, but I will not come to them, because I do not want revolt. I do not like party attitudes and therefore do not want people to form themselves into groups. I want everyone to stay with their wives and children. I do not want revolt. I do not like death. I want life. I want people to feel me. I love God. I love life. I love everyone, and I do everything for other people. I do not like begging. I do not like any society for the poor. I consider everyone poor. I do not like giving money. I will help spiritually. I want a spiritual and not a bodily love. I like the body because it is necessary for the spirit, and therefore I will eat little. I do not want starvation. I do not want people to have the habit of eating a lot. I do not like meat, because I like animals. I weep when I see people eating meat. I choke when I am given meat. I eat it because I want to be understood. I know many people will say that they eat meat because they want to be understood. I understand the meaning of these words. I do not want people to force others to read my books. I want people to influence others to read my books and go to the theater and see my performances. I want theaters to be free of charge. I know that today it is impossible to do anything without money, and therefore I will work hard so that everyone can come and see me without paying for it. I will work hard for money because I must show people that I am a rich man, not a poor one. Today people think that anyone who has no money is stupid and lazy, and therefore I will make money, although I will weep in my heart, and then I will show people who I am. I want to publish these two books so that people understand my actions. I want to work by myself because I can earn money more quickly that way. I want to become rich. I will gamble on the Stock Exchange. I will do everything to become rich, because I understand the meaning of money. I will go to Zurich with Oscar and gamble on the Stock Exchange there. I will buy stocks and shares that I consider good. I know that Oscar will be frightened because he will think that I am gambling. I know that he will beg me to show him my system, but I will not show it to him, because he does not understand the meaning of money. Rockefeller is a good man because he gives money to people, but he does not understand the meaning of money, because he gives money to science. I will give my money to love. To the feeling of God in men. I will buy a theater and perform without charge. Those who want to pay will wait in a line. Those who do not want to pay will make a line on the basis of love. I want a line on the basis of love. I will see the injustices, because I am very perceptive. I will not be deceived, and I will ask the man to leave the theater.* I will ask those who have been unfairly treated to come to me. I will recognize a man's cunning by his face, because I am a great physiognomist. I will show everyone that I know. Come to me, and you will see. I want to write, but my hand is tired because I write fast . . . .

I have had a hearty lunch because I ate quickly. I ate like the others. Oscar sat next to me and saw that I was eating meat. Emma also saw that I was eating meat, but I left almost all of it because I did not want to eat animals that had been killed. People will understand me better if I eat meat. I showed that I was not squeamish, because I ate meat. I have seen Emma's habits. She eats quickly and sometimes, in order to warm her body, as she says, she drinks wine. I realized that this was not

---

* He seems to mean that he will eject line-jumpers. (Tr.)

true, because she felt me and left the wine. She likes coffee out of habit. She is a nervous woman and drinks coffee. She eats everything very quickly, without chewing. Oscar also eats quickly, so does my wife, and I too eat in the way they do. I felt a pain in my stomach. I realized that I was eating little, but because I swallowed the food quickly, without chewing it, I had a feeling in my stomach. My stomach swelled up. I realized it was tired. I felt heat in my stomach and started drinking water. My stomach swelled up even more, but I felt thirsty. I drank a lot. I know that by eating in this way a man soon dies. I let them understand what I had observed, but they did not understand, because I told them this at lunch. I talked to them of the death of animals, but not directly. They did not understand me, because they had eaten a lot. I ate a lot, but I am not tired, because I can write after eating. My wife and Emma, my wife's mother, and Oscar are feeling sleepy. They are lazy, because they do not want to get up from the table. They have noticed that I ate a lot, and therefore they know that I am not stingy. I gave them everything I had. I went to the cupboard for the butter because I know Emma's habit. She likes to have butter at her meals. I gave her the butter, but she did not eat it. She thought I liked butter, because I had eaten a lot of it in the morning. She came back from Hungary, where people are starving because of the blockade imposed on them. I know that the blockade had been imposed by England. I know that Lloyd George wants to continue the blockade because he is afraid of revolt. He knows that if a man eats well, he wants nothing else and therefore is ready for anything. A man who has eaten meat is brutalized and kills people. Lloyd George wants to starve people and therefore considers it necessary not to lift the blockade. I know I will be told that it was not Lloyd George who has imposed the blockade but the English people, because they have elected him as Prime Minister. I will say that it was not the people who had elected him but the rich. I know that all rich people will understand him, because he defends the interests of the rich. I know I will be told that Lloyd George is not a rich man and that he is of working-class origin. I know that all this is lies. I know that Lloyd George has a lot of money. I know that Lloyd George is an ambitious man. I know I will be told that ambition is a good thing. I will say that ambition is a good thing, only you must know how to use it. Lloyd George uses ambition for the rich classes. I use ambition for all classes. I do not belong to the Liberal or any other party. I have no party. I know I will be told, "You belong to the party of the partyless." I know there are people belonging to no party, but I do not belong to that party. I am God. And God is not a party, because He loves everyone. I know I will be told that in my first book I was talking about Wilson's party, and that I approved of that party. To that I must reply that I consider Wilson's party to be more perfect than the other parties. I do not want a party attitude. I want people to love each other. I know I will be told, "You do not belong to anything." I will say that I do not belong to any party. I am God's property and therefore fulfill all His tasks. I know many people will say, "What kind of God orders you to do everything you do? You are deceiving us. You are a primitive man, quite uncivilized." I know all these objections. I will answer them simply. I am man's firstborn, with God's culture and not an animal's. I do not want death. I want life for people. I love other people and not myself. I do not consider selfishness and bestial actions to be culture. I like the working classes and the rich classes and the poor classes. I love everyone. I do not want everyone to be equal. I want love to be equal. I want everyone to love one another. I do not want servants to work for money only. I want to be loved. My servants love me. At first I did not understand life, and therefore I quarreled with the servants. I know that people will tell me that servants are fools and that if you do not show them your fist they will not understand you. I too treated servants in this way, but I have now realized that I was wrong in behaving that way. I do not want the servants to suffer. I know I will be told that servants are not grateful. To that I must reply that servants are just as much human beings as we are, only they have less intelligence. Servants feel when they are not loved, and therefore they are angry. I know I will be told that servants must not be angry, because they are paid. I will say that servants are paid with their own money, because they work for money. People forget that work is money. People think that money is more important than work. Nowadays everyone observes that work is more expensive than money, because there are no workers and there is no money. I am not a Bolshevik. I am a working man. I know that everyone works, but not all work is equal. Good work is a necessary thing. I too work when I write these books. I know many people will say that I do not work, but write for my own pleasure. I will answer that there can be no pleasure when a man gives up all his free time to writing. One must write a lot in order to understand what writing is. Writing is a difficult thing because one gets tired sitting. One's legs become numb, and the writing hand becomes stiff. The eyes are damaged, and one has no air, because the room does not contain enough air. A man soon dies from this kind of life. I know that people who write at night damage their eyesight and wear glasses or pince-nez, and hypocrites wear monocles. I do not wear glasses, pince-nez, or lorgnettes, because I have not written much, but I have noticed that after writing for a long time my eyes become bloodshot. I like people who write a lot, because I know that they are martyrs. I like martyrs for God's sake. I know many people will say that one must write for money because without money one cannot live. I will say with tears in my eyes that these people are like Christ on the cross. I weep when I hear things like that, because I have experienced this in a different way. I danced for money. I almost died because I was overtired. I was like a horse that is forced with a whip to pull a heavy load. I have seen draymen whipping their horses to death because they did not realize that the horse had no strength. The drayman was driving his horse downhill* and whipping it. The horse fell, and all its guts dropped out of its behind. I saw that horse and sobbed in my heart. I wanted to sob aloud, but I realized that people would take me for a crybaby, and therefore I wept inwardly. The horse was lying on its side and screaming with pain. Its scream was like a low moan. I wept. I felt. A veterinary surgeon shot the horse with a revolver because he was sorry for it. I know a story about a dog. I met a French sportsman, Monsieur Raymond. I told him that his dog was very beautiful, but he told me with tears in his voice that he was going to shoot that dog because he felt it was better the dog should die than suffer from starvation. I realized that he had no money, and therefore I wanted to help him. I knew he was an ambitious man, because he liked winning silver cups in the Skeleton Race. Skeleton racing is the name given to a sport in which a man lies on his stomach on a toboggan made of steel and uses all his strength to gain speed.† Such a speed is very dangerous. Many sportsmen are killed accidentally. These sportsmen are affected by wine or tobacco, and therefore their nerves are upset at the slightest provocation. They go down the track at full speed. They become nervous and get killed. I said this to M. Raymond, and he understood me. He fell during a race and was almost killed. I told him that I thought he was nervous today

* "downhill": Nijinsky clearly means "uphill." (Tr.)
† Nijinsky himself participated in St. Moritz's skeleton races, at considerable danger to himself. According to Romola Nijinsky (*Nijinsky*, p. 352), he sometimes took Kyra on the sled with him. (Ed.)

because he had smoked a lot. I made him realize that he was suffering. I noticed his tears, but did not show him that I did, because I was afraid he might weep. He told me he would shoot his dog. I wept, and he did too, in his heart. He felt that I liked the dog, and he went away, leaving my wife and me. I went away feeling sad. I have noticed that when I eat meat and swallow it without chewing, my excrement comes out hard. I have to strain so much that my veins almost burst on my neck and face. I have noticed that all the blood rushes to the head. I realized that this sort of strain could give a man apoplexy. I am not familiar with that illness, but I know cases that I want to talk about. My excrement would not come out. I suffered because I had a pain in my back passage. My back passage was not large, but the excrement was big. I strained again, and the excrement moved forward a bit. I began to sweat. I felt hot and cold all over. I prayed God to help me. I strained once again and the excrement came out. I wept. It was painful, but I felt happy. When all this business was over, I wiped my bottom and felt pain in it. I noticed this bit of gut that had come out, and I got frightened. I started to push it back in. I thought the gut would be sucked in, but it was not sucked in. I wept. I was afraid for my dancing. I knew what it was, a piece of gut that had come out of my bottom. Then God told me not to eat meat and to chew my food for a long time before swallowing it. I did this and noticed that my excrement came out more freely. I began to eat less. My piece of gut was sucked in. I was happy. I know people who have a long gut and cannot either sit or walk, and they have to use suppositories and other methods to make their excrement come out. But no doctor, at least none I have ever heard of, has ever told people to stop eating meat and swallowing their food whole. I know Oscar suffers from that illness. His doctor advised him to have an operation. He is afraid. He scratches his bottom. I saw this when I shared my bedroom with him, for my wife is still afraid of me because Dr. Frenkel told her that I have sick nerves. I know that people die of "cancer," and therefore I think that cancer is nothing other than the decomposition of blood. People feed on all kinds of canned foods and meat, and their blood therefore secretes unnecessary substances. My wife and everyone is afraid of "cancer." I too am afraid of it, but I realize how one can get rid of cancer. Dr. Frenkel laughed when I told him about cancer. He laughed because he thought I understood nothing about medicine. I showed him an example, and he became interested, but he was tired from eating and therefore let that conversation drop. We ate at the same time because my wife had invited him to our house. He was observing me because he wanted to understand whether I was insane or not. He is still convinced that there is something wrong with me. I know there is "something wrong" with him, because he is a nervous man. He smokes a lot, for he picked up this habit in school. I think that many people smoke because they think they look impressive that way. I have noticed that people who smoke have a proud bearing. I visited the mayor of St. Moritz, Mr. Hartmann. I wanted to cheer them up a bit and therefore went in to have a talk. Oscar started talking to the mayor. I noticed that the mayor assumed a dignified attitude, and so did Oscar, and they lit cigarettes. I was looking at the mountains through a telescope, for they told me that one could see deer. I looked and saw nothing and said that I preferred not seeing the deer because it was them, the Hartmanns, that I had come to see. They laughed, but I felt that they were not interested in me. They were interested in Oscar. I left them and started looking for a deer. I set the sights of the telescope and saw a deer. The deer was not frightened of my stare, and I could see it

well. I saw an old, fat deer. It reminded me of Mayor Hartmann. I told them that the deer had turned its back on me.
I wanted to make them feel my presence, but they had no
time for me. I told Oscar that we had to go and eat since the
soup was waiting for us and we were waiting for the soup.
Hartmann and his wife laughed, but they had no time for
me. I felt that they were thinking and not feeling, and I felt
hurt. I noticed that they thought I was insane, because when
the mayor's wife asked me about my health, I answered that
it was always good, and she smiled. I felt hurt and wept in
my heart . . . .

Having nothing else to do, my wife's mother and my wife,
together with Oscar, came into the salon. My wife asked me
to show them my drawings. I pretended that I did not want to.
I showed them the drawings that they had already seen. My
wife asked me to show them the other drawings. I took a batch
of drawings I had been working on continually for two or three
months and threw them on the floor. My wife's mother, my
wife, and Oscar felt that I did not like my drawings. I told
them that nobody was interested in the drawings and so I had
taken them off the wall. They said they were sorry and began
looking at them. I explained to them the meaning of these
drawings. I said that I would be understood in Paris because
people were very sensitive there. I said this on purpose, because
I wanted to show them I was angry. They felt this and said
that they too understood. I made no reply. I showed them some
of the drawings because I wanted them to feel, but I was aware
of what they were thinking and therefore left them with tears
in my soul. I am a man with a soul, and therefore I weep when
I feel that I am not being understood. I knew that I would not
be understood and therefore took all these drawings off the
wall of my room. I hid my manuscripts in the bottom half of
the piano. I knew that nobody would understand my manu-

scripts, but I felt that Dr. Frenkel would send people to take my manuscripts and keep them for a while in order to have them translated. I did not want to show my manuscripts, because I was sure that Dr. Frenkel would not understand them and would take me for a madman. I was afraid for my wife and therefore hid the notebooks. I have hidden all my set designs because I feel that they will not understand them. I will not hide the drawings, because they have seen them. I do not want to create ill will when my wife's mother is here, because I do not want her to take my wife away with her. I know she loves money. I know she invited us to stay with her because she hoped to get my wife's money. I have no money and was therefore afraid that I would be committed to a lunatic asylum. Oscar and other relatives of my wife's mother have shares in a lunatic asylum. I understand without words what people are after. I have a feeling of disgust. I am not angry, but disgusted. I am afraid of Oscar and Emma. They are both dead. I want to help him, because I have noticed that he feels me. I noticed last night when we lay down next to each other that he still feels, for I felt that he also felt. I made this experiment when he fell asleep. Oscar started moving a finger when I thought of God. Oscar turned over when I felt God. I noticed this but failed to understand. I felt that it was God who did it. I discovered it only now. It occurred to me that I had to write but could not. God does this on purpose, because he wants to show me what God is. I wrote "he" with a small "h" because I have noticed that God does not mind what sort of letter one writes his name with. The Germans have equated god with nouns substantial, or, as grammar books put it, nouns substantive.* Germans think that the substantial is god. I think everyone is equal . . . .

* German rules of spelling require every substantive, or noun, to be capitalized. (Tr.)

I have realized that paper will go up in price, and therefore I will buy a lot of it in Zurich, because I intend to write a lot. I know that people are malicious and will not give me what I need. Therefore I must look after my interests. God has looked after my interests. He has promised me that I will win on the stock exchange. I wanted to write stock exchange with a capital letter, but felt offended and wrote it with a small letter. God does not like stock exchanges, but he wants me to gamble. He wants me to fulfill his purpose. He often tells me that I will lose, but I am sure I will win, because I want to give this money to the fulfillment of His purpose . . . .

I get tired of writing with a fountain pen, but I will write, because I want to leave my manuscript. I want to finish these books with a pen. I will look for an improved fountain pen. Tomorrow I will go to Zurich with Oscar, my wife, and her mother. I do not like calling my wife's mother by her name, because I feel that she is a bad woman. I do not like bad people. I have called Lloyd George, Diaghilev etc., etc., by their names because people find it easier to recognize people that way. I purposely made a mistake in writing out Diaghilev's name,* because I want him to see that I have forgotten how to spell his name.

I want to continue writing along the same line, but God does not want me to write on the same line as Diaghilev. I noticed my mistake, as I wrote the name of god and of Diaghilev with a capital letter. I will spell god with a small letter because I want to make a distinction . . . .

I want to go out for a walk, because I am tired of sitting,

---

* The sound *ia* in Diaghilev's name written in Latin characters represents a single Russian vowel, "я." On this occasion Nijinsky misspells Diaghilev's name in Russian by keeping the *ia* of the first syllable and adding the letter "я" to it: "Дiая." He is able to do this because he uses the pre-reform Russian alphabet, which still included the letter "i." (Tr.)

but I will go by myself unless I am noticed. Everyone will think that I am working, and I will go out into the street through the back door. I will go up high and look down, because I want to feel the height. I am off . . . .

I went out into the street through the back door and felt a blast of cold air. I knew that everyone was sitting in the dining room, and therefore I went past the door without making a noise. I know that people have nothing to do, and therefore they prevent other people from living. I do not want to prevent other people from living. I left the dining room because I felt that they did not like me there. I ran into Dr. Frenkel. He seemed bored. I shook hands with him, but first said: "Everyone is ill." I felt a coldness in my soul and therefore left the room.

Oscar came and asked me to come and have tea. Oscar felt that Dr. Frenkel was offended, and therefore he wanted to reconcile us. I did not want to be reconciled, so I stopped him. I told Oscar the object of my great work, saying that my nerves did not get tired as a result of the work. It seemed to me that he understood me, because he agreed with me. Oscar agrees very quickly with my arguments. I wanted to prove to him that God's writing does not tire nerves. I am not afraid of being tired by God . . . .

I had tea together with Dr. Frenkel, Oscar, my wife's mother, and my wife. I drank quietly, but after a while I felt the conversation and started to amuse them all. I amused them with a purpose. I said things that they understood. I joked. Everyone felt cheerful and happy. I noticed that Dr. Frenkel thought I wanted to laugh at him, and therefore I changed the subject. My conversation was about the Bolsheviks in Russia. I wanted to tell a certain story, but could not, because God wanted my wife to tell it. She could not talk, because she did not feel him. I helped her by reminding her. I did not want to speak much, but God wanted me to stimulate everyone. I stimulated every-one and left. I felt Frenkel because he wanted to speak to my wife. I left because I thought that I was not wanted. Frenkel is leaving, and I am staying. I do not want to see him to the door, because I want to make him feel that his opinion is not wanted by anyone . . . .

Dr. Frenkel has come to say goodbye to me. I shook hands with him. He asked me not to write a great deal. I told him to have no fear for me. He asked me if I wanted to see a doctor in Zurich. To that I said I didn't know but that if my wife wanted it, I would see him. He told me that it would be ex-cellent if I could see him, because he was a very good doctor. I told him I would see him if this would help my wife not to worry. Dr. Frenkel understood me. I shook hands with him, and he told me that he was a student of that doctor. I felt he was lying, because he understands nothing about nerves. He himself drinks tea and wine and smokes a lot, and therefore his nerves are strained. I know that Dr. Ranschburg* does not smoke, because he does not smell of tobacco . . . .

I am getting a headache because I have eaten a lot. I ate a lot because I did not want my wife's mother to think that I was stingy. She feels that I am not stingy. Oscar likes me, for he is worried about my health. He has been induced to believe that it is bad for me to work a lot. I will make Oscar feel that I am in good health because I work a lot. I understand why people get tired. They eat a lot, and food makes blood rush to the head when a person thinks. I feel sick and want to belch, and at the same time I have a slight headache. I will not eat a lot tonight, and I know that by morning I will feel all right again . . . .

* Dr. Paul Ranschburg was a neurologist who examined Nijinsky in Budapest in 1914. (Ed.)

I will go to Zurich sometime after six tomorrow morning, and therefore I will go to bed earlier, because I want the nerve doctor to see me in good condition. I will speak to him about nerves, for that specialty interests me. I know a little about this specialty already but will describe it later. I will not be writing in Zurich, because I am very interested in that town. I will go to a brothel because I want to have an intuitive understanding of tarts. I have forgotten tarts. I want to understand the psychology of a tart. I will go to several of them if God wills me to. I know that God does not like it, but I feel that he wants to test me. I feel a great spiritual strength and therefore will not make a mistake. I will give the tart money, but I will do nothing with her. I feel lecherous but afraid at the same time. I feel a rush of blood to the head. I feel that if I start thinking, I will have an apoplectic fit. I do not think, because I do not like to. However, I know what an apoplectic fit is, because of a certain occasion. My friend Serge Botkin cured me of typhoid fever the year I made my debut in Paris.* He cured me of typhoid fever. I drank water from a jug because I was poor and could not buy mineral water. I drank quickly, without suspecting that the contents were contaminated. I went off to dance, but when I came back in the evening, I felt a weakness in my body. Diaghilev called in a doctor, Botkin, for he knew him well. Serge Botkin

---

* In Paris in June 1909, immediately after the Diaghilev troupe's first season, Nijinsky came down with typhoid fever. The offer that Diaghilev made at his bedside was that Nijinsky should live with him and be supported by him. Sergei Botkin (1859–1910), who diagnosed Nijinsky's illness, was a ballet lover and art collector (see Nijinsky's later description of his paintings) as well as a physician. Wealthy and well-connected, he was part of Diaghilev's circle and contributed money and advice to Diaghilev's enterprises. Nijinsky says below that Sergei Botkin was the tsar's doctor. In fact, the court physician was Sergei's brother Evgeny Botkin, who was murdered with the Imperial family in 1918. But according to various sources, Sergei Botkin also treated the Imperial family. (Ed.)

was the tsar's doctor. I felt feverish and was not afraid. I did not know what the matter was with me. Serge Botkin looked at me and understood everything. I felt afraid. I noticed the doctor and Diaghilev exchanging glances. They understood without words. I also understood without words. Botkin looked at my chest and saw spots. I realized that he was frightened. I got frightened too. He became nervous and called Diaghilev into another room. That house has been torn down by now. I wept when I saw it had been torn down. It was a miserable house, but on my money I could not live better. Diaghilev made me an offer in that house when I was lying in a fever. I agreed. Diaghilev realized my value and was therefore afraid that I might leave him, because I wanted to leave even then, when I was twenty years old. I was afraid of life. I did not know that I was God. I wept and wept. I did not know what to do. I was afraid of life. I knew that my mother too was afraid of life, and she transmitted this fear to me. I did not want to agree. Diaghilev sat on my bed and insisted. He inspired me with fear. I was frightened and agreed. I sobbed and sobbed because I understood death. I could not run away, because I had a fever. I was alone. I was eating an orange. I was thirsty and asked Diaghilev to give me an orange. He brought me an orange. I must have fallen asleep with the orange in my hand, for I woke up with the orange all squashed and lying on the floor. I slept for a long time. I did not understand what was the matter with me. I lost consciousness. I was afraid of Diaghilev and not of death. I knew that I had typhoid fever, because I had had it in childhood and remembered that it could be recognized by the spots on the body. My spots were not from measles, because I know what measles is. I will write about measles later . . . .

Dr. Botkin once visited Tamara Karsavina, the well-known

dancer.* Tamara Karsavina was a married woman. She had married Mukhin. Mukhin was not rich, but he could give her an apartment. They had no children. Dr. Botkin visited Karsavina, and when he came back that night, he fell down dead in his room. I noticed that Karsavina was nervous. His death was unpleasant for her because he died after leaving her. I felt that Karsavina was to blame for his death because she had excited him. Serge Botkin liked to eat well, for I noticed that he had a thick neck and an apoplectically red face. I realized that he had a lot of blood. I noticed that everyone was nervous. I noticed everyone's taunts. I am sure that Karsavina flirted with him because he was a man received at Court. Court means the Imperial family. Karsavina flirted because she thought that she would improve her situation that way. Botkin paid compliments because he thought that one could always court ballerinas. I felt love for Karsavina. I did not wish her any harm. Botkin did not wish her any harm either, but he thought that one had to court ballerinas. I am convinced because I know what Karsavina is like . . . . .

Botkin died from an apoplectic fit because he was irritated. His irritation was obviously due to her flirting with him. She flirted, and he lusted. I know that Karsavina is an honest woman, for I noticed that. I too lusted after her a little because she has a beautiful body. I felt that one could not court her, and therefore I felt irritated. I courted her in Paris. My courting consisted of making her feel that she appealed to me. Karsavina felt that but did not respond, because she was married. I sensed my mistake and kissed her hand. She felt that I did not want anything, and therefore she was pleased. I know Karsavina well be-

* Tamara Karsavina (1885–1978) was the leading female dancer of the early Ballets Russes and one of the most admired ballerinas in Europe in the 1910s and 1920s. Nijinsky was her frequent partner and her friend. Vassili Mukhin was her first husband. (Ed.)

cause I worked with her for five years. I was young and did a lot of stupid things. I used to quarrel with Karsavina. I did not want to say I was sorry. I did not want to say I was sorry, because I felt hurt. I realized that Diaghilev had influenced Karsavina against me because he noticed that I was courting her. Karsavina picked a quarrel over some trivial matter, and I was irritated. I wept bitterly because I loved Karsavina as a woman. She felt that I had offended her, and therefore she wept . . . . Serge Botkin died. Everyone wept because they loved him . . . . My wife came and kissed me. I felt glad, but God did not want me to show my joy to my wife, because He wants to change her . . . .
. . . .

Botkin died. I saw his corpse from afar. He was lying on a catafalque. I understood death and was frightened. I left without kissing his corpse.* Everyone kissed the corpse. I could not see the whole business. Relatives wept, and acquaintances pretended to be sad. They looked around the apartment at the paintings and tried to figure out their value. I know that after his death all these things were sold because Serge Botkin's wife did not like any of his whims. Serge Botkin liked buying pictures because he had been told that he had to buy old paintings. His apartment was filled with old paintings. I have noticed that people are not interested in new pictures, because they think that they do not understand art. They buy old pictures in order to show that they have a love for art. I realized that people like art but are afraid to say to themselves, "I understand art." People are very timid because critics frighten them. Critics frighten people because they want people to ask them their opinion. Critics think that the public is stupid. Critics think

---

* It is the custom in the Russian Church to expose the body in the coffin so that friends can come up and kiss the hands or forehead of the dead person. (Tr.)

that they must explain pictures to the public. Critics think that without them there would be no art, because the public would not understand these things. I know what criticism is. Criticism is death. I once spoke to a man on a ship, coming back from New York to Boston. I spoke to him with some heat because he had provoked me. I noticed that he was a Russian detective dealing with disturbances at home. He thought I was an anarchist. I do not know why he thought I was an anarchist. He had an evil face. He did not like me, and I felt it and therefore distrusted him. I was interested in my problem about criticism and therefore talked about criticism. He wanted to have a heart-to-heart talk and drew me into a conversation about domestic policy. I realized this and decided to annoy him by explaining to him the question he had asked me. I spoke loudly because I wanted to impress him. He thought that I was getting irritated, and he pretended that he too was irritated. I noticed that his face was not alive when he spoke to me. He was not nervous when he made himself out to be nervous. I realized that I was acting better than he was. I took to explaining to him about criticism. He listened to me because he was tired of contradicting me. He kept interrupting me because he wanted to change the subject, but I would not let go of it, because I liked that subject. He did not like it and became nervous. I noticed that he did not like my conversation and that he went away leaving my question about criticism unanswered. I discovered afterward that he asked my wife whether I was a "nihilist." I do not know what a "nihilist" means. I know little about "nihilism." I do not understand all these names, because I am not a scholarly man. I was educated in the Imperial School, where I was not taught all these names. I was a pupil of the Imperial School. I did not understand domestic policy until I got married. I understood when I was married because I was afraid of life and I had to live. I will write about politics later. I want to talk about criticism, because I have touched upon this question. I do not like criticism, because it is an unnecessary thing. I know I will be told that criticism is essential because without it people will not understand what is necessary and what is not. I know that critics write because they want the money. I know that with the kind of life we lead nowadays, money is essential. I know I will be told that critics work hard writing what they do. I will say that critics work little, because they do not produce art, but write about art. An artist sacrifices his whole life for art. The critic inveighs against him because he does not like his picture. I know I will be told that a critic is an unprejudiced man. I will say that a critic is selfish, because he writes about his own opinion and not about the public's opinion. Applause is not opinion. Applause is a feeling of love for the artist. I like applause. I realize the value of applause. I will speak about applause later. A critic does not feel applause. A critic likes to duplicate applause, because he wants to show that he has more understanding. People in Paris pay no attention to criticism. Paris critics are angry with the public because they cannot influence it. Calmette is a great critic because he wrote theater criticism and political criticism. He lashed out at "The Faun" and said that the ballet was obscene.* I did not think about obscenity when I was composing that ballet. I was composing it with love. I thought out the whole ballet by myself. I gave the idea for the scenery, but Léon Bakst failed to

---

* In Nijinsky's first ballet, *The Afternoon of a Faun*, which had sets and costumes by Bakst, a faun (Nijinsky originated the role) attempts to seduce a nymph. She escapes, and he consoles himself by lying down on her scarf, ending with a convulsive movement suggestive of orgasm. When the ballet was premiered in Paris in 1912, Gaston Calmette, editor of *Le Figaro*, wrote a front-page article denouncing the ballet as pornographic. At Diaghilev's urging, Auguste Rodin then wrote an article in a rival newspaper, *Le Matin*, praising the ballet. Nijinsky posed for Rodin in 1912. Nijinska (*Early Memoirs*, p. 443) claims that it was Diaghilev who called an end to the sittings, out of jealousy. (Ed.)

understand me. I worked for a long time, but I worked well because I felt God. I loved that ballet and therefore transmitted my love to the public. Rodin wrote a good review, but he was influenced in writing it. Rodin wrote it because Diaghilev asked him to. Rodin is a rich man and therefore did not need money, but he was influenced, because he had never written criticism. He wanted to make a drawing of me because he wanted to make a marble statue of me. He looked at my naked body and found it was wrongly proportioned, and therefore he crossed out his sketches. I realized that he did not like me, and I left . . . .

Calmette wrote his review the same day. I understood from Diaghilev's conversation with Bakst that Calmette had become a general laughing stock. Calmette lost the public's trust as a theater critic . . . .
. . . .

Svetlov, a Petersburg critic, wrote a review about "The Faun" in the "St. Petersburg Gazette" without having been at a performance of it. He wrote because he read "Le Figaro," and "Le Figaro" is the newspaper with the biggest circulation. He wrote under the influence of Calmette's criticism. That he was not in the theater I know from the fact that Diaghilev wanted him to come and help in the work of the Ballets Russes. Svetlov thought that the Ballets Russes had failed, and therefore he hastened to inform the Russian public for fear that the other newspapers would publish this before him. I knew that Svetlov read "Le Figaro," and therefore I realized that he had received that paper before he had left Petersburg. He did not read the Paris newspaper "Le Matin," and so he had not read Rodin's review. If he had read Rodin's review, I am more than certain he would not have written a review like Calmette's but would have written a review like Rodin's. I noticed how worried Svetlov was when he arrived in Paris. He realized his mistake and

therefore avoided me. I was not afraid of him, because I knew that he was malicious. I am not afraid of malicious people, but on the contrary I fight them. I fought with Svetlov so much that I never greeted him when I saw him. He felt this and pretended that he did not like my ballets. He no longer wrote about me. He wrote a history of the ballet knowing nothing about it, because my life was not described in it.* I was not noticed. I wept, because I had worked hard for the Ballets Russes. Diaghilev was angry, but did not show it. I think that Svetlov wrote this book on purpose, because he wanted to show Diaghilev that he had not copied Calmette's review. Svetlov noticed that everyone was laughing at him and therefore wrote this book in order to justify himself . . . .
. . . .

I want to describe my life as an artist. I was nervous because I had masturbated a lot. I masturbated because I saw many beautiful women who flirted. I lusted after them and masturbated. I noticed that my hair started falling out. I noticed that my teeth began to rot. I noticed that I was nervous and began to dance worse. I took to masturbating once every ten days. I thought that ten days was a necessary interval of time, that everyone should come once every ten days, for I heard older people say so. I was no more than nineteen years old when I started masturbating once every ten days. I liked lying in bed thinking about a woman, but I came afterward and decided to make myself the object of my lust. I looked at my own erect prick and felt lust. I did not like it, but I thought that "once I had started the machine running, I had to finish." I came quickly, with a feeling of a rush of blood to my head. I did not

---

* Nijinsky is complaining about Svetlov's *Contemporary Ballet*, which was published in St. Petersburg in 1911 and in Paris in 1912. The book's text deals only briefly with Nijinsky, but other Ballets Russes stars are treated likewise, and the reason it does not discuss Nijinsky's ballets is that it predated them. (Ed.)

have a headache, but I felt a pain in my temples. I now have a stomachache because I have eaten a lot, and I have the same kind of pain in my temples as when I used to masturbate. I did not masturbate much when I danced, because I realized it was death to my dancing. I started preserving my strength and therefore gave it up. I started "chasing tarts." I had difficulty finding tarts, because I did not know where to look for them. I liked the tarts in Paris. They excited me, but, having done it once, I did not want to do anything anymore. I liked those women because they were good people. I felt bad every time after copulating. I am not writing this book to show that people should feel lust. I do not like lust. I do not feel lust when I write these lines. I am weeping bitterly. I feel everything I have lived through, and therefore I write about lust. My lusting almost destroyed me. I felt weak. I could not compose "Jeux."* I composed this ballet on the subject of lust. The ballet was not a success, because I did not feel it. I began it well, but then they started hurrying me, and I never finished it. In that ballet you can see three young people feeling lust. I understood life at the age of twenty-two. I composed that ballet by myself. Diaghilev and Bakst helped me write down the subject of the ballet, because Debussy, the famous musical composer, insisted on having the story on paper. I asked Diaghilev to help me, and he and Bakst together wrote down my story on paper. I told Diaghilev my ideas. I know that Diaghilev likes saying they are his, because he likes praise. I am very pleased if Diaghilev says it is he who has thought up these stories, that is, "The Faun" and "Jeux," for these ballets were

---

* *Jeux* ("Games"), Nijinsky's second ballet (1913), had a score by Claude Debussy and a set by Léon Bakst. It was a light-toned, modern-looking ballet in which three young people—a man (Nijinsky) and two women (Tamara Karsavina and Ludmila Schollar), all dressed in sports clothes—flirted with one another in various configurations. (Ed.)

composed by me under the influence of my life with Diaghilev. "The Faun" is me, and "Jeux" is the kind of life Diaghilev dreamed of. Diaghilev wanted to have two boys. He often told me about this desire of his, but I showed him I was angry. Diaghilev wanted to make love to two boys at the same time and wanted these boys to make love to him. The two boys are two young girls, and Diaghilev is the young man. I camouflaged these personalities on purpose because I wanted people to feel disgust. I felt disgust and therefore could not finish that ballet. Debussy did not like Diaghilev's idea either, but he was given 10,000 francs for that ballet, and therefore he had to finish it . . . .

I know that I must go to Zurich tomorrow and will therefore go to bed now . . . .

. . . .

I did not go to bed, because God wanted to help me. I have a slight headache and heartburn. What I call heartburn is when my stomach is inflamed. I do not like stomachaches, and therefore I want the pain to disappear. I asked God to help me. He told me I must not go to bed. I have noticed that my digestion does not work when I am lying down, and therefore I decided not to go to sleep. I will sleep on the train because I am bored by Oscar and my wife's mother. They have been here for only one day. I do not want to talk to them. I told my wife, in such a way that her mother heard, "that I do not want to talk, because I have to finish my work, as I will not be writing in Zurich." My wife understood and therefore answered nothing, but I do not know what her mother felt, because I did not see her face. She is a cunning woman. I noticed this today at lunch and dinner. At dinner I gave her a tangerine left over from my portion. She wanted another tangerine and therefore started talking about tangerines. I gave her my tangerine and said that I did not care whether I ate a tangerine or an orange. She took the tangerine and said nothing. I scowled at her. Oscar stood up for her. I showed her once again that I was angry by taking the tangerine away from her nervously and giving part of it to Oscar and offering another part to my wife. My wife refused because she thought that I liked tangerines. I put the tangerine on the mother's plate, but she did not eat it. I then showed her once more that I was angry by saying that she was like Tessa. I also told her about the butter. She understood me, because she said nothing. I spoke to her in this way in order to make her understand me. She felt this pinprick, but did not show it in the slightest. She is a very clever woman. She reminds me of Diaghilev. She is a very good actress and therefore knows how to act. I understand acting because I feel. I know I will be told that all artists feel, for without feeling one cannot act. To that I must reply that all artists feel, but not all artists feel well . . . . I am scratching my nose because I feel the hairs moving in it. I have noticed that nerves make hairs move. I have no hair on my head because I used to be nervous . . . .

I know I will be told that my wife's mother is a great artist. To that I will say that I understand what an artist is, because I am an artist myself. I know her as a human being and therefore can judge her attitude. I noticed when I was interned that she would playact in life. I know everyone will tell me that I also playact in life, saying that God wills it. I will say that I playact because God commands me to, while my wife's mother playacts for selfish reasons. She does not like the fact that I have invited her to live with us, because she likes to tyrannize servants and has noticed that I like servants. She knows that I do not flirt with maids. She quarrels with the servants out of habit. I do not want people to send me to bed. I will go to bed when God wills it. I told my wife that I would go to bed soon, but I know that I will be writing for a long time. I do not like to be disturbed when I work. I know, myself, what I need. I am asking for help, and not disturbance. I am not disturbance. I am help . . . .

She quarrels with servants out of habit. I do not like quarreling with servants. I like sharing. My wife's mother does not like servants, because servants scowl at her. Servants scowl at her because she does not understand them. I like them and therefore do the things they like. I do not want to pamper servants. I am not the act of pampering. I am love. I will write on love for servants later . . . .

. . . .

I want to write a lot about the life of my wife's mother. I know everyone will say that I am as much of an actor as she is, the only difference being that she is a woman and a dramatic artist, while I am a man and a dancer. I realize that people do not trust dancers, and therefore I want to show what a dancer is . . . . I like my wife's mother as a human being, but I do not like her as a person in actual life. She is a malicious woman. She is very insensitive. She is selfish in the extreme. She likes only herself. I understand why her first husband, my wife's father, shot himself. I understand why a woman who was my wife's mother's maid shot at her.* I understand why she did not want to have a lawsuit. She was afraid that the court would discover she was in the wrong. She was always frightened when that woman went past her house. I understand that a person cannot be afraid for no reason. I know that the reason was simple. She did not like that woman because that woman drank liquor. My wife's mother scolded her so much that the woman's entire nervous system almost burst

---

* According to Tamara Nijinsky (personal correspondence), the woman who tried to shoot Emilia Márkus was her dresser from the Hungarian National Theater. Some people theorized that the woman was in love with Emilia, or jealous of her. In the sentence "I understand why she did not want to have a lawsuit," "she" is clearly Emilia Márkus, not the dresser. (Ed.)

and she had delirium tremens. I know what delirium tremens is. A person becomes insane for a certain time. All drunkards are subject to that illness . . . .

My wife's mother got frightened and locked the door. My wife told me that story, and therefore I know everything. That woman shot at the door, but before that she hid behind a piece of furniture in the room. When my wife's mother entered the room, the woman showed her the revolver. My wife's mother rushed around from one corner to another and then ran out of the room and shut the door. The woman became angry and started shooting at the door. I felt that woman's sense of hurt. I was not speaking the truth when I defended my wife's mother, saying that she and not that woman was in the right. I have only now understood this story because God has helped me. I love God, and therefore he helps me . . . .
. . . .

The nerves in my nose are calming down, but the nerves in my skull disturb me because I feel the blood draining away from my head. My hair is moving, for I feel it. I ate a lot and therefore feel death. I do not want death and therefore am asking God to help me . . . .

I want to write in a beautiful hand because I feel beauty. My wife's mother used to be a beautiful woman. She has spoiled her beauty because she is always angry and says that there is something wrong with her gallbladder. I told her in Budapest that her gallbladder hurt because she was always quarreling. She does not believe me. She does not believe anyone. She is a bad woman. She is up to all sorts of tricks because she wants publicity. She pretends to like simple people. She shakes hands with streetcar conductors just for show. She does this awkwardly, for I have noticed that the conductors blush. They feel uncomfortable because they think she is laughing at them. She smiles at them with a Lloyd Georgian smile. I know I will be told that she is a good woman because she weeps when she sees people whose feelings have been hurt. I know I will be told that she does charitable works by getting jobs for women who have no jobs. I myself have thought for a long time that she was a good woman, but by a chance occurrence I discovered that she does not like my wife. The first day we met, she wanted to please me and therefore showed me old photographs of my wife. My wife began to weep because she felt offended.* I also felt offended and wept. From that day I no longer trusted my wife's mother. I hated her, but I pretended I did not. She felt I was strong, because she noticed that I did not pay any attention to her. She irritated me, and I quarreled with her. She was afraid that I would be speaking unfavorably about her, and therefore she said that I was horrible and did not like her. I discovered this because people started turning their backs on me, so that those who used to kiss me before no longer greeted me. My wife's mother was blissful because she thought that I had been defeated. I was not defeated, because I was not angry with her. I pretended to be, because I wanted her to improve. I snarled at her every day. And she snarled at me twice as much. I doubled my snarling and she tripled hers, and in that way we quarreled for eighteen months on end. Those were difficult months, when I was an internee.

My wife's mother is a hypocrite. She reminds me of Lloyd George. She is a wicked woman. I do not like wicked people and therefore want to disarm them by writing about their lives. She will be furious when she reads these lines, but I will be delighted because I will have taught her a good lesson. I want her to realize before she dies that she has wronged people, and

---

* In a footnote in her edition of the diary (p. 144), Romola Nijinsky explains: "These were photos in which the mother looked lovely and the daughter looked sick; she was at an awkward age." (Ed.)

I want her to say she is sorry. I do not want her to say so publicly, but I want her to feel it. I want her to regret her whole past life. I know that all the Hungarian critics will be aroused and will blame me, and therefore I will ask God to disarm the critics. I will reply if God orders me to. I know that people will understand me, and therefore I will thank god for his love. I know he loves me and will help me in everything. I am poor. I am destitute. I have no shelter or food, for I have nothing. My wife's mother has a three-story house with marble pillars. She likes that house because it is expensive. I do not like that house, because it is stupidly built. I know many people will say that I do not understand the beauty of that house, for it contains many old pictures and tapestries. I will say that I do not like anything old, because old things smell of death. I know that many people will say that I am a man without a soul because I do not like old people. I will say that I like old people but I do not like the old in spirit. I am young in spirit. Tolstoy was young in spirit. Wagner and Beethoven were young in spirit, etc., etc. I do not want to speak about others, because I do not know them well. I love everyone. I wrote about Tolstoy because he is God. Wagner is not God. Beethoven is God. Bach is not God . . . .

My wife's mother is a horrible woman. I do not like her. I want God to remove her from the face of the earth. I know I will be told that I am a malicious man because I am asking God to "remove her from the face of the earth." I will reply that I love everybody and want to love that woman too, and am therefore asking God to kill all bad feelings in her, and in that case her whole former life would end. This is what I call "remove her from the face of the earth" . . . .
. . . .
. . . .
. . . .

I am going to Zurich. I do not want to do anything for my departure. Everyone is feeling nervous. The servants have become stupid, because they feel God. I also feel him, but I have not become stupid. I do not want to boast. I want to tell the truth. Oscar is telephoning Zurich. He is afraid that they will not understand his name. He feels that no one knows his name, and therefore he wants to force them to understand it. His name is Párdány. He pronounces his name with a stress on every syllable. I realize why he wants his name to be known to everybody. He wants to show that he is rich. He does not want people to think that he is poor. He does not like poverty. I like poverty. I do not care whether people know my name or not. I am not afraid that people will not like me if they realize I am poor. I know that "poverty is no crime." I know everyone will say that I have good eyesight, because I can write small.* I must say that my eyesight gets tired from this sort of writing. I have only been writing this page, and already I feel that my eyes are tired. My eyes smart. I have completely healthy eyesight because I have read little. I always used to read in the morning and in the afternoon. I realized that reading was work. In school I used to lock myself in, pretending to be ill, and read. I lay in bed and read. I liked to read while lying in bed because then I felt at peace. I did not like to lie in bed, but I had to because everyone considered me ill. I no longer feel that my eyes are smarting, because God has helped me. I do not want people to interfere with me. I want to write about the departure for Zurich. Everyone was nervous. I was not nervous, because I did not care. I considered this trip silly. I will go because God wills it, but if God did

---

* This page of the manuscript is written in very small handwriting. (Tr.)

not want it, I would stay home. I do not like pretense. I want God. I want everyone to understand me, and therefore I crossed out those words on purpose, just for show.* I have noticed that I have pins and needles in my left leg and arm. I call "pins and needles" the feeling when the blood stagnates. I cannot move my foot. I cannot write, because the blood in my whole body has stopped moving. I am beginning to understand God. I know that all movement comes from God, and therefore I am asking Him to help me. I do not want to write with this pen, because the pen is dying. It scratches the paper and takes bits of paper with it. This pen is bad, because I am repairing it and it is not getting any better. I will look for another pen in Zurich. I will take ordinary ink and an ordinary pen. I never write on the move, and therefore I do not need a fountain pen with ink in it. I am not angry, but I am sorry for people, because a fountain pen is expensive. I know that everyone likes to have a good fountain pen. I have understood my mistake. I will write with the pointed end because I know that then I will be able to write better, as the pointed end has become blunted. I thought that gold was harder than paper, but paper turned out to be harder. I started writing with the sharpened end. I understand the death of the fountain pen. The Waterman's Ideal Fountain Pen† is a fraud. I understand how men become rich. Men become rich by fraud. I understand what the stock exchange is. I will swindle the stock brokers. Tomorrow I will visit the stock exchange with Oscar. I will be

---

* Three sentences earlier, after "I would stay home," Nijinsky crossed out a phrase that seems to be something like "after making up an excuse." He substituted "I do not like pretense." (Tr.)

† The phrase "Waterman's Ideal Fountain Pen" is in Latin characters except for the word "Ideal," in which the final "l" is Russian, followed by the Russian soft sign "ъ." (Tr.)

watching Oscar. He will be nervous, and I won't be. I will not be nervous and will take note of all the swindling that I am writing about . . . .

I want to write about the journey. My journey was called off because everyone forgot about the train. Oscar, together with my wife's mother and my wife, had believed silly Louise. Louise forgot the time that the man at the station had told her. She forgot because she was nervous. My wife and my wife's mother were angry with her. I explained to them, laughing, that it was not her fault, but I felt the look on my wife's mother's face and changed what I was going to say. I said that trains often changed their schedules because there is a war on. The mother understood me. She thought that I wanted to defend Louise. I gave her to understand that I understood her. She felt it, but did not understand me. I abandoned the conversation because I did not want a quarrel. My wife's mother is in a bad mood, and so is my wife. Oscar is nervous. I am sitting quietly and looking around. I see everybody's faults, because God wants me to be calm. I have noticed that people suppress their nervousness and grow pale. I have noticed this in my wife's mother and in my wife. They were pale and trembled a little. I was not pale, and I did not tremble. I think that Lloyd George finds it very difficult to conceal his nervousness. I think that he resorts to all kinds of subterfuges in order to give his face a good color, thinking that good color betokens calm. I know that good color appears when a person is nervous. I know that Lloyd George is a nervous man, because he has a set smile. He can hold his smile for a long time, for a photographer can photograph it. I know everyone will say that I have also photographed my smile . . . .

My wife came to me and told me that I should tell Kyra I would not be coming back. My wife felt tears welling up and said in some agitation that she would not leave me. I did not weep, because God did not want me to. I said if she was not afraid of me, I would not remain in Zurich but that if she was afraid of me, I would prefer to be in a lunatic asylum, because I am not afraid of anything. She wept in her heart. I felt a pain in my soul and said that if she was not afraid of me I would come back home. She wept and kissed me, saying that she and Kyra would not leave me, no matter what happened to me. I said, "Good." She felt me and left . . . .

I spoke of my smile in a photograph. I have a sensitive smile because I feel God. Wilson's smile is sensitive because he feels God. However, Lloyd George's smile is silly because he does not feel God. I know many people will say that Lloyd George is God in politics. I will say that Lloyd George has not proved it, because all his politics are at the expense of other nations. He does not like other nations. He likes his party, which pays him a lot of money. I know everyone will say that he has no money. I know Lloyd George's tricks. Lloyd George is good at hiding money. Someday he will be exposed, because he has hidden it so that he thinks God will not find it. I will find his money and take it. I will prove to everyone that I will find it. I will not look for it myself. I hope that the people will find it. I will rely entirely on God. I do not want him to be killed, for he is god's creature. I love all God's creatures. I do not want to write "God's creature" with a capital letter about Lloyd George, because I feel offended . . . .*

I want my manuscript to be photographed, because I feel that my manuscript is alive. I will transmit life to people if my manuscripts are photographed. I will recognize the journalists sent up to me for what they are, because I am a

---

* Two sentences earlier, in "he is god's creature," Nijinsky began the name of God with a capital letter, then crossed it out and wrote the word without the capital. (Tr.)

physiognomist-God. I can recognize people by their physiognomies. I know that people do not feel nervous if they are not guilty of anything. I will live in big hotels because I want everyone to see me. I do not want expensive hotels, because Lloyd Georgians live in expensive hotels. I will go into a simple hotel if my wife lets me. I will be afraid for myself if my wife says that she cannot live in a poor hotel. I will resort to cunning in order to avoid getting into a big, expensive hotel. I prefer to live in an apartment. I will take an apartment if I notice that I am not liked. I will show them all how angry I can be. I do not want malicious people, but I will show them how angry I can be, for God will show them too. I am not afraid of malicious people. I am brave and rich. My men will not be bribed. I am a physiognomist-God. I will show Lloyd Georgians that I am man-God. Come on out! Come on out and fight with me. I will defeat everyone. I am not afraid of bullets and poison. I am afraid of spiritual death. I will not go insane, but I will weep and weep. I am a man. I am God. I am man in God. I have faults because God wills it so. I will show faults and perfection because I do not want people to be afraid of me. I am a man with love, and men with love are simple. I am not afraid for Clemenceau. I will show him my manuscripts. I know that he will translate them. I know that he will understand them. I will go to him without announcing it. I will show my card, and I will be allowed in, because people will understand me. I will show them my sensitive smile, and they will let me in because they know that a man with a sensitive smile is good. Lloyd Georgians will not be able to pretend, because a sensitive smile is from God. God is not with Lloyd Georgians, but with Wilsonism. No artist can deceive God. I know what the combination of artist and God is, and therefore I am not afraid for myself. I will go to Clemenceau immediately after my arrival because I wish him good. I want to be allowed in, and therefore I will resort to a trick. I will deceive the Lloyd Georgian police, saying that I am a Lloyd Georgian. I will tell them that I am an "inveterate" Pole. They like "inveterate" Poles because they can steer them according to the wind. I know where the wind comes from, and therefore I will be able to blow against it. I like Clemenceau because he is a man who has faults. He corrects his faults, and therefore God is with him. I am God in Clemenceau. Clemenceau feels God, and God feels Clemenceau. I know that Clemenceau will understand me, because he feels me. I will go to him with open arms, and he will not be afraid of me. I will tell him in bad French that I like him and that I wish him well . . . . I must improve. I have realized that Clemenceau has been shot and his shoulder pierced, and he has been shot from behind and his respiratory organs have been pierced. I have understood that Lloyd Georgians are evil, because I know that a man with his lungs shot through goes on living for a long time, but suffers. Clemenceau will suffer, but I hope that he will understand the whole band of bandits and will know how to protect France. I like France and therefore do not wish her harm. I understand the whole clique that started the war. I know that Clemenceau is a rich man and does not need anything, and therefore I feel that he has not been bribed. Lloyd Georgians bribe not only with money, but also with promises. Clemenceau thought that it was good for France to take Alsace and Lorraine. I realized that this problem must be settled peacefully. Clemenceau felt Wilson and therefore agreed with his aim. I realize that the French like the Alsatians and that many families are weeping because they think they are being hurt because they do not belong to France on the map. I realize that the French do not like the Germans. I realize how the dislike for Germans develops. I know what a German is. I know who has taught France to say "Boche." I am not an evil man. I love everyone. I do not want war, and therefore I want everybody to live in peace. There must be no quarrels. There must be no quarrels. I am love. I am a man with love. I know that German children read about their fathers. I like Germans. I am not a German. I am a man. I do not belong to any party. I am without party. I am a human being, and all people are human beings. I understand people's love. I want people's love. I do not want horrors. I want heaven on earth. I am God in man. All people will be gods if they do what I tell them. I am a man with faults, because I want people to correct their faults. I do not like people who have faults they have not corrected. I am a man who has tried to improve himself. I do not think of past faults. I am not an evil man. I am not an animal but a man. I like animals, but not the predatory ones. Predatory animals should not be killed, because life has been given to them by God. I know many people will say that man has come out of the seed of his father and the womb of his mother. But I must say that the seed has come not from first-born man but from God. I realize that many people will say that man is descended from an ape, but I must say that the ape is descended from the seed of God. I know many people will say that the ape seed is descended from something else. I will then say that that something else is descended from God. I know I will be told that that something else is descended from something else again. I will then say that what you call something else is God. I am infinity. I am everything. I am life in infinity. I am mind, and mind is infinite. I will never die, but man's intellect dies with his body. Man's intellect is limited. I know many people say that the intellect has created everything. The airplanes and zeppelins, etc., etc., have been created by the intellect. I must say that airplanes and zeppelins have been created by the mind, for there is life in them. There is movement in an airplane, there is movement in a zeppelin. I

know that the airplane was created by a Frenchman-God. I know that Frenchmen feel God, but they do not understand him yet, and therefore they make mistakes. A zeppelin is a thing of the intellect, for the zeppelin was invented with the airplane as model. I know many people will say that the airplane was invented in imitation of a bird. I will say that a bird is a living thing and an airplane is a thing made of steel. I know everyone will say that a zeppelin is also made of steel. I will say that a zeppelin is a copy of an airplane, but in a different form. Scientists admired the zeppelin because they understood its power. They realized that a lot of people could be put in it and that therefore it was well adapted for war. The Germans commissioned Zeppelin to produce many zeppelins. They thought they would get chickens, but they got dead people* . . . .
. . . .

My wife's mother came into my room and said she was sorry. I answered her loudly because I wanted her to understand that she should not have said she was sorry, because everyone can come into my room without asking. I was not afraid of noise and shouting. I could work in spite of it. She thought for a while and said she understood that I was accustomed to noise and that this was very good. I felt in that "very good" that she was thinking of something else and therefore did not understand me . . . .

My wife came and kissed me. I thought it was God. I realized that god† is contained in love. I do not want to spell "god" with a capital letter and will therefore spell it with a small letter. I heard the voice of my little Kyra. She loves me, because

---

* A play on words: "zeppelin" in the Russian pronunciation (*tsepelin*) bears some resemblance to the Russian word for chicken (*tsyplyonok*). (Tr.)

† Here Nijinsky starts by capitalizing "God" and then changes the capital to a lowercase letter. (Tr.)

Nijinsky in the title role of *Le Spectre de la Rose*, Paris, 1911

*Photograph by L. Roosen. Courtesy of the Dance Collection, The New York Public Library
for the Performing Arts, Astor, Lenox and Tilden Foundations*

Nijinsky in "Danse Siamoise" from *Les Orientales*, Paris, 1910

*Photograph by E. Druet. Courtesy of the Dance Collection, The New York Public Library
for the Performing Arts, Astor, Lenox and Tilden Foundations*

Nijinsky as the Golden Slave in *Scheherazade*, London, 1911

*Photograph by Baron Adolphe de Meyer. Courtesy of the Dance Collection,
The New York Public Library for the Performing Arts, Astor, Lenox and Tilden Foundations*

Nijinsky, as the Faun in *The Afternoon of a Faun*, carries the nymph's scarf to his rock *(opposite)* and lies down on it *(above)*. London or Paris, 1912/13

Photographs by Baron Adolphe de Meyer. Courtesy of the Dance Collection, The New York Public Library for the Performing Arts, Astor, Lenox and Tilden Foundations

Nijinsky as Albrecht in *Giselle*, Paris, 1910

Photograph by Bert. Courtesy of the Dance Collection, The New York Public Library
for the Performing Arts, Astor, Lenox and Tilden Foundations

Nijinsky in the title role of *Petrouchka*, Paris, 1912
*Photograph by Bert. Courtesy of the Dance Collection, The New York Public Library
for the Performing Arts, Astor, Lenox and Tilden Foundations*

Nijinsky in the title role of *Petrouchka*, London, 1913
*Photograph by Dover Street Studios. Courtesy of the Dance Collection, The New York Public Library
for the Performing Arts, Astor, Lenox and Tilden Foundations*

she wept when I told her that I was going away forever. She
felt me and started weeping . . . .

I went to the bathroom to piss and saw that it was dirty. I
realized that Oscar was a sick man because his excrement was
soft. He had spattered it all over the toilet. I did not want dirt
and therefore took a brush and cleaned the dirt out. After that,
I felt that the brush was dirty and therefore put it into the bowl
and flushed the toilet. The water poured out with a rush and
got rid of the dirt on the brush. I noticed that the brush was
bad because people do not take care of brushes. The brush left
its bristles in the bowl. I left the bristles because I felt that
Louise would understand it was me and would love me more.
I want to show Louise this book in German and show her the
place where I write about her. She is a woman from Zurich,
and she is called Louise Hamberg. The man who sees her will
show her the place where I write about her. I love Louise, and
she loves me too. I have never flirted with her, and she has
therefore grown even fonder of me. She has never said anything
to me, and I understood because I felt love . . . .

I write in small handwriting because notebooks are expensive. I have understood the tricks of shops. Shops take ad-
vantage of the war because they are afraid it will end. Shops
resort to tricks, saying that the war forces them to demand
high prices. I was in a shop in St. Moritz that is called "The
Road." I went in at God's command. I had no money. I asked
for notebooks. There was one woman there, thin, with black
hair and a pince-nez on her nose. The pince-nez had a gold
chain. I realized that the woman had shares in that shop, for
the simple reason that she mentioned one price and a
woman* in the shop another. The woman with the pince-nez
mentioned a high price and the woman without the pince-
nez a low price. I followed the woman without the pince-nez.

* Clearly, "another woman." (Tr.)

I noted the nervousness of the woman with the pince-nez. I knew this shop from before, because I had bought paints and paper for my set designs there. I did not spare money. The paint and the paper were very expensive. I realized\how expensive they were, and I almost gave up my work, but God helped me because he told me he would help me. I believed him and bought a lot of paints. I knew that paints dry up, but I have understood the mistake that people make and therefore am not afraid of paints drying up. I know how to melt dry paints. I take a little hot water and put a piece of dry paint into that hot water. Shops charge high prices for everything they sell, saying that this is the war. I understood the trick of the shops because I lived for a long time in St. Moritz together with God. I lived with God for over a year and worked every day. I slept and thought of God. I know that many people will say that a person cannot sleep and think. I will say that he who tells me so is right, for I do not think when I sleep, but feel. I made a mistake on purpose in writing this because I want people to understand that I do not think when I write, but feel . . . .

The shop was deceiving people. I was also deceiving people. I understand the faults of shops, and therefore I know what I need. I will not write in large handwriting but in small handwriting because that way I will economize on paper. Shops think that people are stupid because they have a lot of money. I must say that it is not people who are stupid but shops, for they sell things for money and not for people. I like people and therefore do not deceive them. I realize who starts wars. Wars occur because of commerce. Commerce is a terrible thing. Commerce is death to mankind. Unless people change their way of life, commerce will destroy everything. I know that many people will say that no life is possible without commerce. I know that commerce is an empty thing. I know that people

engaged in commerce do not feel God. I know that god* does
not like people engaged in commerce. I know that god loves
working people. I am not a Bolshevik. I do not want murders.
Bolsheviks are murderers. I am a man of love. I want love for
everyone. I want life for everyone. I like things if I need them.
I do not want things if I don't need them. If I like a thing, I
take care of it. I bought three big notebooks for a very high
price. I realized that the woman with the pince-nez and chain
had swindled me. I want to swindle her and will therefore write
in a small handwriting. I do not like shops. I would like factories to be destroyed, because they spread dirt on the earth. I
like the earth and therefore want to protect it. I do not want
pogroms. I want people to realize that they must give up all
rubbish, because there is not much time left to live. I feel the
suffocation of the earth. The earth is suffocating. It produces
earthquakes. I know what an earthquake is. I know that everybody hates earthquakes and asks God that there be no more
earthquakes. I want earthquakes because I know that the earth
breathes. I know that people do not understand earthquakes
and that therefore they blame God. People do not understand
that they themselves have started earthquakes. I know that
many people will say that earthquakes are produced by earthquakes, for the earth has not cooled down yet. I know the
mistakes people make, and therefore I must say that an earthquake is the result of a suffocating earth. People will probably
tell me that I am mistaken, because I have not studied the earth.
I will say that I have studied the earth because I feel it and do
not think. I know that the earth is a living thing. I know that
the earth was a sun. I know that all stars that twinkle are suns.
I know that the moon and other planets, for example, Mars,

---

* Again Nijinsky starts writing the word "God" with a capital letter and then changes
the capital to a lowercase letter. (Tr.)

are not suns. I know that there are no men on Mars. I know
that people will be afraid of me because I speak of things I have
not seen. I must say that I can see without eyes. I am feeling.
I feel. I know that the blind will understand me if I explain to
them that eyes are an obsolete thing. I will say that people on
Mars have no eyes. That on Mars people live with love and
that they do not need eyes, because they have no sun. I know
that all astronomers will exclaim that Nijinsky is a stupid man
and does not understand astronomy. I will say that all astronomers are stupid. Astronomers have invented telescopes to ex-
plore the atmosphere. Astronomers are the most boring people
in the world. I know I will be told that astronomers are god. I
will say that astronomy is nonsense. I know I will be told I am
insane because I speak of things that I do not understand. I
know that I understand. I am the spirit in man that carries
Nijinsky's body. I have eyes, but I know that if my eyes were
gouged out, I would be able to live without eyes. I know a
French general* who goes out for a walk with his wife every
day and feels life. He thinks he is unhappy and therefore smiles
at everyone he meets. I noticed him because he walked in a
strange way and held his head thrust back. I realized he was
unhappy, and I was sorry for him. I liked him and felt the need
to tell him that I was not afraid of being blind. But I realized
that he would not understand me, and therefore I left this task
for later. I know there are no people on Mars, because I know
that Mars is a frozen body. Mars was like the Earth, but many
billions of years ago. The Earth will also be like Mars, but in
several hundred years' time. I feel that the Earth is suffocating,
and therefore I ask everyone to abandon factories and obey me.
I know what is needed for the salvation of the earth. I know
how to light a stove and will therefore be able to light up the

* The implication is that the general is blind. (Ed.)

earth. My stove-setter is stupid, he drinks and imagines it is good for him, but he is killing himself. I am the Divine savior. I am Nijinsky and not Christ. I love Christ because he was like me. I love Tolstoy because he is like me. I want to save the whole terrestrial globe from suffocation. All scientists must abandon their books and come to me. I will help everyone, for I know many things. I am a man in God. I am not afraid of death. I beg people not to be frightened of me. I am a man with faults. I too have faults. I want to reform. I am a man with faults. I must not be killed, for I love everyone equally. I will go to Zurich and will study Zurich with God. I will write about Zurich. Zurich is a commercial town. I will understand its faults. I will describe about Zurich in order to prove to you that I am right. I am reason, and not intelligence. I am God, for I am reason. Tolstoy speaks a lot about reason. Schopenhauer also wrote about reason. I too write about reason. I am the philosophy of reason. I am the true, not invented, philosophy. Nietzsche went mad because he realized at the end of his life that everything he had written was nonsense. He became frightened of people and went mad. I will not be frightened of people if people attack me, gnashing their teeth. I understand the crowd. I know how to lead it. I am not a military commander. I am a man in a crowd. I do not like a crowd. I like family life. I do not want children to be bred in great numbers. I know what breeding children in great numbers leads to. I love all children. I am a child. I like playing with children. I understand children. I am a father. I am a married man. I love my wife, for I want to help her in life. I understand why people constantly chase after girls.* I know what a girl is. I will write a lot because I want to explain to people what life is and what death is. I

---

* "girls": Russian euphemism for "prostitutes." (Tr.)

cannot write quickly, because my muscles get tired. I cannot bear it anymore. I am a martyr because I feel a pain in my shoulder. I like writing, because I want to help people. I cannot write, because I am tired. I want to finish, but God will not let me. I will write till God stops me . . . .

I had a good dinner, but I felt that I should not eat soup. It was canned soup . . . . I wanted to run and get some money, for I thought it was necessary, but God proved to me that I should not. I took a checkbook. I want to take a checkbook and not money, because I want to show on the Stock Exchange that I have credit. The stockbrokers will believe me and will lend me money. I will win without money. I know that everyone will be frightened, and therefore I will go to the Stock Exchange by myself. I will put on a bad suit because I want to see the whole life on the Stock Exchange. I will deceive the stockbrokers. I will take my good suit and pretend to be a rich foreigner, and I will visit the Stock Exchange. I am afraid of the Stock Exchange because I do not know it. I went there once with Diaghilev, who knew a man who was a stockbroker. Diaghilev gambled for low stakes and therefore won. I will gamble for low stakes because I too want to win. I know that little people lose because they get nervous and do silly things. I will observe everyone with complete detachment, and I will understand everything. I do not like knowing everything in advance, but God wants to show me the way people live and therefore is warning me. I will go to the railway station on foot and not in a cab. If everyone is going in a cab, I will too. God wants to show people that I am the same kind of person as they are . . . .

I will go now . . . .

I am waiting . . . .

I do not want . . . .

I will go to my wife's mother and talk to her because I do

not want her to think that I like Oscar more than her. I am checking her feelings. She is not dead yet, because she is envious

. . . .

. . . .

. . . .

THE FOURTH
NOTEBOOK

While writing his diary, Nijinsky broke off at a certain point (possibly at several points), took up another notebook, and wrote in it letters to his friends, family, and other people— sixteen letters in all. The first six are in readable prose, French, Russian, or Polish, and were all written for a practical purpose, though it is doubtful that any of them was ever copied out and sent. In the remaining ten, most of which are written as verse (and all but one in French), Nijinsky yields increasingly to the seductions of wordplay, taking the syllables of his words apart, fashioning new words, and again and again juxtaposing words on the basis of sound, or "clanging." These letters are similar to the poems in the diary.

Nijinsky did not date any of the letters. (Nor did he number them. The numbers have been added for the reader's convenience.) But in the diary, on page 121, he clearly indicates the point at which he interrupted his narrative, opened a new notebook, and wrote the first of the letters, to Jean de Reszke. It is likely that in that one break he also wrote all the remaining letters. This is indicated by certain statements that he makes when he returns to the diary: "I wrote a letter to Diaghilev and his friends" (p. 121); "I wrote in the same way in French . . . I know they will laugh when they get these letters" (p. 126). The increasingly manic qualities of the writing—the forced jocularity, the insistent rhythms, the rush and excitement—also suggest that all the letters were part of a single, ever-accelerating impulse. The hours passed; still he remained at his desk. "I write write write" (p. 122). By the final letters, what we have, much of the time, is something barely readable—simply a sequence of sounds. Even in these letters, however, Nijinsky is not out of control. In Letter XIII, for example, he twice stops what seems a runaway train of sounds to explain punctiliously, in parentheses, that he has used a Russian word and to say what the word means. Furthermore, many apparent nonsense lines seem to contain elaborate puns. However difficult they are to read, these letters are very careful sound constructions, something like scat singing.

The wordplay poses serious translation problems. (It is obviously for this reason that no edition of the *Diary* prior to this one has included the complete fourth notebook.) The last six letters are not translatable. They are reproduced here in the original French, much of it spelled phonetically.

Nijinsky thought enough of the fourth notebook to give it a title page, calling it an "exercise book." Preparing to write in Polish to Reszke, he gave his last name in the Polish spelling. (Ed.)

WATZLAW NIŻYŃSKI

1919, ST. MORITZ DORF

EXERCISE BOOK

I

To Jean de Reszke*

Dear Mr. Reszke,

I cannot write well in Polish, and I am very sorry. I like the Poles, and that is why I write to you in Polish. I know that you know I am a Pole. I do not want anything from you, only that you help me with my papers. It is very difficult today to obtain papers, and that is why I address you with this request. I ask you to inquire with the French authorities about the possibility of getting the papers for me. My wife loves me, and that is why she would like to be with me. I too want her to come with me. I also have a daughter, whose name is Kyra. I gave her this name because I liked Greece. I liked Greece because I thought

---

* Jean de Reszke, a Pole, was one of the great operatic tenors of the late nineteenth century. Romola Nijinsky, in her edition of the diary (p. 66), explains that Kyra was an old Byzantine name; hence Nijinsky's connecting it to Greece. Adam Mickiewicz, poet and playwright, was the leading figure in Polish literature of the early nineteenth century. On the question of Nijinsky's two baptisms, see the footnote on page 122. Jean de Reszke's brother, Edouard de Reszke, another famous singer, had died in 1917. The dancer Bonislawsky, from whom Nijinsky claims to have learned his Polish, has not been identified. Nijinsky presumably spoke Polish, mixed with Russian, at home as a child, but as he points out to Reszke, he was educated in Russia, and he spent much of his adult life in French-speaking countries. Therefore he had little remaining command of Polish. This and the one other letter written in Polish in the fourth notebook (Letter VI, to his mother) are full of misspellings, grammatical errors, and Russianisms. (Ed.)

up "L'Après-midi d'un faune." I know that you love me, and that is why I am approaching you with this wish. You saw me very little in life, but you have a friendly disposition toward me. I cannot speak well, because I was not allowed to speak Polish. I like the Poles, and that is why I turn to you with this request. I have learned the Polish language from a dancer from Warsaw, whose name was Bonislawsky. I loved this man because he gave me the opportunity to know the poems by Mickiewicz. I am a writer too, but I cannot write as nicely as Mickiewicz. I also know Polish literature, but in Russian translation. I know Russian better, because my mother and my father left Poland in their youth. I was born in Kiev, and I was baptized at the Church of the Holy Cross in Warsaw. I was born in 1889, and my mother had me baptized in Kiev. I was registered twice, because my mother did not want me to serve in the army. She had me registered in Warsaw, because she wanted me to serve in Warsaw. My mother gave me her milk and the Polish language, and that is why I am a Pole. I was brought up in Russia, where I was like a Russian boy. I am a Pole because my father was a Pole. I love Russia, but I do not love bolsheviks. I see their victories as horror. I consider bolshevik victories godless. An animal without God is a beast with sharp teeth. I want to call those animals from the forest by their name, but I forgot it. I pity people, because I love them. I am myself a man, and that is why I pity people. I cry when I hear that a bolshevik killed a man. I am not a bolshevik, because I am not of their party. My party is to love everybody. I am not Paderewsky. I love Paderewsky, but I do not love his politics. I love Wilson's politics, because I feel that he wishes well for everybody. I do not want politics where people quarrel and kill one another. I do not like partisanship, because I see people kill one another. I love everyone. I am a Pole. I speak Polish. I love my mother and my father. I also know that you feel I love you. I know, because I feel it, that you love me. Your wife expressed her friendship for me many times. I have not forgotten you during that time when I did not see you. I cried when I heard that your brother died. I was very sorry for him. I did not know him, but I could feel him. I knew you loved him, and that is why I was sorry. I cannot write clearly, because I did not occupy myself with languages. I occupied myself with dancing, and that is why I dance well. I want to dance in Paris, therefore I want you to help me obtain transit to France. I have no connections, because I spent all my time in Switzerland. I occupied myself with dance and with dance theater. I love singing, but I cannot sing. I know you can sing, although you lost your voice, and I will be happy to hear you sing. I am an artist whose voice is dance. I have not lost my voice yet, because I am very young. You have sung a lot in your life. I know the Marchioness of Ripon. She told me about you. I know that you sang in England with great success. You were a great artist. Everybody knew you. You knew everybody, and that is why you can help me. I have many friends in Paris, but I am not acquainted with them. I want to know many people, and that is why I ask you to tell all your acquaintances that I will dance for them in your home. During the war I occupied myself a lot with dance, and that is why I was very successful. I want to show the public how successful I am, but I do not want to work with Diaghilev, because he caused me a lot of unpleasantness. I know you do not love him either, and that is why you will help me. Diaghilev thinks I have died for the art. I am more alive than ever. I love French artists, and therefore I want to dance for them. I know that French artists were murdered during the war, and many fathers left their wives and children without a piece of bread. I know that the government cannot give them everything, and that is why I will dance for the poor artists in France. I will also dance for the

Poles when I go to Poland. I cannot write well, but I write to you because I know you are a Pole. I love the Poles, and that is why I love France. Poles love France because France gave them her soul. The Pole also gave his soul and died in the battlefield. The war brought the Poles and the French together. France knows Polish heroic deeds. I do not know Polish words, but I can feel them. That is how I can write. I did not write for over ten years, because I did not have anyone to write to. My father died ten years ago in Kharkov. I always wrote to him in Polish. My father left my mother with her children to bring up in Petersburg. The Russian government gave me education. Diaghilev brought me to Paris. I love Paris. Paris is the heart of France, and I want to have a place in the French heart. You will be the intermediary. You will get me papers. You will get me Polish papers, and I will get the others myself.

I thank you for your kindness, and I hope to see you soon.

With love,

Watzlaw Niżyński

Translated from the Polish by Jaroslaw Anders

II

"Dear Madam" (To Ottoline Morrell?)*

Dear Madam,

I am very happy to receive your letter. I felt that you wanted to let me know that the Ballets Russes is now bad. But I felt that Massine is good because you write that he is kind when he speaks. You have said that he speaks very well of me. I believe that he speaks very well of me, but I feel that this is playacting. I do not know how many acts this play will have.

---

* This letter and Letter III are probably two parts of one letter, to the same person. Nijinsky ended the one and began the next on the same page, rather than turning to a new page, as he did to separate the other letters. Letter III thus seems to be a postscript to Letter II. In her edition of the diary (pp. 89–91), Romola Nijinsky includes abridged versions of both letters. She identifies the addressee of Letter II only as "Lady X." She says that Letter III was to the Marchioness of Ripon. But Nijinsky's friend Lady Ripon was dead by this time, as he notes in the diary. In fact, Letter III appears to have been written to another English friend of Nijinsky's, the Bloomsbury hostess Ottoline Morrell, for in it he asks the favor (that the addressee help Dmitri Kostrovsky's wife get to Russia) which in Letter IV he will tell Kostrovsky he asked of Ottoline Morrell. As for Letter II, it contains a response to a point (Massine's goodwill toward Nijinsky) that in the diary Nijinsky says was made in a letter he has received from a lady who seems on other grounds to be Ottoline Morrell. When Nijinsky states in Letter II that Diaghilev almost had him put in prison, he is referring to an actual event. In 1917, when he was dancing with the Ballets Russes in Barcelona, he again fell into a contract dispute with Diaghilev and decided to pull out of the tour. Diaghilev, claiming that Nijinsky was in breach of contract, had him met by two policemen at the train station as he was attempting to leave the city. The episode is related by Romola Nijinsky in *Nijinsky*, p. 322. (Ed.)

I know very well that Massine loves Diaghilev greatly. I know that I detest Diaghilev. Diaghilev detests me because he almost had me put in prison in Barcelona. I am not afraid of prison. I dance in Barcelona with love. I always dance with love. Massine dances without love, because he likes drama. Massine is a nice boy. I love him too, but he does not love me, because he thinks that I harmed Diaghilev. Diaghilev tells him that he does not love me because I take all his money. I take all my money, which I earned with him. Diaghilev does not like to pay. Massine must notice that Diaghilev does not pay right away. I like it when people pay me exactly. I have a mother to whom I must send money because if I don't give it she will die of hunger. Massine likes money. Money likes him. I like money too. I am not jealous that he has taken my place in your heart. I like Massine very much. I embraced him, but he did not respond. That made me sad. I do not want to work for Diaghilev any longer. I will always work without him, because I have ideas entirely different from his. I like Massine, and I hope that he will come and visit me. I hope that Massine is not afraid of Diaghilev and that he will let him. I too was like him. Now I am not the same. I have worked a great deal. I have made great progress, but this progress is different from Diaghilev's. I am not Diaghilev. I am a man with a heart. I work with my heart and hope that I will develop my spirit very greatly. I am no longer Nijinsky of the Ballets Russes. I am Nijinsky of God. I love God and he loves me.

I would like you to see my dances without a troupe, and therefore I want you to come and see me in Paris. I am coming soon. Until then,

With friendship, Vaslav Nijinsky

Translated from the French by Joan Acocella

240

III

"Dear Madam" (To Ottoline Morrell?)*

Dear Madam, I ask you to give this letter to an artist named Dmitri Romanovich Kostrovsky. This artist is epileptic, but he is a very intelligent man. I like him very much, and therefore I am writing him this letter. I am leaving this letter open because I have no secrets. I ask you to send this letter in your name because the Ballets Russes people steal my letters. I would like very much for you to show this letter to the English authorities, because I don't want this letter to get lost. I want to ask you to allow Kostrovsky to write using your address, because I am afraid the agents of the Ballets Russes will steal this letter. I want to ask you a favor. I would like you to take care of this man. This man is very poor. He has his wife with him. His children are in Russia. I think that his wife is suffering because she cannot see her children. I do not want Kostrovsky to leave with her. I want him to remain, and his wife to leave for Russia. His wife is not an intelligent woman. I know that the English authorities are afraid of Bolsheviks. I too am afraid of Bolsheviks. My mother has escaped from the Bolsheviks and gone to Kiev. My mother suffered very much. I know that the English authorities will understand me, and therefore I want to show them my letter. I know that Lloyd George is an intelligent man,

* On this letter, see the footnote to Letter II. (Ed.)

and I know that he will allow Kostrovsky's wife to travel to Russia. I thank you in advance. With friendship, Vaslav Nijinsky

Translated from the French by Joan Acocella

IV

To Dmitri Kostrovsky*

My dear Dmitri, I love you and am therefore writing to you. I know you miss me. I miss you. I am sorry for you. I pity myself. You have understood me. I have understood you. I want you to come here. I want to see you. I shall take care of your health. I love you. I don't want you to dance. I don't want to tire you. I wish you health. I kiss your notebook and weep, for it hurt me to take this notebook away from you. I am weeping at the moment, but am holding back my tears, for I am a strong man. I want you and your wife to be happy. I know your wife loves you. I love her too. I wish you both happiness. I want to help her. I am aware of her grief. I shall help her. I have requested Lady Morrell to ask the British authorities for permission to let your wife into Russia. I don't want you to fall into the hands of the Bolsheviks, for that party wishes everyone evil. This party loves itself. I love everybody. I am not a Party. I am the people. The people is God. I speak of God. I love God. I love Tolstoy. I do not like bolsheviks. The bolsheviks can kill me as much as they wish. I am not afraid of death. I know that death

---

* On Nijinsky's fellow Ballets Russes dancer Dmitri Kostrovsky, who converted him to Tolstoyanism, see the footnote on page 32. Kostrovsky and his wife were in London, but their children were in Russia. See Letter III, in which Nijinsky asks his correspondent, presumably Ottoline Morrell, to help Kostrovsky's wife obtain papers so that she can travel to Russia. (Ed.)

is a necessary thing. I know that everyone must die, and therefore I am always ready for death. I love you and don't want you to die. I am sorry for you. I love living with you. I am a good man. I have no ulterior motive. I am a man up front. Diaghilev is a man who has ulterior motives. I don't like people who have ulterior motives. I want you to come to me. I will send you the money for the journey if the government lets you come to me. I will ask the government to give you the right of entry. I am a powerful man. I have many connections. I know England likes people who have connections. I know England's love for people. I know that you love England. I know that men are Gods. I know that you are God. You don't understand God and therefore don't know that you are God. I have studied my own self a great deal. I did not leave my room for months. I liked being alone. I have apprehended God. I realize his significance. People will understand me if you understand me. I write a lot. I draw a lot. I dance a lot. I talk a lot. I am bored a lot. I weep a lot.

I want you to reply to my letter. I know that the authorities will not forbid this letter, for it speaks of God and not of bolsheviks, and I am not a bolshevik. I am God. I love everybody.

I am awaiting your answer. I will think you have died if I don't get an answer soon. I know that the body dies, but the spirit does not die. The spirit is God. God lives if the body lives. I am God. I am the spirit in the body.

Kisses to you and your wife. Your friend,
Vaslav Nijinsky.

Translated from the Russian by Kyril FitzLyon

V

To the President of the Council of the Allied Forces*

Dear sir, I am a Polish subject. I want nothing from you. I want to ask you to forward this letter. I love my mother, and I want her to know that I am alive. I know that you have a great deal of business to do, but I know that you are a man. You will understand me if you have seen my dances. I know that dancers do not understand business. I understand very well. I am very rich, because I understand business. I ask you to be so kind as to send this letter to my mother under your protection. I know very well that this depends on you. I know very well that you have to show this letter to other authorities. I ask you once again to give me the happiness of sending this letter to my mother. My mother is a sick woman. She has lost one son. She suffers because she cannot see me. She is not a Bolshevik. She is almost seventy years old. She loves me very much. She knows that I am very famous. She knows that I am loved everywhere. She knows that I have very grand connections. She thinks that I am dead because I have not written to her in a year and a half. She thinks that I am dancing in England. She is afraid that people will harm me, thinking that I am a Bolshevik. My

* Romola Nijinsky, in her edition of the diary (p. 91), identifies the addressee of this letter as the President of the Council of the Allied Forces. It was because of the revolution and civil war in Russia that Nijinsky had not communicated with his mother in a year and a half. (Ed.)

mother knows very well that I am not a Bolshevik. She knows
my love for people. She knows that I do not like violence. She
knows that I do not like this fighting with schoolboys. She
raised me, and therefore she knows me. I am a man, not a
savage animal. I do not like savagery. I do not like Bolsheviks.
They can kill me, but I am not afraid. They wanted to kill my
mother because she is a bourgeois. I am not a bourgeois. I am
a man. I love everyone. I do not want people to die. I love my
wife. She is a Hungarian. I traveled with her during the war. I
was in France. The French authorities allowed us through. I
went through several times. I love France. I wish France very
well. I love England. I love Poland. I love Russia. I love Italy.
I love the whole world. I am a man, not a savage animal.

I thank you in advance.

Vaslav Nijinsky.

Translated from the French by Joan Acocella

VI

To Eleanora Nijinsky*

My dear Mother, I love you always. I am in perfect health. I did not have any news from you. I wrote to you but received no reply. They sent my letters back. I am happy. I am unhappy because I cannot see you. I love you and ask you to come to me. I am renting a house where I have installed myself. I have this house for you. I love you because you brought me up. I have a daughter, and I want you to bring her up. I know you have God in you, and I want you to give Him to my daughter. My daughter is a wonderful child, because she listens to those who love her, and therefore I know that she will listen to you. God wants you to be with my daughter. I want you to be with me. I am asking you to come right away. I will send you money for your trip. I do not want politics. I am not politics. I am a man of God. I like everyone. I do not want murders. I am young and strong. I work a lot. I do not have a lot of money, but I have enough to give you for your whole life. I want to see Brońcia and Sasha. They are with you. I know they love you. I know it is very difficult for them to get money. They are

<hr />

* This is the letter that Nijinsky asked the President of the Council of the Allied Forces to forward in Letter V. Nijinsky's mother, Eleanora, was living in Russia with her daughter, Bronislava, and Bronislava's husband, Alexander (Sasha) Kochetovsky. "Wacio" and "Brońcia" are the Polish diminutives of Nijinsky's and his sister's first names. (Ed.)

tired. I want to help them. I love everyone. I do not want money for myself. My wife loves you and wants you to come here. I too want you to come. Please write to me through the English authorities. My address is the English authorities. I know they will love you when they see you. I want you to go to them alone, without Sasha. They are afraid of bolsheviks, and that is why they do not want young boys. I do not know Sasha, because I have not seen him for a long time. I am young, and I do not want bolsheviks, because they kill people. I love Kerensky, because he did not want people's death. Today I do not know him, because he does not reveal his thoughts. I reveal my thoughts because I want people to know me. I do not like partisanship. I am without a party. I know God likes people and does not want their death. The bolsheviks did not understand Tolstoy. Tolstoy is not a bolshevik. I often read Tolstoy. I can see that he loves everyone. Tolstoy loves God, not the party. I love God, and not the party. God is my party. God is with me, and I am with Him.

I kiss you, my mother, and ask you to kiss everybody who loves me.

Your son, Wacio.

Translated from the Polish by Jaroslaw Anders

VII

To André de Badet*

Dear friend André,

Please tell all your friends that I love them and that I want to meet them. I am a man and I want to write as I can. Before, all the letters were written by my wife. She understood me and wrote. I could not write all alone because I did not learn [French]. Now I know a little. I love you very much and therefore I want you to see my thoughts. I am not the same as before. I am a man with soul. I want to prove to you that I have soul. I am a God. I am Dance. I am love. I am God. I don't want you to think that I am a madman, and therefore I want to prove to you. I am a man with God. I love God, and therefore I am a madman. I like mistakes because I want people to understand me. If I write without mistakes, people will think

* André de Badet, a diplomat and writer living outside Montevideo, became a friend of the Nijinskys when the dancer was touring South America with the Ballets Russes. Badet helped Nijinsky arrange his last public performance, the Red Cross benefit in Montevideo in September 1917. This letter indicates that Nijinsky had corresponded previously with Badet from St. Moritz but that those letters were written by Romola, whose French was excellent. Here, writing without her help, he worries about the mistakes he will make. He complains that his writing does not "feel rhythm"—a problem that he will solve by writing most of the remaining letters in verse. He ends the letter by drawing a line across the page; presumably, this is the border that he says he has added. (Ed.).

that I am a madman. I am not a madman, because I have consciousness. I am not a madman, because I am a God. I am a God because I love him. I am not afraid of evil. One can write what one wants. I love love because it is God. I love God because he is love. I cannot write well, because it does not feel rhythm. I am rhythm with meaning. I am rhythm with love. I love love with meaning. I love love with God. I love God because he gives. I love God because he lives. I am life. I am a God. I love God. I love life. Without life, no God. I love my wife because she gives life. My child is a life. I give life to my child. I love children because they live. I love life because *He* lives. I am God for love. I love my wife and she loves me. I am a man for God. I am a man for Him. I love Him very much. I am a man. I am a man.

Your friend Vaslav Nijinsky.

Just now, I made a border because I do not like the borders [in this notebook]. My borders are not so pretty, but they give life. You love life because I give life.

Translated from the French by Joan Acocella

VIII

To Rawlins Cottenet*

Dear friend Cottenet,

I am happy to receive your letter.
I am happy that you are well.
I love it very much that you are well.
I am well because you are well.
I like to write in rhythm,
Because you are a rhythm.
I love very much for you to love,
But I am a rhythm to love
I love rhythm without you,
Because I love my wife very much.
I love very much to show you
What rhythm is, what rhythm is.
I love very much the rhythm of God
I the rhythm, I the Dance.
I am Dance, I am a God.
I love dance as you loved

---

* Rawlins Cottenet, a member of the board of directors of the Metropolitan Opera, was an American friend of the Nijinskys. It was he who suggested Robert Edmond Jones as the designer for Nijinsky's *Till Eulenspiegel*. The letter contains extensive, untranslatable play on *pas* (Fr., "not"), *pattes* (Fr., "paws"), and *fauttes* (Fr. *fautes*, "mistakes"). (Ed.)

I am Dance for you in God.
I am Dance for you in God.
I love love in you of God.
I am God for you love.
I love love because He love.
I love love for you in God.
I am a man but not paws
I have paws but in Him
I love love without paws,
I love paws with Him.
I am a man but not paws
I have paws but in Him.
I am that because he is
I am that because he is.
I love the world because he does.
I love you because he does.
I am that because he is That.
I cannot be that.
I have great love for you
I have great love for you
I am not a man without paws
I am paw with paws.
Paw, papaws I am a Paw
I love paws but not paws.
I love you very much without anything
I am man, I am man.
I love in you a man without paws
I love in you a man without paws
I am a man because I have faults
I am a man because I have faults.
I love truth very much.
I have written the truth.
I sent my greetings to you and sister

I love you two, you two, very much,
But send my greetings to all mankind
But send my greetings to all mankind
I am man, I am man
I love mankind, I love mankind.
I love you my God you.
I love you my God you.
You are old, I am young
You love young people in me
I love you because you are man
I love you that you are man.
I wrote because He wills
I wrote because He wills.
I send my greetings to you and sister
I send my greetings with my wife.
I am wife, I am wife
I love a wife for you very much
I love in you a man, a man
I am man, I am man.
I send you much love, much love
I love you, I love you.
   Greetings
      Vaslav Nijinsky

Translated from the French by Joan Acocella

IX

To Serge Diaghilev*

To Man,

I cannot call you by name, because you cannot be called by your name. I am not writing to you quickly, because I don't want you to think that I am nervous. I am not a nervous man.

* On Serge Diaghilev, founder-director of the Ballets Russes and Nijinsky's mentor and lover from 1908 to 1913, see the introduction. The letter reflects Nijinsky's continuing bitterness over his shattered relationship with Diaghilev, and it may be the pressure of that emotion that sets off the complicated wordplay in this letter. Often, his choice of words proceeds by association. When he speaks of "declining" in the grammatical sense, as one declines a noun, this makes him think of related words, such as "inclining" or "bowing down," and he takes off in that direction. Elsewhere the association is of sound rather than sense. When he writes of Diaghilev's organizing *truppa*, or troupes, this puts him in mind of *trup*, or corpse, so the next sentence is "I am not a corpse." Often he will use nonsense words, sometimes chaining them off real words. (Thus *muzhay*, or "manhood," in one line produces *vmuzhay*, an invented word, in the next line.) Conversely, invented words, such as *porosh*, *chuy*, and *khul*, will lead him back to real words: *poroshok* ("powder"), *cheshuya* ("scaly skin"), *khuy* ("prick"). In such instances, one is uncertain whether to translate the word, thus tearing it out of its phonic context, or leave it in Russian, thus suppressing a meaning that it may have had for him beyond its sound. Decisions have been made case by case. *Poroshok*, for example, has been left in Russian, since Nijinsky seems to use it primarily for its sound value. *Cheshuya* ("scaly skin"), on the other hand, appears to have been chosen not just for its sound—he arrived at it from *khuy* to *chuy* to *chushuya* to *cheshuya*—but also for some lateral sense. It has therefore been translated. As for *khuy*, or "prick," it comes as no surprise that in a letter to his former lover this word has a meaning for him beyond its sound. In several instances he writes it large and bold, and capitalizes it. (Tr.)

I am able to write calmly. I like writing. I do not like writing fine phrases. I never learned to write fine phrases. I want to write down thoughts. I need thought. I am not afraid of you. I know you hate me. I love you as a human being. I do not want to work with you. I want to tell you one thing. I work a lot. I am not dead. I am alive. Within me lives God. I live in God. God lives in me. I am very busy working on dances. My dances are making progress. I write well, but do not know how to write fine phrases. You like fine phrases. You organize troupes. I do not organize troupes. I am not a corpse. I am a living person. You are a dead person because your aims are dead. I have not called you friend, because I know that you are my enemy. I am not your enemy. An enemy is not God. God is not an enemy. Enemies seek death. I seek life. I have love. You have spite. I am not a predatory beast. You are a predatory beast. Predatory beasts do not like people. I like people. Dostoevsky liked people. I am not an idiot. I am a human being. I am an idiot. Dostoevsky is an idiot. You thought I was stupid. I thought you were stupid. We thought we were stupid. I don't want to decline. I don't like declensions. You like people bowing down to you. I like people bowing down to me. You revile those who bow down. I like those who bow down. I call for declensions. You frighten declensions. My declension is a declension. I don't want your smile, for it smells of death. I am not death and I don't smile. I don't write in order to have a laugh. I write in order to weep. I am a man with feeling and reason. You are a man with intelligence and without feeling. Your feeling is evil. My feeling is good. You want to destroy me. I want to save you. I like you. You don't like me. I wish you well. You wish me ill. I know your tricks. I pretended to be nervous. I pretended to be stupid. I was not a kid. I was God. I am God within yourself. You are a beast, but I am love. You do not love those people now. I love those people, every-

255

one, now. Don't think I don't listen. I am not yours. You are not mine. I love you now. I love you always. I am yours. I am my own. You are mine. I like declining you. I like declining myself. I am yours. I am my own.

You are mine. I am God.
You have forgotten that God is.
I have forgotten that God is.
You are within me, and I am within you.
You are mine, and I am yours.
You are the one who wants death.
You are the one who loves death.
I love love love.
I am love but you are death.
You are afraid of death, of death
I love, I love, I love
You are death, but I am blood.
Your blood is not love.
I love you, you—
I am not blood, but I am the spirit
I am the blood and the spirit in you.
I am love, I am love.
You do not want to live with me.
I wish you well.
You are mine, you are mine.
I am yours, I am yours.
I love writing with a pen.
I write, I write
You do not write you tele-write
You are a telegram, I am a letter.
You are a machine. I am love.
You are a woodpecker, I am a woodpecker.
You reach manhood, I reach manhood,

You are a *vmuzhay* I am a *vmuzhay*
We are *vmuzhai*, you are *vmuzhai*
You are a male, I am a male
We are males, you are males
Your *muzhay* is not my *muzhay*
You are a *vmuzhay*, I am a *vmuzhay*.
You are a male, I am not yours
Yours is he, but mine is not you,
You are yours, but I am He
He is mine, he is not yours.
I want to tell you that you cannot be so.
I want to tell you that you cannot be so.
I am yours, you are mine,
We are we, we are not you—
We are we, we are not you
You are the one who calls for death
You are the one who calls for death
I am yours, but you are not mine
Mine is one's own, but one's own is not yours
You are a woodpecker, I am not a woodpecker,
You knock and I knock
Your knock is your knock, but mine is a knock
Knock-knock, knock, in a knock there is a knock
I am a knock, but I do not knock
You knock, knock, knock
I knock, knock knock
I am knocking in your soul
You knock in your brain.
I love you my knock
I am a knock, a knock, but you are not a knock,
I want to knock within the knock
You knock in the brain, in the brain.
I want to knock for you, knock, knock, knock

A knock is a cockerel.
I am a cockerel, but not a cockerel
You are a cockerel, but not a cockerel
I sing, sing, sing
You sing sing, sing
I drink drink drink
You drink drink drink
I am a cockerel a cockerel a cockerel
I am a cockerel a cockerel a cockerel
My cockerel sings sings
Your cockerel drinks drinks
I am a cockerel but you are not mine.
I am a cockerel but you are not yours.
We sing in the cockerel.
I sing without the cockerel.
We sing of the cockerel.
I sing without the cockerel.
Sing cockerel, sing cockerel.
Your cockerel will die, will die
I sing, I sing, I will die, I will die
I sing, I sing, I will die, I will die
You will die without the Cockerel
I will die with the Cockerel
Your cockerel is death, is death
My cockerel is life, is life.
I love you cockerel.
I love you cockerel.
You sing and I sing.
We sing, but I am not yours
I sing well.
You sing badly
I sing, sing, sing
You sing, sing, sing

We sing, but I am not yours
You are not mine and I am not yours,
You do not love me, one's own
I love you not one's own.
You are not mine and I am not yours
We are Yours, you are not theirs
I am Yours, but you are not mine
Mine is Yours, mine is Yours
Poro, poro, poro, tok
I *poro*, I *poro*
I *poro, poro, poro*
You *porosh*, you *porosh*
I *porosh*, you *porosh*
I am *tok* but you are *tok*
Tok, tok, tok, poroshok
I am *porosh* but you are *oshok*
I am *poshok* but you are *dushok*
I am *toshok*, but you are *tushok*
We in *prokh* are *poroshok*
I am *porosh*, but you are *oshok*.
We make a noise, we make a noise
You are not noise, but I am noise
I am young, but you are old.
We are death, but I am young
Lolod is life, but not a sledgehammer
I am a sledgehammer not a hammer
You are *tok* and I am *tok*
I am *tok, tok, tok.*
Tok, tok, tok, and not *tok.*
We are *tok, tok, tok*
You are not *tok*, but I am *tok*
I am *tok, tok, tok*
I wish you *tok, tok*

You are not *tok*, you are not *tok*
I am *tok*, I am *tok*
I *tok* every day
You *tok* every day
We *tok*, we *tok*
You *tok*, I am not *toch*
We are *toch*, but not *chech*
Chech is *toch*, I am not *toch*
We *chech* and I *chech* I *chech*
Chech, *chech*, *chech* is not *chech*
I *chech ul khul*
I *chech* I am *ul khul*
Chul chul you are their *chul*
Mul chul you are *khul*
I am a prick, but not yours
You are mine, but I am not yours
Mine is a prick because the Prick
I am the Prick, I am the Prick
I am God in my prick
I am God in my prick.
Yours is a prick, not mine not mine
I am a prick in His prick.
I prick, prick, prick
You are a prick, but not the Prick
I can prick, prick
You cannot prick a prick
I am not a prick in your prick
I am a prick in His prick.
Chuyu, chuy, I am not *chuy*
You are *chuy* not mine in *chuy*.
I am *chuy, chuy*, you are not *chuy*.
We are *chuy*, not not *chuy*
Chuy, chuy, chuy, not *chushuya*.

I am not a *chuy* in a scaly skin
I am a *chuy*, I am a *chuy chuy*
Chuy chuy chuy, but not *uy*
Uy is intelligence, but not mine
I am intelligencing I love
Mine is the intelligence in the *chuy* intelligence
I am *chuy*. I love.
Chuy, chuy, chuy not scaly skin.
I am God not in a scaly skin.
A scaly skin is intelligence in *chuy*
I am *chuy*, I am *chuy*.

I want to write a lot to you, but I cannot work with you, for your aims are different. I know that you know how to pretend. I don't like pretending. I like pretense when a person wants the good of others. You are a spiteful man. You are not king. But I am. You are not my king, but I am your king. You wish me harm, I do not wish harm. You are a spiteful man, but I am a lullabyer. Rockabye, bye, bye, bye. Sleep in peace, rockabye, bye. Bye. Bye. Bye.

Man to man

Vaslav Nijinsky.

Translated from the Russian by Kyril FitzLyon

X

To Misia Edwards*

Dear Madam,

You are a friend of Diaghilev.
Diaghilev is your friend
I am not Diaghilev
You are not a Diaghilev
I am one of the—a man
I am not Diaghilev
You are what I am
I am not what you are

* Misia Edwards (later, Misia Sert), the estranged wife of the very wealthy publisher Alfred Edwards, was a close friend of Serge Diaghilev's and a patron of the Ballets Russes. See the footnote on page 43. This poem to Misia is the first in a series of five letters to people (José-Maria Sert, Jean Cocteau, Reynaldo Hahn, and Gabriel Astruc, in addition to Misia) who were or had been closely associated with the Ballets Russes, the circle from which Nijinsky felt he had been banished. Therefore the bitterness with which he wrote to Diaghilev overflows into these letters too, as does the insistent wordplay. Letters XI–XVI, untranslatable, are printed in the original French. (There may be some copying errors. Nijinsky ordinarily makes corrections by writing on top of the original, and this makes the corrected word hard to decipher.) The present letter is translated, but with many words left in French, to preserve the verbal gymnastics and also because a number of the words are neologisms, with no English equivalent. Nijinsky rings changes on three groups of words or sounds. The first includes *or* (Fr., "gold"), *toréador* (Fr., "toreador"), *trésor* (Fr., "treasure"), *toro* (Sp., "bull"), *amour* (Fr., "love"), *mor* (probably from Fr. *mort*, "death"), *tor* (possibly from Fr. *tort*, "harm," "wrong"), *cor* (Fr., "horn"; also from Fr. *corps*, "body," and Fr. *encore*,

You give me a pencil
I do not give a pencil
Your pencil is of *or*
My pencil is without *or*
You give me an *or*
I give you an *or*
This an *or* not an *or*
Or and *or* not an *or*
Your *or* not of *or*
My *or* is *or*
I do not *or* of *tor*
My *tor* not a *tor*
Tor is *tor* is *tor* not *tor*
I am *tor* you not of *or*
My *tor* is an *or*
Your *ore* is a *tor*.
Tor is *tor* it is a *tor*
Tor tor tor is *toredor*
Toreodor, toreodor tor
Tor is an *or tor*
Tor is *or* is not *l'or*
L'or is *tor* is not an *or*
Or and *or* and *or* and *or*.

_____

"still"), and *coeur* (Fr., "heart"). The second consists of *fou* (Fr., "mad") and *fouillé* (Fr., "elaborate"); the third of *argent* (Fr., "money," "silver") and *argenterie* (Fr., "silverware," "silver plate"). Though the language is dizzying, its meaning is not unclear. The silver, gold, and treasure refer to Misia's material wealth; the death, lack of love, and lack of heart, to what he sees as her spiritual poverty. The toreador and bull are associations to the fact that Misia's lover, José-Maria Sert, is Spanish. The madness of course refers to his concerns about his sanity; the dwelling on things *fouillé*, or "elaborate," to his worry that his writing is simple and uncouth. This letter, then, reiterates the main theme of the diary, the superiority of spiritual to material values. I have retained Nijinsky's spelling. (Ed.)

Or and *or* and *or* and *or*
Or deor deor deor.
I am *or* but not an *or*
Or and *tor tereodor*
Tor tresor is *l'or* my *or*
Or is *l'or* is not an *or*
My *tresor* is an *or*
Or, or, or, or, or, or, or
I am *l'or* but not an *or*
Or is *or* is *or* is *or*
Or is *or* is *or* is *tor*
Tor, tor, tor, tor, tor, tor, tor,
Tor, tor, tor, tor, toredor.
I am beef but not a *tor*
Tor is *tor* but not a *tor*
Tor, tor, tor is not a *toro*
I am *toro* but not a *tor.*
To Madam Edwards with *l'amour,*
To Madam Edwards with *l'amour.*
With *l'amour,* with *l'amour*
My *amour* is an *amour*
Your *amour* is an *argent*
My *amour* is not *argent*
Argentries is *argentries*
I am not an *argent*
My *argent* is your *argent*
You *argent* is we *argent*
You *argent* in my *argent*
You *argent* is a *l'amort*
Mor is *or, or* is *mor*
Mor is *tor, tor* is *mor*
I am not a *fouillole*
I am *fou* but not a *fouille*

Fouille is *fouille*, I am a *fouilles*
Fouille is *fouille* is *fouille* is *fouille*
Fouille is *fouille* is a *fouille*
I am *fouille* but not a *fouille*
You are *fouille* but I am *tor*
I am *tor* a *toredor*
Toredor I am a *tor*
Tor is *or* not an *or*
Or my *or* my *ors* are *or*
Tor is *tor* is *or* is *or*.
Coeur is *cor*, is *cor* is *cor*
I am *cor* but without *or*
Tor is *or* but not a *cor*
I am *cor* but not a *tor*
Tor my *tor*, I am a *tor*
Tor is *tor* it is a *cor*
Cor my *coeur*, but not a *cor*
Cor is *cor* is not a *cor*
Cor my *coeur*, my *coeur*, my *coeur*
I am *coeur*, I am *coeur*.
You are *cor* but not a *coeur*
You are *coeur* but not a *coeur*
You are *coeur* without *coeur*, without *coeur*
My *coeur* is a *coeur*.
You *coeur*, my *coeur*, your *coeur*, his *coeur*
We *coeur*, all *coeur*. I have *coeur* without *or*
Your *coeur* is *l'or*. My *coeur* without *l'or*.
Lor, *lor*, *lor*, *lor*, *lor*, *lor* not *coeur*.
Coeur, *coeur*, *coeur*, *coeur*, *coeur*, *coeur*, *coeur*, *coeur*
Coeur, *coeur*, *coeur* is *coeur*.
My *coeur* a *coeur*.
Your *coeur* a *cor*
My *cor* not *coeur*

Coeur, coeur, coeur, coeur
Coeur, coeur, coeur, coeur.

My *amour* is a *coeur*, but your *amour* is without *coeur*.
Friend with *coeur* Vaslav Nijinsky

Translated from the French by Joan Acocella

XI

To José-Maria Sert*

Chèr Monsieur.

Mont or n'est pas un tor
Tor sent or nes pas un or
Or a tor, tor est or
Vous ette tor mes pas un or
Or et or et or et or
Or deor or deor
Mon tresor est une l'or
L'or est tor n'est pas tresor
Mon tresor n'est pas tereur

---

* The Spanish painter and Ballets Russes designer José-Maria Sert was Misia Edwards's lover and, later, her husband. This letter is an extension of the preceding one,
to Misia, but whereas the letter to Misia contained a great deal of clanging, this one
consists almost entirely of clanging, in a combination of French and invented Spanish.
To the vocabulary already listed for Letter X, Letter XI adds the following words,
together with variations on them: *tereur* (Fr. *terreur*, "terror"); *coro* (from Fr. *corps*,
"body," and *cor*, "horn," and possibly also from Sp. *corrida*, "bullfight"); *coeurro*
(from Fr. *coeur*, "heart"), *moro* (from Fr. *mort*, "death"); *terodapo* (apparently a mix
of French and Russian spellings for "toreador"); *ponte* (perhaps from Fr. *pont*,
"bridge," or from "Pontius," see below); *monte* (perhaps from Fr. *mont*, "mountain");
Dieuso (from Fr. *Dieu*, "God"); *homme* (Fr., "man"); *pomme* (Fr., "apple"); *Pilatus*
(Lat., Pontius Pilate; probably also Mt. Pilatus, in the Swiss Alps); *matromonio*, *patromonio*, and *monotonio*, self-explanatory. The letter ends, "With friendship to Sert as
a man, Man Vaslav Nijinsky." (Ed.)

Tor est tor c'est tereur
Tor tereur pas tresor
Mon tresor n'est pas tereur
Tor tor tor toreodor
Je sui or sent tereur
Je sui or sent tereur
Mon tresor c'est un or
Votre tor pas un or
Tor et tor toreodor
Tor et torop pas un tor
tor et tor toreodor.
Toro, toro, toro, toro
Toro, toro, toro, toro.
Toro, toro, toro or
Oro toro c'est un toro
Toro oro, oro toro
Moro toro c'est un toro
Loro-toro, moro-toro
Oro-coro, coro toro
Toro moro c'est un coro
Coro moro c'est un toro
Toro-coro, coro toro
Loro, loro loro loro
Loro moro moro toro
Moro coro soro moro
Moro, moro, moro, coro
Coro moro, moro coro
Coro coro pas un coeuro
Coeuro, Coeuro, Coeuro, Coeuro
Coeuro, Coeuro c'est un toro
Toro moro, coeuro moro
Moro, moro, moro coeuro
Coeuro, Coeuro, coeuro, coeuro

Moro toro terodapo
Toro moro terodapo
Loro moro coeuro moro
Moro coeuro toro moro
Corro, corro, corro, corro
Corro, corro, corro, corro
Corro Corro, Corro corro
Corro corro corro morro
Votre corro morro morro
Coeurro Coeurro morro morro
Morro corro, corro, corro
Votre coeurro morro morro
Ponte morro ponte morro
Ponte morro, ponte morro
Ponte coeurro ponte coeurro
Coeurro ponte, ponte coeurro
Votre ponte n'est pas coeurro
Coeurro ponte monte, monte
Monte ponte, ponte monte
Monte coeurro, monte coeurro
Coeurro, coeurro pas un corro
Corro, corro pas un coeurro
Coeurro-corro, corro monte
Monte coeurro-corro monte
Dieuso monte, Dieuso monte
Monte, ponte Dieuso coeurro
Coeurro ponte Dieuso monte
Avec mes amour pour un homme
Avec mes amour pour un homme
Homme un home est un home
Home mon home est un homme
Pomme, pomme n'est pas un pomme
Pomme, pomme, pomme nes pas popom

Popo, pompo pas Pilatus
Pitou latous pas Pilatous
Latous, latous pas un catous
Catous patous pas Pilatous
Latous, latous, latous, latous
Catous, catous, catous, latous.
Matous patous, latous ratous
Ratous, ratous tatous matous
Tous, tous, tous, tous, tous, tous tous, tous
Je suis patous pas Pilatous
Latous patous pas Pilatous
Latous latous patous patous
Matous patous mon Pilatous
Latous patous catous catous
Caktous, caktous, caktous, caktous
Tous, Tous, Tous, Tous, Tous, Tous, Tous, Tous
Matromonio, patromonio, patromonio matromonio
Matromonio patromonio, patromonio matromonio
Monio tonio tonio monio, monio tonio monotonio
Monotonio tonio tonio
Monio bonio, bonio monio
Avec mes amitie a Sert pou un homme.
    homme Waslaw Nijinsky

XII

To Jean Cocteau*

Homme.

Je suis un homme
Je suis un homme
Vous ette un homme
Vous ette un homme
Votre homme est une home
Votre home est un homme
Je suis homme
Je suis homme
Vous ette homme mes pas un homme
Je suis homme mes pas un home
Vous ette home mes pas un homme

* In 1909, during the Ballets Russes' first season in Paris, the nineteen-year-old Jean Cocteau became a fan and friend of the company. Soon he was working for it as well. With Frédéric de Madrazo, he composed the libretto for *Le Dieu Bleu* (1912), which starred Nijinsky. He was also the librettist for *Parade* (1917) and *Le Train Bleu* (1924). Just as Nijinsky accused Misia Edwards of having no heart, here he describes Cocteau as a man "without light." He then takes off on a long flight of associations. Near the end of the letter he says, "I write very badly but I want to tell you that I love you. I love you, my dear Cocto." Then the sound *coc* (Fr. *coq*, "rooster") launches him on another flight of associations, including Russian words. As in the poems within the diary, he brings in *mia* and *tia*, Church Slavonic for "me" and "thee," respectively. *Mia* becomes *miaou* (Fr., "meow"), which then takes him to *chat* (Fr., "cat"). He ends, "With friendship for a man but not Cocto, Vaslav Nijinsky." (Ed.)

Homme ne home me home me home
Home un homme mes pas un homme
Vous ette home, je suis un home
Vous ette home sens lumièr
Je suis home avec lumièr
Je suis homme avec un coeur
Vous ette home sens lumièr
Je suis home avec lumièr
Votre home ne pas un homme
Hom est homme ne pas un pomme,
Pomme est pomme est pomme est pomme
Pomme est pomme est pomme est pomme
Pomme est pomme ne pas un pont
Pont est pont pas un pomme
Pomme pomme pone pone pone
Ponee nonee nonee ponee
Lonee ponee nonee ponee
Ronee ronee ronee ronee
Ronee ponee ponee ponee
Monee ponee ponee monee
Jonee jonee ioyonee
Jonee jonee iouonee
Jy iy ioudonee
Donee jonee ioydonee
Monee jonee ioudonee
Donee jonee ioudonee
Ronee ponee ioudonee
Monee tonee ioudonee
Tonee tonee monotonee
Monotonee, monotonee
Ponee, tonee, ponee, tonee
Jonee tonee ioudonee
Joydonee jonee honee

Honee, Honee mojodonee
Mojodonee ioudonee
Donee, donee ioudonee
Ioudonee, ioudonee
Ioudonee monotonee
Ponee pontee pontee piousse
Ponte piousse mono piousse
Piousse, piousse, piousse, piousse
Piousse, piousse, piousse, piousse
Jiousse, iousse, piousse piousse
Piousse iousse ioudonesse
Ioudonesse ponte piousse
Piousse tiousse miousse iousse
Miousse iousse tiousse piousse
Piousse tiousse ioudonesse
Ioudonesse tiousse piousse
Miousse tiousse pontee piousse
Pontee piousse tiousse iousse
Miousse iousse, iousse, iousse
Tiousse piousse miousse iousse
Iousse miousse pontee iousse
Ponte tiousse, ponte piousse
Piousse, piousse, piousse, piousse.
Piousse, piousse, piousse, piousse.
Je suis iousse mes pas piousse
Iousse, iousse, iousse, iousse
Miousse, miousse, miousse, miousse
Je suis iousse, je suis iousse
Je suis miousse, je suis miousse

Je ecris tres malle mais je veux vous dire que je vous aime. Je
vous aime mon chere Cocto. Coc, coc, to, ne pas le coc. Je suis
coc vous ette un coc. Ne pas coc, ne pas coc coc, coc, coc ne

pas un coc. Je suis coc, je suis coc. Coc, coc, coc, je suis un coc. Coc, coc, coc, je suis un coc. Mon coc et ton coc tu un coc mais pas un coc. Je suis coc tu un coc. Nous ommes coc, vous ette un coc. Coc, coc, coc, cet un coc. Coc iyage ne pas un coc. Coc, coc, coc, ne pas un coc. Coc, coc, coc, cette un coc. Je suis coc mes pas un coc. Pas un coc est un moge. Mogi, cogi, togi, jogi. Migi, gigi, gi gi, rigi. Tchigi, tchigi, tchigi, rigi. Tchigi, rigi, rigi, tchigi. Migi, tigi, tigi, tigi. Jagi, jagi, jagi, jagi. Je suis russe pour ça je dis que je suis ja. Ja, moi, moi est ja. Iia, jia, jia, jia. Tia, tia, tia, tia. Mia, mia, mia, mia. Mia, mia ne pas miou. Miou, tiou, miou, tiou. Tiou miou, tiou miou. Miaou, Miaou, miaou, mia. Mia ou mia ne pas miaou. Miaou miaou pas mia. Tia miaou mes pas moi. Toi moi est un chat. Chat un chat mes pas toi. Je suis chat mes pas toi. Toi un pate mes pas moi. Mois un pate sent toi. Toi, toi, toi, toi. Je suis chat me pas toi.

Avec mes amitie pour un homme me pas Cocto.

Waslaw Nijinsky

XIII

To Reynaldo Hahn*

Chèr ami Reinaldo.

Je suis homme mes pas lui
Lui homme mes pas je suis
Je veux ça par ce que je suis
Suis je suis, je suis, je suis
Lui suis, je suis, je suis, je
Mi, re, do, si, do bemol.
Mol be mol et sent bemol
Bol est mol est mol, sent mol
Col est tol, est mol sent ol
Ol est tol, tol est mol.
Tu veux ça moi pas ça
Tu veux ça je suis un ça
Ça pas ça je suis un ça
Ça un ça, je suis un ça
Ti un ça, mais mi ne ça

* Like his friend Cocteau, the French composer Reynaldo Hahn was one of the Parisian friends of the Ballets Russes. He composed the score for *Le Dieu Bleu*. In the parts of the letter that can be read, Nijinsky, as in previous letters, protests that he is a human being and questions whether his correspondent is. He apologizes for his handwriting and his French. He uses some Russian words and explains them. Since Hahn is a musician, the wordplay at the opening is sprung from "Mi, re, do, si, do." (Ed.)

Ça gi ja gi gagi cagi
Cagi, cagi, cagi, cagi
Gagi, gagi, gagi, gagi
Jagi, jagi, jagi, jagi
Miagi, miagi, miagi pagi
Pagi, pagi, pagi, pagi
Biagi, biagi, biagi, biagi
Tagi, tagi, tigi, tagi.
Gagi, gagi, gagi, gagi
Cagi, cagi, cagi, cagi

Tigi, tagi, tigi, tagi, tagi, tagi, tagi, tagi. Magi, magi, magi, nogi.
Nogi, togi, nogi, togi. Tigi tagi, tigi, tagi. Ragi, ragi, ragi cagi.
Tigi tagi ragi ragi. (Ragi est en russe geusser.) Tigi ragi pagi
dogi. Dogi, pougi, pougi, pougi. Jagi, magi ne pas cagi. Je suis
caqui me pas taki. Taki, taki, taki, taki. Jiaki, jiaki ce moiki.
Maki, noki, noki, joki. Joki, boki, coci, joki. Tiki, taki, tiki,
taki. Miaki, biaki, piaki, raki. Raki, raki, raki, raki. Mouki,
mouki, mouki, mouki. (En russe mouki ça veux dir soufrensse.)
Je suis homme est ça je sais. Je suis homme pour ça je suis. Je suis
homme, mais pas un home. Home et homme ne pas un homme.
Homme ce homme, tu pas un homme. L'homme un homme
avec le coeur. Tu un cor mes pas un coeur. Tu un coeur mes
pas un cor. Cor est cor c'est un cor. Cor pas cor est sent cor.
Mon ecritur n'est pas bon, mes espie est très bon. Si tu sens tu
comprent, si tu pensse je suis baitte. Je ne conai pas ècritur
françai ét pour ça j'ai les faute.

J'ai fait faute par ce que je faute.
Tu est faut par ce que sent faut.
A toi de moi, Moi, toi, toi, Moi.

Waslaw Nijinsky votre ami est homme.

XIV

To Gabriel Astruc*

Chèr Astrugu.

Je suis astrugu, sent astrugu
Tu astrugu avec astrugu
Astro, astro, astro, a
Astro, astro, astro, ca
Ca, ca, ca, ca, ca, ca, ca
Ta, ca, ta, ca, ta, ca, ca
Et tu et tu est pas tu
Tu ba tu, tu ba tu
Ba tu ba tu ba tu tu
Tu, tu, tu tu tu tu tu
Je ne suis pas tu tu tu
Tu me tu, tu me tu
Tu un coro, tu un cor
Cor cor cor cor cor cor cor

---

* On Gabriel Astruc, the impresario who presented most of the Ballets Russes' pre–World War I seasons in Paris, see the footnote on page 10. By associations of sound and sense, Nijinsky in this letter goes from the name of Massine to *singe* (Fr., "monkey"), to *pattes* (Fr., "paws"), to *ongles* (Fr., "claws"), to *aigle* (Fr., "eagle," the image that he used for Diaghilev in the diary), to *corschoune* (Russ. *korshun*, "hawk"). This is followed by a chain from *Dieu* (Fr., "God") to *Di* to *pi* to *pipi* (Fr., "pee-pee") to *papa*. (Ed.)

Tu fait ça pour ça je sai
Sai ça ce ça tu est ça
Massa massa massa in
Tu ma ssine ma ssine massine
Tu un massin tu est ça
Je suis ça mes pas un singe
Singe un singe mes pas un singe
Je suis singe mes pas beaucoup
Tu un singe beaucoup, beaucoup.
Tou est singe avec les pattes
Patte patte patte patte patte patte patte
Patte patte patte patte son tes pattes
Je suis patte mes pas des pattes
Patte sont patte mes pas des pattes
Pattes les pattes sont cent pattes
Tout tes patte sont avec ongles
Tout mes patte non pas des ongles
Ongles et ongles ne sont pas ongles
Tu un ongles tu un aiglle
Tu un aiglles pou un aiglles
Tu un corro tu un corro
Corro corro corro corro
Corro corro corro corro
Corro corro corro corro
Corro corro corro corro . . . .
Tu un corro mes pas corro
Tu un cor pas un cor
Cor cor cor cor cor cor cor cor
Cor cor cor cor cor cor corschoune
Corschoune corschoune est un russe
Est un russe un corro corro.
De Waslaw Nijinsky a Corro Astrugu
Je ne suis pas un astrug.

Pou l'amour de Dieux je suis.
Je ne suis pas un Di—eux
Di—eux Di—eux Di—eux Di
Je suis Di mes pas un pi
Pi pi pi pi pi pi pi
Je suis pipi pas un pi
Tu un pi mes pas un pi
Je suis pi mes pas pipi.
Pipi, pipi, pipi, pi
Pipi, pipi, pipi, pi
Pipi pas pi papi pa
Papa, papa papa pa
Je suis papa tu aussi
Je suis papa tu aussi
Je veux papa je veux pa
Pa pa pa pa pa pa pa
Papa pa pa papa pa
Tu ne pa moi un pa
Pa un pa un pa papa
Papa papa papa pa.
Je veux dir que vous ette un Papa.
Je veux dir que je Papa
Tu papa moi papa
Tu un tu un tu papa
Tu un corro tu papa
Papa papa pas un cor
Cor est mor mes pas papa
Papa papa pa pa pa.
Avec amitie pou Gabrielle Astruc.
Avec amitie de Waslaw Nijinsky

XV

To mankind*

Au hommes

hommes, hommes, hommes
home   home   home
hommes, hommes hommes
home   home   home
Je suis homme est un home
Je suis homme est un home
Je suis home avec lumièr

---

* This is Nijinsky's longest and most elaborate letter. In it he again protests that he is a man, that he has a heart, that his spirit has light. To the vocabulary of the preceding letters he adds other French words, or variations thereon, including *pied* ("foot"), *finir* ("finish"), *souci* ("care"), *enfant* ("child"), *vivre* ("live"), *rat* ("ballet student"), *biffstek* ("beefsteak"), *rire* ("laugh"), *santé* ("health"), *sage* ("wise"), *bon* ("good"), *bombe* ("bomb"), *mauvais* ("bad"), *barbare* ("barbarian": Romola sometimes called him this in jest), *tombeau* ("tomb"), *tambour* ("drum"), *bourse* ("stock exchange"), *tousse* ("cough": Kyra had respiratory infections), *foi* ("faith"), *corbeau* ("crow"), *automobile* ("automobile"), *son* ("sound"), *saucisson* ("sausage"), *cactus* ("cactus"), *mouvement* ("movement"), *temps* ("time" or, in ballet, "step"), *battu* ("beaten"), *tuba* ("tuba"), *anglais* ("English"), *français* ("French"), and the name of his cook, Marie. Near the end, he brings in Lloyd George and Clemenceau again. At times there are words concealed in apparent nonsense lines. In "Co cot co cot co cot co" he is obviously playing on *cocotte* (Fr., "prostitute"). Other cases are less easily decided. In "Je suis tu mes pas tu tu," "tu" may be "you" (*tu*) or "killed" (*tué*) or part of "tutu," a garment he was familiar with. Or it may be all of these. Though the salutation of the letter is "Au hommes"—to mankind—some lines are clearly addressed to Romola: "I love you you you," "You do not love me anymore," "I am not bad, I am good." (Ed.)

Je suis homme avec lumièr
Je suis hommes je suis hommes
Je suis hommes je suis hommes
Je suis homes je suis homes
Je suis homes avec lumièrs
Mes lumièrs sont tes lumièrs
Tes lumièrs sont mes lumiers
Tu un homme avec un coeur
Je suis coeur avec lumière
Ton lumièr est mon lumière
Tu lumièr avec lumièr
Je lumiè est tu lumiè
Nous lumiè est vous lumiè
Piè est piè piè, piè, piè, piè
Je suis piè je suis piè
Mi et mi, re, do est sol
Je suis sol je suis sol.
Ma fa sol est ton sol
Sol sol sol sol sol sol sol
Je suis sol avec un sol
Je suis sol avec ton sol
Sol est sol sont pas un sol
Je suis sol mes pas un sol.
Mi re do fa sol si do
Je suis do avec un sol
Sol avec un sol sent sol
Je suis sol avec un coeur
Sol mon sol est ton sol
Je suis sol avec le coeur
Coeur pas coeur pas coeur pas coeur
Je suis coeur avec un coeur
Vous ette coeur avec un coeur
Je suis coeur avec un coeur

Tu te tu te tu te tu
Tu tu tu tu tu tu tu
Tu ne pas un coeur un coeur
Je ne tu pas avec coeur
Je suis coeur mes pas un cor
Je suis cor avec un coeur
Patri patri pas un coeur
Je suis patri avec coeur
Coeur et coeur ne pas un coeur
Je suis coeur dand un coeur
Tu un coeur sent coeur sent coeur
Je suis coeur avec un coeur
Tu veux coeur moi aussi
Tu veux coeur moi aussi
Tu sent coeur par ce que tu cor
Cor, cor, cor cor cor sent coeur
Je suis cor avec un coeur
Tu un cor cor cor cor cor
Cor cor cor cor cor cor cor
Je suis cor avec un coeur
Je suis coeur avec un cor
Je esprie avec un coeur
Mon esprie est un coeur
Ton esprie est sent sent coeur
Sent sent sent sent sent sent sent
Je suis sent mes pas un sent
Tu un sent avec le sent
Je suis sent vec le coeur
Coeur mon coeur mon coeur mon coeur
Je suis coeur je suis coeur.
Ce mon coeur que j'ai un coeur
Je suis coeur pou ça je homme
Homme homme homme homme homme homme homme

Je suis homme et un home
Tu un homme et home sent home
Je suis home avec un homme.
Tu me dis que tu fini
Je ve dir que je fini
Tu fini est moi fini
Nous fini et vous fini
Fini, fini, fini ki
Ki ki ki ki ki ki ki
Ki ki co ki co ki co
Co co co co co co to
Co co co co co co to
co cot co cot co cot to
To tu to tu to tu tu
Tu te tu te tu te tu
Je suis tu mes pas un tu
Tu est tu te tu te tu
Je suis tu toi moi
Nous nous somme nous somme avec
Je suis si isi isi
Je suis si isi isi
Je isi isou si si
Je isi isou si si
Pas sousi sousi sousi
Je suis si isi isi
Ioussi si ioussi si
Si si si si si si si si
Je suis si si si si si si
Je suis si si si si si si.
Mon enfant isi si si
Je suis si je suis isi
Je suis si si je suis si
Tu est si si pas sousi

Je suis si si je suis si
Tzi tzi tzi tzi tzi tzi tzi
Tu veux tzi tzi tu veux tzi
Je veux tzi tzi tzi tu veux ça
Je suis ça et je suis ça
Je suis ça suis ça je ça
Ça ça ça ça ça ça ça
Je suis ça je suis ça
Tu est ça moi aussi
Tu veux ça moi aussi
Je suis ça je suis ça ça
Ça ça ça ça ça ça ça.
Ça ce ça mes pas un chat
Je suit chat avec le coeur
Coeur mon coeur mon coeur est chat
Je suis ça je suis je ça
Il va voir que je suis ça
Il va voir que je suis ça
Je veux vivree je veux vivree
Je veux vivree je vivrai
Je vivrai je vive je vive
Tu vivra moi aussi
Tu tu tu tu tu moi
Je suis ça je suis je ça.
Tu veux tu moi tu a
Je suis tu toi moi
Je suis ça je suis un chat
Tu un chat moi aussit
Tu veux ça moi aussi
Tu veux ça moi aussi
Tu te ça te ça te chat
Chat chat chat chat chat chat chat.
Je suis chat mes pas un chat

Je suis chat mes pas un chat
Tu te tu avec un chat
Je me tu avec amour
Mon amour est ton amour
Je suis ça je suis je ça.
Je suis ça mes pas un chat
Chat et chat ne pas un chat
Je suis chat avec un chate
Chate et chat cet un marie
Marie marie marie chate
Je suis chat je suis chat
Je veux chate je veux une chate
Je suis chat je suis un chat.
J'aimrai chate par ce que je chat
Si me chate ne pas un chat.
Je suis chat avec les pattes
Je les pattes avec les ongles
J'ai les ongles mes avec ça
Je suis ça je suis je ça
Je suis ça je suis je ça
Mi ou ça mi ou ça mi
Mi mi mi mi pi pi pa
Pa pi pa ti pa pi ti
Ci ci ci ci ci ci ci
Je suis ci ci je suis ça.
Je veux dir que je suis ça
Je veux dir que ce comme ça
Je comme ça et vous comme ça
Je suis ça et vous aussit
Aussit aussit aussitaux
Aussitaux que je suit to
To to ro to rat to rat
Rat et rate sont rats sont rats

Je suis rats je suis je rats
Je suis rats je suis je rats
Tu un rat et moi un rat
Tu est ra tu est un rat
Ra tu ra tu ra tu est rat
Je suis ra sent tu un rat.
Mia ou mia ou mia ou mia
Je suis mia je suis un mia
Mia ou mia ou mia ou mia
Tu te mia ou tu te rat
Tu te tu te tu te rat
Je suis rat je suis un vie
Je vivee en vie en vie
Je suis vie je suis je vie
Vie eu vi eu vi eu vi
Vivreu vivreu vivreu vi
Vi ia vi ia vi ia vi
Vi sa vi sa vi sa vi

——— ——— ——— ——— ——— ———

Je suis boeuff mes pas biffstek
Je suis stek sens boeuf en biff
Je suis biff mes pas un stek
Je suis stek je suis stek
Stek et stek ne pas un biff
Biff et biff ne pas un stek
Biffstek, biffstek, biffstek biff
Je suis biff mes pas un stek
Je suis biff mes pas un stek
Je suis biff mes pas un stek
Je suis sent sent sent sent sent
Je suis sent je suis sent

Tu est sent moi aussi
Je suis sent je suis je sent
Je suis biff mes pas un sent
Je suis biff mes pas un sent
Tu un sent je suis un boeuff
Bee bee bee bee bee bee bee
Je suis bee je suis un bee
Bee et a ne pas un bee
Je suis bee je suis un bee
J'aime les bee je bee je bee
Je suis bee je bee je bee
Tu te tu te tu te tu
Je suis tu mes pa je tu
Tu te tu te tu te tu
Je suis tu je suis je suis
Je me tu pour tu te tu
Je me tu pour tu te tu
J'aime toi toi toi
Je suis ta je ta je ta
Ta je ta je ta je ta
Je ne jeta tu te ta.
Je ne veux pas rire de ta
Je veux ta je veux te ta
J'aime toi tu pas toi
Je me ta me ta me ta
Je te ta tu ta tu ta
Je suis ta mes pas toi.
Je suis ça je suis je ça
Je jeusue je suis je sue
Je me tu pour ta sentee
Je suis ça je suis je ça.
Tu ne m'aime plue je sai ça
Tu ne sai pas que je ça

Tu te ça je suis je ça
Ça je ça je ça je ça.
Ça je ça je ça je ça
Je suis ça je ça je ça.
Tu me tu et tu et tu
Je suis ça je ça je ça.
Tu te tu pour ça je ça
Je suis ça je ça je ça.
Tu veux ça moi aussi
Je suis ça je suis un singe
Je suis singe mes pas un singe
Je suis singe sent ettree singe
Singe et singe ne pas un singe
Singe et sage ne pas un singe
Sage sage et sage et sage
Je suis sage je suis un singe
Singe et singe ne pas un singe
Je suis singe mes pas un sent
Sent sent sent sent sent sent sent
Sent je sent je sent je sent
Je suis sent mes pas un sent
Sent et sent ne pas un sent
Je suis sent mes pas un sent
Sent avec esprie de bonne
Je suis bonne je suis je bonne
Je suis sent je sent je bonne
Je suis bonne je suis je bonne
Bonne et bon ne pas un bon
Bon bon bon bon pas un bon
Je suis bon mes pas un bombe
Je ne bombe pas je ne bombe
Je suis bonne je suis je bonne
Bonne et bombe ne pas un ça

Je suis ça je suis je ça
Ça je suis ne pas un bombe
Bomba bomba bomba rdée
Bomba rdée bomba rdée bon
Bon bon bon bon bon bon bon
Bon bon bon ne pas mauvai
Mais bon bon est sont mauvai
Je ne suis pas un mauvai
Je suis bon bon bon bon bon
Bon bon bon ne pa bon bon
Je suis bon est bonne en bon
Bomba rdée bardée bardée
Je suis bonne je suis je bonne.
Je ne suis je bombardée
Je ne suis je bombardée
Je ne suis je bon bon bon
Je ne suis je barbarée
Bon ton bon ton bon tombaux
Je suis bon mes pas tombaux
Je suis tombaux pour tombaux
Je suis tombaux pour tombaux
Je ne suis je tambourin
Je ne suis je tambourin
Je ne suis je tambourin
Je ne suis je tambourin.
Mon tamboure est un tamboure
Cette tamboure est un tamboure
Je ne suis je un tamboure
Je ne suis je un tamboure
Tu tambourre ta bourre ta boursse
Tu ta boursse ta boursse ta boursse
Boursse ta boursse est boursse est boursse
Boursse et boursse ne pas un boursse

Tu un oursse sent boursse sent boursse
Je ne suis je oursse sent boursse
Tu est un homme avec le coeur
Tu est un homme avec le coeur
Tu un homme un homme n home
Tu un home avec lumière
Tu lumière est tu le coeur
Tu un coeur sent que tu sasche
Sasche Sasche sasche toi que tu
Tu ne tu pas tu ne tu
Tu ne pas un tu et tu
Tu ne pas un tu tu tu
Je ne suis pas tu tu tu
Tu ne pas un tu tu tu.
Je veux diree que tu tu
Je veux diree que tu tu.
Tu ne c'est pas ça ce que tu
Tu ne c'est pas ça ce que tu.
Tu te tu te tu te tu
Je ne tu pas tu pas tu
Tu ba tu ba tu barbare
Je ne tu pas les barbare
Tu te tu te tu toujour
Je ne tu pa te toujour
Je ne suis pas un tueur
Je ne suis pas un tueur
Je suis homme je suis un home
Je suis home avec un homme
Je veux bien toi mon homme
Je veux bien toi mon home
Je ne veux pas tu te tu
Je ne veux pas tu te tu
Je venue chez toi chez toi

Je venue chez toi chez toi
Je ne peux pas dir tous a
Je ne dit pas tous a tous
Tous a tous a tous a tous
Je suis tous mes pas un tous.
Tousse pas tousse pas tousse pas tousse
Je suis tous je suis tous
Je veux tous tous tous en bien
Je veux tous tous tous en bien
Je ne veux pas mort la mort
Je veux vie la vie la vie
Je veux vive re vive re vi
Je suis vie je vie un foi
Foi je vie une foi je vie
Je suis vie mes pas la mort
Tu lamor mes pas l'amour
Je l'amour tu te tu te
Te tu te tu te tu te
Tu te tu te tu te tu . . . .

Je veux dire que vous l'amour,
Mes vous ne senti senti sent
Sent sent sent sent sent l'amour
Je suis mour me pas la mor
Je suis mor me pas la mor
Jc suis mor me pas la mor
Je l'esprie en cor en cor
Je l'esprie avec l'amour
Tu te tu te tu te tu
Tu l'amor l'amor l'amor
Cor cor cor cor cor cor cor
Car car car car car car car
Car car car car pas un car

Je suis car mes pas l'amor
Je le cor le cor corbaux
Je suis cor cor cor corbeaux
Tu te tu te tu te tu
Je suis tu je suis je tu
Tu ne peure moi du tous
Je suis tous je suis je tous
Mon amour pour tous pour tous
Je suis je suis je l'amour.
Je suis je suis je suis je
Je suis je suis je suis ça
Ça, ça, ça, ça, ça, ça, ça
Je suis ça je suis je ça.
Je me tu qante tu te tu
Je me tu qante tu te tu
Tu te tu te tu te tu
tu tu tu tu tu tu tu.
Je veux ça sent ça sent ça
J'aime toi toi toi.
Tous a tous a tous a tous
Tous a tous a tous a tous
Tu a tu a tu a tu
Je suis tu te tu je suis
Tu me tu je suis je tu
Tu te tu te tu te tu.
Tu car tu car tu car car
Tu car tu car tu car car
Car car car car car car car
Je suis car mes pas un cor
Cor cor cor cor cor cor cor
Cor cor cor cor cor mourra
Cor mourra est tu mourra
Je suis ça je suis je ça

Tu te tu te tu te tu.
Je suis ça je ça je ça.
Ça je ma je ta je *ca*
Ca ca ca ca ca ca ca
Je ne ca mes ca un ca
Cet un ca mes pas un ca
Je suis venue pour ça pou ça
Je suis venue pour ça pou ça
Je ne suis je Dieux en Dieux
Je suis je Dieux, Dieux, Dieux
Je suis je Dieux Dieux Dieux
Je suis je Dieux Dieux Dieux
Je suis homme mes pas monsieur
Je suis je pas monsieur
Mon sieur mon sieur mon sieur mon
Mon ton ton mon mon ton mon
Moto moto moto bile
Je suis bile mes pas oto
Oto oto mo bilee
oto oto mo bilee.
Je suis bile mes pa oto
Oto mo bi lèe bi lèe
Bi lée bi lée bi lée bi
Je suis bi mes pas un pi
Pi pi pi pi pi pi pi
Je suis pi et tu un pi
Pi pi pi pi pi pi pi
Je suis pi je suis pigont
Je pigont pigont pigont
Je pigont pigont pigont
Tu te tu te tu pigont
Je ne tu pas les pigont
Tu me tu te tu pigont

Je ne suis je un pigont
Pigont pichont tu pichont
Je pichont je ne pichont
Ne pichont pas tu pigont
Je pigont mes pas pichont.
Pa pi chont pi chont pi chont
Je pi je pi pas pichont
Pas pi pas pi pas pas pi pi
Je pi pi mes pas pichont
Chot pi chont pi chont pi chont
Je pi chont mes pa pichont
Pas pi chont est chont pi chont
Je suis chont me pas pichont.
Mon pigont ne pas pichont
Je suis chont je suis je sont
J'aime les sonts les sonts les sonts
Sont pas sont je suis je sont
Sont tu sont tu sont sont sont
Je suis sont avec le sont
Sont sont sont sont sont sont sont
Je suis sont mes pas un sont.
Sonne pas sont je suis un soo
Soo soo soo soo soo soo soo
Soo pas ça mo pas ça soo
Soo soo soo soo mo pa soo
Mon pas soo pas soo ma soo
Mopa soo mo pas un soo
Je suis soo mes pas un soo
Soo soo soo soo soo soo soo
So si so si so si son
Son son son son son son son.
Son si son si co sison
Je sui sont me pas un soo

294

Soo soo soo soo soo soo soo
Je ne suis je sossi sont
Sossi sossi sossi sont
Sossi sossi sossi sont
Je ne veux pas sossisont
Sont il sont il sont il sont
Sont il sont il sont il sont
Je suis sont mes pas ssisont
Tu me tu me tu me tu
Je suis ton ti ton ti ton
Ton ti son ti ton ti ton
Je suis ton je suis je ton
Tu te tu te tu te tu
Je suis tu mes pas un tu.
Je ne veux pas dire toussa a
Je ne veux pas dire toussa a
Tousse a toussa a tousse a tousse
Je suis tous mes pas cactousse
Ca ki ca ki ma ki pas ki
Pa ki ia ki jaki iaki
Ti ki ta ki ti ki ta ki
ta ki ta ki ta ki ta ki . . . .
Je ne suis pas un mouvement
Je ne suis pas un temps
Je ne suis pas un mouvement
Je ne suis pas un temps
Temps et temps et temps et temps
Je ne pas du temps du temps
Tu te tu le temps passera
Tu te tu le temps passera
Je ne suis je que un homme
Je ne suis je que un homme
Homme un home. Homme un home

Je suis home je suis un homme
Je me tu pou tu te tu
Tu tu tu tu tu tu tu.
Tu car cor car tu car cor
Car car car car car car cor.
Je suis cor je suis un cor
Je suis cor je suis un cor
Cor cor cor cor cor cor cor cor
Je suis cor mes pas un cor
Tu un cor cor je suis cor cor
Tu un cor cor je suis cor cor
Je suis cor cor tu ne cor cor
Je suis cor cor tu te cor cor
Cor cor cor cor car car car car
Car car car car car car car car.
Je suis car tu ne pas car
Je suis cor mes pa tu cor
Tu te cor te tu te cor
Je suis cor en bonne sentèe.
Mon sentèe et ton sentèe
Ton santèe est mon sentèe
Je suis cent mes pas toi
Tu te tu ne pas du cent
Cent cent cent cent cent cent cent
Je suis cent je suis je cent
Tu me tu avec le cent.
Je ne suis je que le cent
Je ne suis je que tu sent
Sent toi que tu te tu
Sent toi que tu te tu.
Tu tu tu tu tu tu tu
Je suis tu mes pas tu tu.
Tu tu tu tu tu tu tu tu

Je suis tu tu je suis tu tu.
Mes tu tu mes tes tu tu
Je suis tu tu ne pas toi
Toi tu tu moi pa tu
Je suis batu mes pa tu tu
Je suis tu tu mes pas batu
je suis tu tu mes pas tu tu
Tu te tu je tu te tu
te tu te tu je pas tu tu.
Tu ba tu ba tu ba anglai
Anglai ba ta toi ba tu
La coq anglai mais pas français
Je suis anglai je suis anglai
Tu un anglai je suis anglai
Tu te tu te tu te tu
tu te tu mes pas anglai
Je suis anglai mes pas anglai
Je suis anglai amour anglai
Je suis anglai amour anglai
Anglai trenglai toi anglai
Je sui trenglai je sui trenglai
Je sui trenglai mes pas anglai
Je sui un djordje mes pas un lojd
Lojd lojd lojd lojd lojd lojd nes pas djordjee
Je suis Djordje mes pas djordjee
Jeorge loid jeorge un homme aussi
Je suis loid loid loid loid jeordje
Je suis jeordje me pas un loid
Je suis djordje mes pas un leid
Leid est leid ses sont des leids
Leids leids leids leids leids leids leids leids
Leids leids leids leids leids leids leids leids
Je suis leids mes pas un leids

Tu te tu pou Clemansau
Je suis ça je suis je ça.
Je me tu pour ça je ça
Je ne suis je ça pour ça
Je suis ça sent ça sent ça
Je me tu pour ça pour ça
Tu te tu pour ça sent ça.
Je suis ça je suis je ça.
Tu ne pas un ça je ça
Tu te tu pour ça pour ça
Je ne tu pas je suis ça
Je veux ça par ce que tu ça
Je veux ça par ce que tu ça
Ça ça ça ça ça ça sent
Je suis sent je sui je sent.
Je me sent sent sent sent sent
Je suis ça je suis je ça.
Je ne veux pas cont te tu
Je ne veux pas cont te tu
Tu te tu te tu te tu
Je suis tu est tu te tu.

XVI

To Jesus*

Au Gèsue

Je suis gèsue
Jc suis gèsue
Je suis gesue
Je suis gesue
Je suis un sue
Je suis un sue
Je suis je suis je suis je suis
Suis je suis je suis je suis
Je suis suis je suis suis je
Je ne veux pas sent je suis
Je me suis je suis je suis

* This letter is built on a bit of wordplay that turned up briefly also in Letter XV. He begins by saying that he is Jesus—"Je suis gèsue"—but then becomes more interested in the similarity of the sounds *sue* and *suis*. (Ed.)

NOTE ON THE MANUSCRIPT

Nijinsky's diary was recorded in three school notebooks, the first with grid-lined paper, the other two with unlined paper. In all, there are 314 pages (recto and verso) of diary text, plus a title page for what Nijinsky calls Book II. In each notebook the pages are numbered internally—that is, the text begins with page 1 in each—but the numbering is not in Nijinsky's hand. In the first notebook Nijinsky begins writing with a graphite pencil, then changes to a blue "indelible pencil," then finishes in black ink. In the second and third notebooks all the diary text is in black ink. In the third notebook the end of the diary text is followed by thirteen blank leaves. In the first notebook, the first two leaves have been cut out. These pages seem to have contained drawings; traces of artwork can be seen on the remaining edges. There is no indication that any text has been lost. The first entry of the diary begins with a paragraph indent.

Preceding the diary text of the third notebook are nine pages of pencil drawings, mostly abstract designs, based as usual on the arc. The first of these, reproduced on page 2, features Nijinsky's name, written "Waslaw Nijinsky" (in the Latin, not the Cyrillic, alphabet), with each of the two words inscribed in a separate eye-shape. Within the diary text there are two further drawings. When, in the second notebook, Nijinsky discusses the shortcomings of the ink he is using (page 108), he draws a reproduction of the label on his ink bottle. In the third notebook, when he declares that he is not God, he draws an arc and crosses it out, as noted. See pages 166–67.

The first and second notebooks contain not just the diary text but also some writing on dance notation: one and a half pages (preceded by a title page) in the first notebook, fifteen pages (with no separate title page) in the second notebook. In relation to the diary text, the material on notation is written upside down and back-to-front. In other words, Nijinsky, as he went from one to the other, turned the notebook over and started from the opposite end. It seems likely that the material on notation was finished before Nijinsky embarked on the diary. It is written in a markedly different hand—more rounded, more careful, and therefore, it seems, reflective of a calmer mental state—from what we see in the diary. Furthermore, the title page preceding the notation material in the first notebook carries the date 19–17–1918, which is probably an error for 1917–1918, a period in which he worked extensively on his system of dance notation. (In the Bolshoi Ballet Archives there are five school notebooks containing writings by Nijinsky on notation. Of the three that are dated, one is from 1917, two from 1918.) The notation material in the diary notebooks is not included in our text. The notation experts Ann Hutchinson Guest and Claudia Jeschke discuss it briefly in their book *Nijinsky's "Faune" Restored*, saying that it differs from the thoughts on notation that Nijinsky recorded while he was interned in Budapest in 1914–16. I am indebted to Dr. Guest for the information on the notebooks in the Bolshoi Ballet Archives.

Nijinsky made only one major division in the diary. Two and a half pages into the third notebook, he signed off on the preceding material and then began a new section, calling it "Book II, On Death." He obviously meant all the prior material to be

Book I, and he had a title for it. In the first paragraph of Book II, he writes, "I will call the first book 'Life' and this book 'Death.'" Accordingly, I have inserted a title page, "Book I, On Life." Elsewhere he considers giving the title "Feeling" to the diary as a whole, but it seemed to me that the book should be given its usual name: *The Diary of Vaslav Nijinsky*.

The fourth notebook, containing the letters, is the same sort of school exercise book as the three notebooks containing the diary. Once the property of Igor Markevitch, it is now in the Bibliothèque Nationale, Department of Music, in Paris. In 1994 the three diary notebooks were acquired by the New York Public Library. They are in the library's Dance Collection at Lincoln Center. (Ed.)

BIBLIOGRAPHY

The introduction and notes include information taken from the following works:

American Psychiatric Association. *Diagnostic and Statistical Manual of Mental Disorders.* 3rd ed. (DSM-III). Washington, D.C.: American Psychiatric Association, 1980.

———. *Diagnostic and Statistical Manual of Mental Disorders.* 4th ed. (DSM-IV). Washington, D.C.: American Psychiatric Association, 1994.

Baer, Nancy Van Norman. *Bronislava Nijinska: A Dancer's Legacy.* San Francisco: The Fine Arts Museum, 1986.

———. "Die Aneignung des Femininen: Androgynität im Kontext der frühen Ballets Russes, 1909–1914." In *Spielungen: Die Ballets Russes und die Künste.* Ed. Claudia Jeschke, Ursel Berger, and Birgit Zeidler. Berlin: Verlag Vorwerk 8, 1997. 40–53.

Beaumont, Cyril. *Bookseller at the Ballet: Memoirs 1891 to 1929.* London: Beaumont, 1975.

Benois, Alexandre. *Memoirs.* 2 vols. Trans. Moura Budberg. London: Chatto and Windus, 1964.

———. *Reminiscences of the Russian Ballet.* Trans. Mary Britnieva. London: Putnam, 1941.

Bleuler, Eugen. *Dementia Praecox or the Group of Schizo-*

phrenias. Trans. Joseph Zinkin. New York: International Universities Press, 1950.

Bourman, Anatole, in collaboration with D. Lyman. *The Tragedy of Nijinsky.* New York: McGraw-Hill, 1936.

Bowlt, John. *The Silver Age: Russian Art of the Early Twentieth Century and the "World of Art" Group.* Newtonville, Mass.: Oriental Research Partners, 1979.

Buckle, Richard. *Diaghilev.* New York: Atheneum, 1979.

———. *Nijinsky.* New York: Simon and Schuster, 1971.

Chagall, Marc. *My Life.* Trans. Elisabeth Abbott. New York: Orion Press, 1960.

Drummond, John. *Speaking of Diaghilev.* London: Faber and Faber, 1997.

Garafola, Lynn. *Diaghilev's Ballets Russes.* New York: Oxford, 1989.

Gaspers, Kinga Mária. "Life and Career of Emilia Márkus, the Leading Actress of Hungarian Theatre." M.A. thesis, Arizona State University, 1993.

Guest, Ann Hutchinson, and Claudia Jeschke. *Nijinsky's "Faune" Restored: A Study of Vaslav Nijinsky's 1915 Dance Score "L'Après-midi d'un Faune" and His Dance Notation System.* Philadelphia: Gordon and Breach, 1991.

Haskell, Arnold, in collaboration with Walter Nouvel. *Diaghileff: His Artistic and Private Life.* London: Gollancz, 1935.

Hodgson, Moira. "Nijinsky's 'Diary,' " *Dance Magazine,* December 1974, 37–40.

Karlinsky, Simon. "A Cultural Educator of Genius." In *The Art of Enchantment: Diaghilev's Ballets Russes, 1909–1929.* Ed. Nancy Van Norman Baer. San Francisco: The Fine Arts Museums of San Francisco, 1988. 14–25.

Karsavina, Tamara. *Theatre Street: The Reminiscences of Tamara Karsavina.* New York: Dutton, 1931.

Kirstein, Lincoln. *Dance: A Short History of Classic Theatrical*

Dancing. New York: Dance Horizons, 1969. Reprint of *The Book of the Dance*, 2nd ed., 1942.

————. *Movement & Metaphor: Four Centuries of Ballet*. New York: Praeger, 1970.

————. *Nijinsky Dancing*. New York: Knopf, 1975.

Lieven, Prince Peter. *The Birth of Ballets-Russes*. Trans. L. Zarine. London: Allen and Unwin, 1936.

Lifar, Serge. *Serge Diaghileff: His Life, His Work, His Legend. An Intimate Biography*. 1940. Reprint, New York: Da Capo, 1976.

Macdonald, Nesta. *Diaghilev Observed by Critics in England and the United States, 1911–1929*. New York: Dance Horizons, 1975.

Magriel, Paul, ed. *Nijinsky: An Illustrated Monograph*. New York: Henry Holt, 1946.

Mallon, Thomas. *A Book of One's Own: People and Their Diaries*. New York: Ticknor & Fields, 1984.

Massine, Léonide. *My Life in Ballet*. Ed. Phyllis Hartnoll and Robert Rubens. London: Macmillan, 1968.

Morrell, Ottoline. *Memoirs of Lady Ottoline Morrell: A Study in Friendship, 1873–1915*. Ed. Robert Gathorne-Hardy. New York: Knopf, 1964.

Nijinska, Bronislava. *Early Memoirs*. Trans. and ed. Irina Nijinska and Jean Rawlinson. New York: Holt, Rinehart and Winston, 1981.

Nijinski. "Nijinski," *El Día* (Montevideo), 13 September 1913, 8.

Nijinsky, Romola. *The Last Years of Nijinsky*. New York: Simon and Schuster, 1952.

————. *Nijinsky*. 1934. Reprint, New York: Pocket Books, 1972.

————, ed. *The Diary of Vaslav Nijinsky*. 1936. Reprint, Berkeley: University of California Press, 1968.

Nijinsky, Tamara. *Nijinsky and Romola*. London: Bachman & Turner, 1991.

Ostwald, Peter. *Nijinsky: A Leap into Madness*. New York: Carol Publishing, 1991.

Rubinstein, Arthur. *My Many Years*. New York: Knopf, 1980.

Sert, Misia. *Two or Three Muses: The Memoirs of Misia Sert*. Trans. Moura Budberg. London: Museum Press, 1953.

Snow, William. "Nijinsky's *Notebooks*" [including interview with Christian Dumais-Lvowski], *Ballet Review* (New York), winter, 1996, 33–37.

Sokolova, Lydia. *Dancing for Diaghilev: The Memoirs of Lydia Sokolova*. Ed. Richard Buckle. London: John Murray, 1960.

Stanciu-Reiss, Françoise, ed. *Ecrits sur Nijinsky*. Paris: Chiron, 1992.

Stravinsky, Igor, and Robert Craft. *Memories and Commentaries*. 1960. Reprint, Berkeley: University of California Press, 1981.

Svetlov, Valerian, with the collaboration of Léon Bakst. *Le Ballet contemporain*. Trans. M. D. Calvocoressi. Paris: De Brunoff, 1912.

ACKNOWLEDGMENTS

Joan Acocella wishes to thank Robert Cornfield for advice throughout this project; Robert Gottlieb for doing the preliminary photo layout; Monica Moseley of the New York Public Library (Dance Collection) for assistance with photo research; Richard Howard and Anatoly and Regina Krishtul for help with translation; Nancy Van Norman Baer, Sally Banes, Marion Bastien, Arlene Croce, Christian Dumais-Lvowski, William Emboden, Joseph Frank, Lynn Garafola, Ann Hutchinson Guest, Ivor Guest, Simon Karlinsky, Stephen Kirschner, Alastair Macaulay, Madeleine Nichols, Richard Taruskin, and David Vaughan for answering questions, making suggestions, and providing materials. My thanks are also due to Tamara Nijinsky for permitting us to publish the fourth notebook and for loaning us her family photographs. All new writings on Nijinsky borrow from the existing literature on him, but the introduction and notes to this edition would have been far less informed had I not had, in particular, Peter Ostwald's painstakingly researched *Nijinsky: A Leap into Madness*, together with additional material that Dr. Ostwald gave me before his death. I am also indebted to Séverine Imfeld and Barbara Stettler, Hans Curt Frenkel's daughter and granddaughter, respectively, for providing me with information about Dr. Frenkel.

311

Finally, both Joan Acocella and Kyril FitzLyon thank the staff of Farrar, Straus and Giroux: Paul Elie, Jonathan Lippincott, Susan Mitchell, Karla Reganold, Lorin Stein, Anne Stringfield, Marcela Valdes, and above all our editor, Jonathan Galassi.